Sandscrapers

The U.S. Navy's LSMs (Medium Landing Ships) and LSM(R)s (Rocket Ships) in World War II

Cdr. David D. Bruhn, USN (Retired)

A total of 558 Medium Landing Ships were built in WWII. The modest 203-foot ships had bow ramps like those of much larger LSTs, and a deck house resembling the turret of a medieval castle. So unique were their looks, that it was not uncommon when an LSM entered port, for someone to yell out, "What type of ship is that?" Despite their large numbers, the ships were relatively unknown to the public. Perhaps because they entered service late in the war—after the Navy decided it required a vessel larger than a tank landing craft, but smaller than a tank landing ship—or because they first saw combat at Leyte in autumn 1944. During the launch of the Philippine Islands Campaign, much attention was focused on the Allied invasion of Europe.

Nicknamed "Sandscrapers," the shallow-draft, small LSMs were able to land on beach areas denied LSTs, and did so at Leyte, Ormoc Bay, Mindoro, Lingayen, Zambales, and other island assaults in the Philippines. LSMs were also at Iwo Jima and Okinawa, and supported Australian troop landings on Borneo. Of the dozen LSMs reconfigured as rocket ships, LSM(R)s, for use in naval bombardment, one-quarter were lost to kamikaze attacks at Okinawa while employed with destroyers on isolated radar picket stations. With their decks bristling with explosive rockets, LSM(R)s were particularly vulnerable targets. One hundred seventy-seven photographs, maps, and diagrams; appendices; and an index to full names, places, and subjects add value to this work.

To the officers and men assigned to "sandscapers"
in the Pacific Theater in World War II,
and the Soldiers and Marines carried
into harm's way on board these ships

Sandscrapers

The U.S. Navy's LSMs (Medium Landing Ships) and LSM(R)s (Rocket Ships) in World War II

USS *LSM-51* landing U.S. Army troops on Japanese-held Fort Drum in Manila Bay on the mission to recapture the American fortification.

Cdr. David D. Bruhn, USN (Retired)

HERITAGE BOOKS
2025

HERITAGE BOOKS

AN IMPRINT OF HERITAGE BOOKS, INC.

Books, CDs, and more—Worldwide

For our listing of thousands of titles see our website
at
www.HeritageBooks.com

Published 2025 by
HERITAGE BOOKS, INC.
Publishing Division
5810 Ruatan Street
Berwyn Heights, Md. 20740

International Standard Book Number
Paperbound: 978-0-7884-4711-2

Heritage Books by Cdr. David D. Bruhn, USN (Retired)

Battle Stars for the "Cactus Navy":
America's Fishing Vessels and Yachts in World War II

Beavers: American River College's Running Dynasty, 1964–1979
David D. Bruhn and Al Baeta

Distant Finish
David C. Bruhn and Jack Leydig

Enemy Waters:
Royal Navy, Royal Canadian Navy, Royal Norwegian Navy,
U.S. Navy, and Other Allied Mine Forces Battling the
Germans and Italians in World War II
Cdr. David D. Bruhn, USN (Retired)
and Lt. Cdr. Rob Hoole, RN (Retired)

Eyes of the Fleet:
The U.S. Navy's Seaplane Tenders and
Patrol Aircraft in World War II

Gators Offshore and Upriver:
The U.S. Navy's Amphibious Ships and Underwater Demolition Teams,
and Royal Australian Navy Clearance Divers in Vietnam

Guns Up, Depth Charges Readied:
U.S. Navy, Commonwealth, and Other Allied Escort Ships
Shepherding Convoys, and Battling German and Italian Air
and Naval Forces in the Mediterranean in World War II

Guns Up:
Naval Action in the Yellow Sea off Korea, 1950–1953

Home Waters:
Royal Navy, Royal Canadian Navy, and U.S. Navy
Mine Forces Battling U-Boats in World War I
Cdr. David D. Bruhn, USN (Retired)
and Lt. Cdr. Rob Hoole, RN (Retired)

Ingram's Fourth Fleet:
U.S. and Royal Navy Operations Against German Runners, Raiders,
and Submarines in the South Atlantic in World War II

Intercept:
The U.S. Navy's Intelligence-Gathering Ships
("Cold War Spy Fleet") 1961–1969, 1985–1989

Kissing Cousins:
U.S. Navy Wooden Minesweepers and Variants (YMS, PCS, AGS)
and USN and Royal Australian Navy Bomb and Mine Disposal
Personnel in the Pacific in World War II, 1944–1945

Land Yacht Seaward:
Building a Cozy Wooden Camper for a Small Truck

MacArthur and Halsey's "Pacific Island Hoppers":
The Forgotten Fleet of World War II

Support for the Fleet:
U.S. Navy and Royal Australian Navy Service
Force Ships That Served in Vietnam, 1965–1973

Toe the Mark

Turn into the Wind:
Volume I: US Navy and Royal Navy Light Fleet Aircraft Carriers
in World War II, and Contributions of the British Pacific Fleet

Turn into the Wind:
Volume II: US Navy, Royal Navy, Royal Australian Navy, and
Royal Canadian Navy Light Fleet Aircraft Carriers in the
Korean War and through End of Service, 1950–1982

War Bound from Stockton: U.S. Navy Ships from California's
Central Valley, In Harm's Way in Pacific Waters in World War II

We Are Sinking, Send Help!:
The U.S. Navy's Tugs and Salvage Ships in the African,
European, and Mediterranean Theaters in World War II

Wooden Ships and Iron Men:
The U.S. Navy's Coastal and Motor Minesweepers, 1941–1953

Wooden Ships and Iron Men:
The U.S. Navy's Coastal and Inshore Minesweepers, and
the Minecraft that Served in Vietnam, 1953–1976

Wooden Ships and Iron Men:
The U.S. Navy's Ocean Minesweepers, 1953–1994

Contents

Foreword by Commodore Hector Donohue AM RAN (Rtd)   xvii
Foreword by George H. S. Duddy   xxi
Acknowledgements   xxv
Preface   xxxi
1. USS *LSM(R)-193* Unscathed by Waves of Kamikaze Attacks   1
2. LSM Commissioning, Shakedown, Movement Forward   15
3. Leyte Landings   25
4. USS *LSM-20* Sunk, *LSM-23* Damaged by Kamikaze Aircraft   39
5. Landing Ship Lost, Others Damaged at Ormoc Bay   51
6. Luzon Operation: Mindoro Landings   61
7. Lingayen Operation   71
8. Subsidiary Landings at Zambales, Grande Island, and Nasugbu   89
9. Mariveles – Corregidor   99
10: 1st Filipino Regiment Landed at Catbalogan, Samar   109
11: Assault of Iwo Jima   113
12: Palawan Island Landings   125
13: Mindanao Island Landings   131
14: Operation VICTOR I Amphibious Landings   141
15: Assault Landing on Cebu's Central Eastern Coast   147
16: Assault and Occupation of Okinawa   155
17. Assault on Japanese-held Fort Drum   175
18. Invasions of Sadau and Tarakan Islands, Borneo   183
19. Invasion of Brunei Bay, Borneo   195
20. Invasion of Balikpapan, Borneo   203
Postscript: The RAN's Contribution to Amphibious Warfare   211
Appendices
  A. USS *LSM(R)-188* Casualties   227
  B. USS *LSM(R)-195* Casualties   229
  C. USS *LSM(R)-190* Casualties   231
  D. USS *LSM(R)-194* Casualties   233
  E. USS *LSM-135* Casualties   235
Bibliography/Chapter Notes   237
Index   259
About the Author   273

Photos and Sketches

Foreword-1: Comdr. R. S. Pearson, RAN   xvii
Foreword-2: Wave of landing craft leave HMAS *Manoora*   xviii
Foreword-3: Wounded being carried to the beach at Balikpapan   xx
Foreword-4: 7th Australian Division troops landing at Balikpapan   xx
Foreword-5: Ex-USS *LSM-47* in service as barge *Foss-162*   xxi
Foreword-6: *Arctic Snowbird II* at Tuktoyaktuk, NWT, Canada   xxiii
Acknowledgements-1: *LSM-51* landing troops on Fort Drum   xxv
Acknowledgements-2: Richard DeRosset at Veterans Museum   xxv
Acknowledgements-3: Seaman Richard DeRosset, USN   xxv
Acknowledgements-4: Cmdre Hector Donohue, AM RAN (Rtd.)   xxvii
Acknowledgements-5: George Duddy on board the MS *Volendam*   xxvii
Preface-1: Five LSTs and one LSM at Iwo Jima   xxxi
Preface-2: Naval Amphibious Forces Shoulder Patch   xxxii
Preface-3: Gen. Douglas MacArthur and Adm. Chester Nimitz   xxxiv
Preface-4: Destroyer USS *Monssen* firing her 5"/38 guns   xxxvii
Preface-5: Painting by James Turnbull of troops boarding craft   xxxviii
Preface-6: LCVPs heading for beach at Zamboanga, Mindanao   xxxix
Preface-7: Large infantry landing craft USS *LCI(L)-191* under way   xli
Preface-8: Echelons of LVTs (amtraks) carrying Marines   xlii
Preface-9: A DUKW amphibious truck bringing supplies ashore   xliii
Preface-10: Painting "Philippine Foreclosure" by James Turnbull   xliv
Preface-11: Drawing "The Wave Breaks on the Reef" by Kerr Eby   xliv
Preface-12: Drawing "Marine Fall Forward" by Kerr Eby   xlv
Preface-13: Drawing by Kerr Eby of a tank landing ship   xlvi
Preface-14: Painting "Dry Run" Target Drill by Reginald Marsh   xlvi
Preface-15: Painting "Suicide in Pairs" by James Turnbull   xlvii
Preface-16: Views of an LSM from different aspects   xlviii
Preface-17: Painting "Stern Anchor" by Reginald Marsh   l
Preface-18: An LSM(R) fires a salvo of 5-inch rockets   li
Preface-19: USS *LSM-132* unloading a road grader at Tsurimi, Japan   li
Preface-20: Sign alongside an Army constructed road at Oro Bay   lii
Preface-21: Reginald Marsh's painting "The Navy's Happy Medium"   liv
1-1: Hagushi anchorage and Yontan airfield on Okinawa   2
1-2: USS *LSM(R)-193* under way   4
1-3: Robert A. Studley and William D. Erwin with 40mm gun mount   5
1-4: Japanese "Kate" carrier attack bomber hit by anti-aircraft fire   6
1-5: Japanese "Jake II" Navy reconnaissance aircraft   7
1-6: Japanese "Betty II" Navy land attack plane   8
1-7: Japanese Navy "Zero" fighter launching from the carrier *Akagi*   8
1-8: Damage to USS *Hugh W. Hadley* following Kamikaze attacks   9

2-1: USS *LSM-126* and *LSM-127* at the Charleston Navy Yard   15
2-2: Painting by Reginald Marsh of LSTs and smaller LSMs   16
2-3: Aerial view of Key West, Florida   18
2-4: Aerial view of U.S. Naval Station Coco Solo, Panama   19
2-5: American sailors at a bar in Coco Solo on "Bottle Alley"   19
2-6: Neptune party held on board the aircraft carrier USS *Enterprise*   20
2-7: Shellback Certificate of Raymond Stone   21
2-8: U.S. Navy ships in Teavanui Harbor, Bora Bora   21
2-9: Shipping in the harbor at Noumea, New Caledonia   23
2-10: Ships in anchorage of Manus Island of the Admiralty Islands   24
3-1: Gen. MacArthur and Philippines president Sergio Osmena   25
3-2: USS *LSM-311* and other LSMs prepare to land at Leyte   26
3-3: Troops aboard an LSM cleaning the gun of a Sherman tank   31
3-4: USS *LSM-311* and other sister ships landing cargo at Leyte   32
3-5: Japanese Kamikaze pilot taxies his bomb-laden "Zero" fighter   34
4-1: USS *LSM-20* sinking in Surigao Straits   39
4-2: Eight LCIs nested together, location unknown   42
4-3: Japanese "Oscar" Army type 1 fighter   46
5-1: Rear Admirals Arthur D. Struble and Daniel E. Barbey   51
5-2: Destroyer conducting shore bombardment at Ormoc Bay   54
5-3: Wave of assault craft heads for the beach at Ormoc Bay   54
5-4: USS *LSM-318* afire in Ormoc Bay, Leyte   55
5-5: Japanese "Betty" Navy Type 1 land-based attack aircraft   56
5-6: Lockheed P-38 Lightning fighter aircraft   57
6-1: Light cruiser USS *Nashville* after being hit by a Kamikaze   63
6-2: A "Black Cat," PBY Catalina, over San Pedro Bay   64
6-3: USS *LST-738* burning after she was hit by a Kamikaze   66
6-4: Navy ships fighting fires on USS *LST-742*   67
7-1: Australian heavy cruiser HMAS *Australia* in Lingayen Gulf   74
7-2: Painting by James Turnbull of Navy LVT landing craft   76
7-3: Vehicle landing ship USS *Ozark* under way   77
7-4: U.S. Army DUKW amphibious truck on a Normandy beach   78
7-5: A Sherman M4 tank wading ashore from USS *LSM-168*   79
7-6: USS *LSM-127* beaching on Panay Island, Philippines   83
7-7: USS *LSM-219* offloading equipment   84
7-8: Japanese Shinyo explosive motorboat at Lingayen Gulf   87
8-1: Philippine Army members paddle out to meet U.S. forces   89
8-2: View over lower part of the north side of Grande Island   92
8-3: Aerial photo of the former U.S. Naval station at Olongapo   93
8-4: Piper Cub preparing to take off from the carrier USS *Ranger*   94
8-5: Sub-chaser USS *PC-1129* under way   96
8-6: Destroyer escort USS *Lough* at Hingham, Massachusetts   97

9-1: Japanese troops celebrate atop a U.S. Army coast defense gun 100
9-2: Painting by Dwight C. Shepler of U.S. Navy minesweepers 101
9-3: Minesweeper USS *YMS-48* in port 101
9-4: Destroyer USS *Hopewell* after hit by shore battery rounds 102
9-5: Light cruiser USS *Phoenix* shelling Corregidor 103
9-6: U.S. Coast Guard cutter *Ingram* at Navy Yard, South Carolina 104
9-7: USS *LSM-169* at Mariveles Bay after striking a mine 105
9-8: Rescue in Manila Bay of a sailor from USS *LSM-169* 106
9-9: Entrance to the Mariveles Naval Base, Bataan 108
10-1: Naturalization ceremony for 1st Filipino Battalion soldiers 111
11-1: Five LSTs and one LSM unloading cargo at Iwo Jima 113
11-2: American flag on Mount Suribachi, Iwo Jima 122
12-1: Destroyer USS *Drayton* (DD-366) shelling Palawan Island 125
13-1: Lt. Gen. Robert Eichelberger and Rear Adm. Forrest Royal 132
13-2: Heavily loaded LCMs in welldeck of USS *Rushmore* 133
13-3: Deck load of DUKWs and "J" boats on board *Rushmore* 133
13-4: Yard minesweeper USS *YMS-71* 135
13-5: LCI(L)s with troops approaching the beach at Zamboanga 136
13-6: Painting by Carlos Lopez of Navy commandos 136
13-7: Soldiers from *LCI(L)-771* wade ashore at Zamboanga 137
13-8: USS *LSM-138* and *LSM-18* unloading at Zamboanga 138
13-9: House between beaches at San Mateo Point, Zamboanga 138
13-10: Concrete pillbox near beach east of Baliwasan River 139
14-1: USS *PT-490* with General Douglas MacArthur aboard 141
14-2: Painting by James Turnbull of a Filipino guerrilla 144
14-3: Motor torpedo boat tender USS *Portunus* with PT boats 145
15-1: Americal Division troops on board USS *LST-1035* 148
15-2: Amphibious tractors (LTVs) approaching the beach 150
15-3: Landing craft (LCVPs) approach the Cebu invasion beach 151
15-4: Cebu invasion beach, three hours after the landing 151
15-5: A Sherman tank wades ashore from *LSM-168* 152
15-6: Japanese midget submarine beached in the southwest Pacific 153
16-1: USS *LSM(R)-188* after being damaged by a Japanese aircraft 162
16-2: Painting by Richard DeRosset of USS *YMS-311* 172
17-1: Fort Drum with battleship USS *New Jersey* in the background 175
17-2: El Fraile Island, circa 1909 178
17-3: 14-inch turret for Fort Drum, El Fraile Island 179
17-4: American soldiers embarked aboard USS *LSM-51* 181
17-5: Soldiers gaining access to Fort Drum from *LSM-51* 181
18-1: Lt. Frederick William McKittrick hoists an Australian flag 183
18-2: Troops of 2/4 Commando Squadron going ashore 186
18-3: USS *LSM-151* beaching at Sadau Island 186

18-4: Plane laying smoke off Tarakan Island   187
18-5: Engineers attach demolition charges to beach obstacles   187
18-6: Rear Adm. Russell S. Berkey, USN   188
18-7: Pre-landing naval bombardment of Tarakan Island   189
18-8: LSTs beached in gaps blown in obstacles   190
18-9: Folding assault boats in a South Australian factory   191
18-10: Royal Australian Engineers carrying an assault boat   191
18-11: Infantry landing ship HMAS *Westralia* at Sydney Harbour   192
19-1: General view of the Brunei Bay area, British North Borneo   195
19-2: Light cruiser HMAS *Hobart* guns laying down a barrage   197
19-3: Troops running from beached LCVPs through the surf   198
19-4: USS *LSM-203* and *LSM-68* unloading on beach   199
19-5: 2/17 Infantry Battalion members riding on a Matilda tank   201
19-6: The Sultan of Brunei, his wife, and Wing Commander Kay   202
20-1: Large infantry landing craft discharging troops   203
20-2: Offshore log barricade at low water   208
20-3: Anti-tank ditch and damaged concrete pillbox   209
20-4: Balikpapan Australian War Cemetery at Balikpapan   210
Postscript-1: Training at HMAS Assault   211
Postscript-2: Infantry landing ship HMAS *Westralia*   213
Postscript-3: Landing craft approaching Tanahmerah Bay   216
Postscript-4: HMAS *Kanimbla* and her landing craft   218
Postscript-5: HMAS *Manoora* at Morotai Island   219
Postscript-6: HMAS *Manoora* with LCVPs (Higgins boats)   221
Postscript-7: Troops debarking from HMAS *Kanimbla*   221
Postscript-8: Comdr. Alfred Victor Knight, RANR (S)   223

Maps and Diagrams

Preface-1: Diagram of an LCVP   xl
Preface-2: Diagram of an LCM(3)   xli
Preface-3: U.S. Navy Medium Landing Ship (LSM) drawings   xlix
1-1: Radar Picket Stations at Okinawa   1
1-2: Amphibious landings at Kerama Retto and Okinawa   11
2-1: Florida Keys extending southwest from the Florida mainland   18
2-2: Southwest Pacific   22
2-3: General MacArthur and Admiral Halsey's advancement   24
3-1: Philippine Islands   27
3-2: Landing schedule for LSMs *19*, *21*, and *257* at Red Beaches   30
3-3: Northern Attack Force landing beaches in Leyte Gulf   30
3-4: Southern Attack Force landing beaches in Leyte Gulf   36
4-1: Baybay on Leyte's central west coast   40

4-2: Position of ships and action during an enemy aircraft attack   43
4-3: Later position of ships   44
4-4: Cruising disposition before enemy attack   49
4-5: Disposition of ships after enemy plane attack   50
5-1: Central Philippine Islands   52
6-1: Philippine Islands   61
7-1: Landing beaches at Lingayen Gulf   72
7-2: Philippine Islands   74
8-1: Luzon Island and adjacent areas of the Philippines   90
8-2: Manila and surrounding area of southern Luzon Island   94
9-1: Minesweeping areas associated with U.S. landings at Mariveles   99
10-1: Central Philippine Islands   110
11-1: Portion of Southeast Asia and adjacent Central Pacific   114
11-2: Southern Japanese Islands   115
11-3: Iwo Jima landing beaches and day-by-day frontline positions   118
12-1: Southern Philippine Islands   126
12-2: Central east coast of Palawan Island   127
13-1: Zamboanga assault beaches   134
14-1: Sulu Archipelago, Philippines   142
14-2: Central Philippine Islands   143
15-1: Cebu Island   147
16-1: Southern area of Okinawa Island   155
17-1: Drawing of longitudinal section of Fort Drum, Manila Bay   179
18-1: Movement of Australian assault forces to Borneo   184
Postscript-1: Movement of Allied forces up the New Guinea coast   214
Postscript-2: Borneo   220

Foreword

The latter chapters of *Sandscrapers* relate to the Borneo Campaign where the LSM's interacted with the Royal Australian Navy (RAN). In this foreword I will provide a summary of an also little-known Australian unit, the RAN Beach Commandos, which was part of the Australian contribution to the Amphibious Forces deployed during that Campaign.

In December 1943, the RAN decided to raise a dedicated Naval Beach Commando Unit to work as an element of the Australian Army's two Beach Groups. These Groups were designed to support a division-sized amphibious landing and consisted of pioneers, engineers, transport, medical, military police and naval beach commandos. This composition enabled the Beach Group to manage the force flow through the beach landing site while concurrently maintaining it, establishing store dumps, supporting medical evacuations, handling prisoners of war, and resisting attack if necessary.

The first RAN Beach Commando Unit was formed in January 1944 followed by a further three units shortly afterwards. In November 1944 the four Beach Commando Units were grouped together as the RAN Beach Unit under Commander R. S. Pearson RAN.

Photo Foreword-1

Commander R. S. Pearson, RAN.
Australian War Memorial photograph 115568

Trained in assault techniques, Naval Beach Commando Units were responsible for controlling the waves of landing craft and transforming the confused landing area into an organized beachhead. A Beach Commando Unit consisted of some 20 officers and 150 sailors and included beachmasters, beach parties, a repair and recovery section, and a naval beach signals section. In addition to seamanship skills and boat and landing craft handling, these sailors also received infantry training that included patrolling, field engineering and demolitions. Landing with the first and second waves, the Beach Commandos conducted a quick reconnaissance of the area as they guided subsequent assault waves into shore and provided communications between the army units and the naval landing force.

The RAN Beach Commandos first saw action on 1 May 1945 during the assault on Tarakan Island off Borneo. Two RAN LSIs—infantry landing ships *Westralia* and *Manoora*—carried units of the 9th Australian Division as well as a Naval Beach Commando Unit under the command of Lieutenant Commander Bernard J. B. Morris, RANVR.

Photo Foreword-2

The second wave of the 2/48th Battalion AIF leaves HMAS *Manoora* in landing craft during the invasion of Tarakan, Borneo, on 1 May 1945. Australian War Memorial photograph 090812

The main invasion force landed before dawn on 1 May. The Beach Commandos landed with the first wave of each forward battalion. They carried out reconnaissance, marked beaches, established and maintained signal communications, organised and furthered the unloading of landing craft, salvaged craft that became stranded, and generally organised and conducted all the work on the beaches. The only RAN casualties during this operation were three beach commandos: two telegraphists were killed, and a signalman wounded when a Beach Control Point came under shellfire on 2 May. Lieutenant Commander Morris received the United States Bronze Star Award for his role in the Tarakan landings. This was the only award given to the RAN Beach Commandos.

In the next operation, the rest of 9th Division landed on Labuan Island and Brunei Bay in British North Borneo, commencing 10 June 1945. The Assault Group included a Beach Commando Unit, under the command of Lieutenant Commander Ron McKauge, DSC, RANVR. The main body of the assault group landed on Labuan Island, dubbed Brown Beach, while a smaller force, landed in Brunei Bay - White and Green Beaches, respectively. The selected beaches in Brunei were wide and sandy, much better suited to amphibious landings than those at Tarakan.

When the amphibious fleet departed, the Beach Commandos remained, employed in various duties including patrol and survey. They were withdrawn on 27 June through the Australian Beach Group Camp on Labuan Island.

The Beach Commandos' final action in World War II was during the Australian 7th Division's amphibious assault at Balikpapan on 1 July 1945. All three Australian LSIs, *Westralia*, *Manoora*, and *Kanimbla*, embarked two Beach Commando Units, under the command of the experienced Lieutenant Commander Morris. Three beaches, designated Red, Yellow and Green, were selected for the landing with advance parties from the two RAN Beach Commando Units landing with the second wave. When Morris came ashore 45 minutes after "H" hour, he noted that the Unit's beachmasters had "organised their beaches well" – the shore had been surveyed, exits marked, and the area was kept "comparatively clear" of stores and equipment. They had to work effectively. In the first hour after landing more than 16,500 men were ashore and nearly a thousand vehicles landed.

An article in the *Townsville Daily Bulletin* (Queensland) of 9 July 1954 by war correspondent Douglas Lockwood described their activities during the Borneo landings. He noted they were known as "gypsies" as they regarded themselves lost souls—they worked on the beaches with the army but had little contact with the navy. Lockwood went on to say: "Unprotected, on the fire-swept beaches, they directed all movement from the invasion fleet to the shore of men, tanks, guns, ammunition, food and supplies. During an amphibious landing against an unfortified position, beaches were usually pretty hot—the enemy naturally concentrated his artillery on the point of supply to the disembarked troops. And in the words of the Seventh Division Diggers in the landing at Balikpapan, the gypsies copped it."

Photo Foreword-3

Wounded being carried back to the beach dressing station at Balikpapan.
RAN beach commandos in background. Smoke is billowing over the beach from
oil tanks set on fire by the naval bombardment that pounded the Japanese defences.
Australian War Memorial photograph 111031

The Naval Beach Commando Units were disbanded shortly after the assault at Balikpapan and its men were reassigned throughout the RAN, many remaining in the South West Pacific Area. The RAN Beach Commandos at Balikpapan, and in the other Borneo operations, demonstrated that the beach commando concept devised by the Australians for joint and combined amphibious landings worked well. The Army embraced the Naval Beach Commandos and described their work as essential, being an "integral part of the beach group."

Photo Foreword-4

Balikpapan, Borneo, 1 July 1945: Troops of the
7th Australian Division landing at Balikpapan.
Australian War Memorial photograph 128283

Commodore Hector Donohue AM RAN (Rtd)

Foreword

Ex-USS *LSM-47* in commercial service as barge *Foss-162* (Foss Launch & Tug Co., Seattle, Washington). After World War II, dozens of this class of ship saw service on the Columbia River bordering the states of Oregon and Washington, and in Alaska. Several served on the coast of British Columbia, and one in the frigid north on the Canadian Arctic coast. Medium landing ships (LSMs) converted to lumber/timber barges were used for hauling wood products from remote locations over open waters. Some vessels employed in Alaska remained self-propelled, while others which plied the Columbia River were converted to tugs and barges for the grain trade.

My association with David Bruhn began over ten years ago. At the time he was interested in battles of former naval vessels, particularly wooden ones, while my main interest lay in their post-war deployment in the waters of British Columbia as civilian vessels. Over the years we have become colleagues and good friends. I have helped him with his books, editing, preparing forewords and even writing a chapter; while he was the driving force that encouraged me as an eighty-year-old, to set down my research and interest into marine transportation for the Canadian fur trade into a book and along with others helped me to prepare and publish it. My book *Called by the North, Extraordinary Adventures of the Fur Trade, Shipbuilders, Navigators and Traders in Northwestern Canada and Alaska* was published by Heritage Books Inc. in 2022.

LSM (MEDIUM LANDING SHIP) WAR SERVICE

The Allies could not have prosecuted let alone won WWII without the numerous classes of efficient landing ships and craft including LSMs (comprising thousands of vessels) which deposited their embarked soldiers with their equipment on distant shores to fight the enemy.

As evidenced by the late Tim Colton's numerous shipbuilding tables, hundreds of yards throughout North America produced these and other vessels used in the war. Even interior yards like the Pullman Standard Car Manufacturing Company's shipbuilding division on Lake Michigan cranked them out, all efforts amazingly organized and managed to the single goal.

Although appearing late in the war and only used in the Pacific, the 558 LSM and LSM(R) versatile vessels described in this book played a key role in the Philippine Islands Campaign and subsequent drive toward the Japanese home islands. In addition to putting troops ashore while under fire and Kamikaze attack, they and their larger cousins the LSTs brought bulldozers, graders and rollers for grading and compacting the landing fields needed to base aircraft to combat the Japanese and bomb their defences. During the Battle of Okinawa, Allied aircraft bombed the enemy homeland.

POST-WAR CIVILIAN SERVICE

The service of many former LSMs extended well beyond that spent sailing under the "Stars and Stripes." Demilitarized ships—functioning as forerunners of modern RO-RO (roll on, roll off) vessels—could put supplies from Seattle on remote Alaskan beaches. With their shallow drafts and powerful engines, they could also be used as river tugs for pushing grain barges on inland waterways such as the Columbia River. When their propulsion wore out, and stripped of superstructures and engines, they became readymade barges for hauling lumber and timber to distant ports and mills.

Such vessels were ready for use in helping reestablish civil economies that had been stripped of marine infrastructure during the war. Their availability at "fire sale" prices is what I referred to as a "Maritime War Dividend" in my 2016 Nauticapedia.ca article "Western Canada's Maritime War Dividend – Military Vessels Converted for Civilian Use." While the article is narrowly geographically focused, this same benefit extended to maritime nations around the world.

Photo Foreword-6

Arctic Snowbird II at Tuktoyaktuk, Northwest Territory, Canada, 1949.
NWT Archives/McCall family/N-2002-022-0375

A compelling employment of a former LSM was the three-year deployment of the *Arctic Snowbird II* to the western Arctic. Initially, privately-owned, she was purchased by the Canadian Government for service as a Royal Canadian Air Force vessel. Her role was to distribute supplies, mainly aviation gasoline, from 1948-1951.

Following WWII, heightened by the looming Cold War and the needs of Arctic surveillance and defence, the RCAF vigorously resumed their important activity of providing photography for mapping the vast Arctic regions, started before the war. In my book, I document the huge difficulty in supplying communities in Canada's western Arctic in the first half of the twentieth century.

The Air Force in their resumed project also experienced these difficulties, particularly as they were attempting to do all supply by air. It was reported at the time they were using five gallons to land one gallon of gas at their field locations. This statistic was reported, along with the larger story of how a former LSM was first used to alleviate the Air Force's problem in the 1948 article "The Voyage of the *Snowbird II*" by S.E. Alexander.

In a harsh, geographical area where there were no docks or landing facilities, the vessel's reinforced bottom, ramp and ability to land and retract from beaches was highly advantageous. What is particularly interesting to me is that the successful voyage of the *Snowbird II* was inspired by one related in my book. This was the seemingly improbable voyage, Arctic activities and return of the former rum runner *Audrey B.* between 1935 and 1939, by three trappers with little marine experience.

These men sailed her from Vancouver around Alaska and then as far east as Cambridge Bay, nosing their frail craft through ice-infested waters. Contracted to the Hudson's Bay Company after their supply vessel *Fort James* was crushed in the ice flows and sunk, they managed to get supplies through as far as Cambridge Bay and saved the area from privation. The return of the vessel to Vancouver in 1939 directly across the Pacific through a huge atmospheric depression is another remarkable chapter of the vessel's story.

In his usual role of searching out the stories of "less glamorous" ships, David has thoroughly described the important contributions of LSMs and their crews in World War II. Canada benefited greatly from the post-war availability, and acquisition of some of these great little amphibious ships for civilian maritime uses.

George H.S. Duddy P. Eng. Ret., White Rock, British Columbia

Acknowledgements

Photo Acknowledgements-1

USS *LSM-51* landing U.S. Army troops on Japanese-held Fort Drum in Manila Bay on the mission to recapture the American fortification.

Photo Acknowledgements-2

Photo Acknowledgements-3

Left: Richard DeRosset being honored at the San Diego Veterans Museum and Memorial Center.
Right: Seaman Richard DeRosset, USN
USS *Paul Revere* (APA-248) Western Pacific 1974 cruise book

I am greatly indebted to renowned maritime and aviation artist Richard DeRosset for the masterful painting which graces the cover of this book. The fine art depicts the medium landing ship USS *LSM-51* being held alongside Fort Drum in Manila Bay by LCVP landing craft ("Higgins boats"), as embarked U.S. Army troops leapt aboard the concrete American fortification from a makeshift wooden ramp hinged to and deployed (lowered into position) from the top of the ship's tower-shaped superstructure.

This special operation, involving mounting an assault on the Japanese-held American fort at the entrance to Manila Bay, is the subject of Chapter 17. A caption below the painting on the front cover explains to viewers that what appears to be a very crudely-built vessel is in fact, a U.S. Army fort (constructed in the early 1900s). After blasting away the top of the small islet, Army engineers built thick concrete walls circumscribing the shoreline of the islet, topped by a thick slab of concrete. This structure, after being fitted with gun turrets, resembled a battleship, albeit, an unsinkable one.

In the early 1970s during his naval service, Richard visited the, by then abandoned, decrepit Fort Drum. He described it as "very creepy," owing to the great damage wrought to it during World War II by precursor aircraft and naval bombardment, which was followed by intense fire that swept through the fort's interior after 3,000 gallons of a gasoline/diesel oil mixture was pumped into it, and ignited.

DeRosset has created over a thousand paintings and murals during his illustrious career, but this one had special meaning owing to his personal knowledge of Fort Drum. Much time spent at sea—first as a Navy "bluejacket," later as crewmember of the fishing boat *Petrel* which caught fire and sank seventy-five miles off the southern California coast, and subsequently master of the small merchant tanker MV *Pacific Trojan*—in conjunction with his considerable talent and extensive research for each painting, ensure authenticity of his superlative work.

Many thanks to Commodore Hector Donohue AM RAN (Retired), who has generously penned forewords and provided material for many of my books. He has shared valuable Royal Australian Navy-related material from his own published articles and books, and undertaken new research specifically to assist me, and my sometimes co-author Rob Hoole, a retired Royal Navy Mine Clearance Diving Officer.

Donohue began his career in the RAN in 1955 as a seaman officer and subsequently sub-specialized as a clearance diver and torpedo and anti-submarine officer. His service in the RAN included command of the destroyer escort HMAS *Yarra* and the guided missile frigate HMAS

Darwin. Ashore, he held a number of senior positions in Defence policy and force development prior to retirement in mid-1991.

Photo Acknowledgements-4

Commodore Hector Donohue, AM RAN (Rtd.)

Canadian George Duddy, a retired professional engineer and maritime expert who resides in British Columbia, with family lineage leading eastward across the Atlantic to the UK, and backward in history to the Royal Navy's age of sail, has served as content editor for nearly two dozen of my books. He has also kindly penned forewords for some of them, including this one.

Duddy authored *Called by the North: Extraordinary Adventures of the Fur Trade, Shipbuilders, Navigators and Traders in Northwestern Canada and Alaska* in 2022. Readers wanting to vicariously experience Canada's Great North in the early 1900s, may review the cover art and synopsis of his book on the following page.

More recently, George joined Rob Hoole and me in authoring *Rarely Idle: U.S. Navy Sub-chasers and Royal Navy Motor Launches and Canadian-built Drifters Combating German U-boats in World War I.* An overview of this book follows that of *Called by the North.*

Photo Acknowledgements-5

George Duddy in Glacier Bay aboard the MS *Volendam* during an Alaskan cruise in 2019. A contributor and U.S. Military & Naval Vessel Correspondent for Nauticapedia.ca Project, he is sporting an organization ballcap.

Following the collapse of whaling in Canadian western Arctic waters at the start of the 1900s, vessels facing the perilous voyage around the Alaskan Peninsula came in pursuit of Arctic fur trade. They came initially from the old whaling ports of California and settled locations in Alaska, but after 1914 also from Vancouver on Canada's west coast. The vessels included those owned — or in support of — large fur trading companies and also those of adventurers bent on making their fortunes in the rich trade. Arctic transportation was also provided by expansion of the existing Mackenzie River system from the interior of Canada through the Boreal Forest and Mackenzie Delta. This book provides a fascinating account of the ships, shipbuilders and navigators of these waterways, and how the Arctic fur trade, pioneered by American entrepreneurs, was finally taken over by the Hudson's Bay Company. Expanding eastward, the Company achieved many Arctic "firsts." In 1930 a relay of company vessels successfully made the first west to east transit of the Northwest Passage; and several fur trading posts developed into permanent northern settlements. These, and many other intriguing stories, are enriched through 193 photographs, maps and diagrams; appendices; a bibliography; and an index to full names, places, and subjects, all adding value to this unique work.

Called by the North

Extraordinary Adventures of the Fur Trade, Shipbuilders, Navigators and Traders in Northwestern Canada and Alaska

George H. S. Duddy

Rarely Idle

U.S. Navy Sub-chasers and Royal Navy Motor
Launches and Canadian-built Drifters
Combating German U-boats
in World War I

Cdr. David D. Bruhn, USN (Retired),
Lt. Cdr. Rob Hook, RN (Retired),
and George H. S. Duddy

During World War I, while the British and German battleship forces, and later an American one, kept each other "in check," German submarines waged war on Britain's merchant fleet, which before the war was the largest in the world. With the island nation needing not only to fight the war on an industrial scale, but also to feed its population, large numbers of anti-submarine vessels were desperately needed. The Admiralty, lacking sufficient naval units to conduct anti-submarine patrols off Britain's expansive coastlines, requisitioned, armed, and employed hundreds of fishing vessels in this role, or as minesweepers. Requiring many additional purpose-built ships and craft, the Royal Navy acquired 75- and 80-foot motor launches built in American and Canadian shipyards, and 86-foot Canadian-built Admiralty drifters; and was strengthened by U.S. Navy 110-foot sub-chasers dispatched to Europe. By war's end, 135 chasers were operating in European waters, based at the Azores; Plymouth, England; Queenstown, Ireland; Gibraltar; Brest, France; Corfu, Greece; and Murmansk, Russia. "Eagle boats" constructed by auto builder Henry Ford arrived at Murmansk after the war for duty following that of the sub-chasers. One hundred forty-three photographs, maps, and diagrams; appendices; and an index to full names, places, and subjects add value to this work.

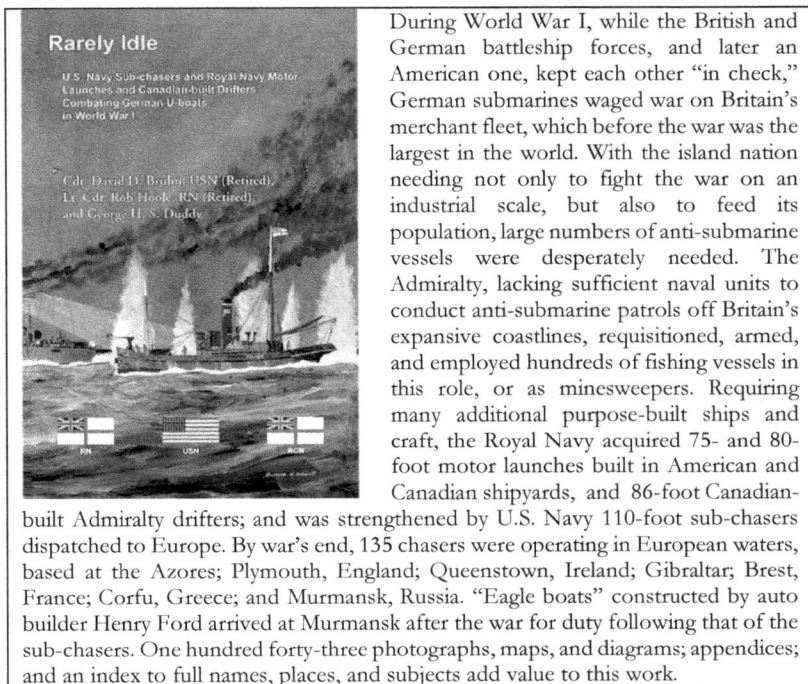

Finally, a tip of the hat and crisp salute to Lynn Marie Tosello, my stalwart, long-serving editor. She has joined me on many vicarious voyages on board a variety of relatively small ships that sailed the deep, and made my accounts of the important contributions of their crews much crisper, more eloquent, and more easily understood by readers who have not trod the pitching decks of steel or wooden vessels.

Preface

Of all the fighting forces of the Navy, one of the least understood are the Amphibious Forces. In a general way, of course, the public is aware that special craft, large and small, are designed to hit enemy beaches, disgorge their cargoes of men and material and then back off under their own power.... The Amphibious Forces are in a very real sense "the infantry of the Navy," with their personnel and equipment, along with their front-line duties, [they] form one of the "fightingest teams" afloat.

—Naval History and Heritage Command.[1]

Photo Preface-1

Five LSTs and one LSM nose into the dark sands of Beach Green One at Iwo Jima, with Mount Suribachi in the background, 24 February 1945. The landing ships are (from bottom to center): *LSM-264, LST-724, LST-760, LST-788, LST-808* (with an LCT embarked), and *LST-779* (carrying a pontoon causeway).
Naval History and Heritage Command photograph #NH 65314

Many, if not most, Americans of a certain age are familiar with the LSTs (tank landing ships) of World War II. Probably the most famous of the amphibious ships, they were an improved alternative to the assault ships, which primarily carried troops, later to be lowered in landing craft, a long operation, sometimes dangerous. Some may know that crewmen of these ships commonly referred to them as "large, slow targets," because they were large, ponderously slow and, normally carried tanks with assault troops. As such, they made inviting targets for enemy forces wanting to sink assault force capability at sea, not fight it ashore.

LSMs (medium landing ships) are much lesser known, perhaps because they came into the war relatively late and only in the Pacific Theater. Photos of 328-foot, 4,080-ton LSTs discharging their loads on hostile beaches frequently appeared in the press, while those of their smaller sisters, the 203-foot, 740-ton LSMs, rarely achieved this distinction. The preceding photograph of the five LSTs and one LSM beached at Iwo Jima, nicely illustrates the relative differences in their length, girth, and displacement. Details about the medium landing ships follow the next several pages devoted to an overview of amphibious warfare.

Before readers delve into this background information in advance of progressing into the text, a brief explanation of U.S. Navy ship designations may be in order. Acronyms are normally used to distinguish ship types and classes. For example, a modern guided missile cruiser is designated CG, meaning "cruiser, guided missile," but is referred to by sailors in conversation as guided-missile cruiser. Similarly, while "landing ship, medium" might be found in formal documents, LSMs were termed medium landing ships in the Fleet.

NAVAL AMPHIBIOUS FORCES "BADGE OF HONOR"

Photo Preface-2

Naval Amphibious Forces Shoulder Patch.
Naval History and Heritage Command #NHHC 2018.052.001

To distinguish them and in recognition of the critical and dangerous work of Naval Amphibious Forces in transporting soldiers and Marines to shore, often under heavy enemy fire, the Naval Amphibious Forces shoulder patch was authorized in June 1944. Similar in design and function to the shoulder insignia worn by Army and Marine Corps personnel, it identified sailors who wore it on the left shoulder of their uniform above their rating badge as a member of the Naval Amphibious Forces.

It was authorized to be to be worn by enlisted personnel who either:

- Completed training in amphibious warfare at bases of the Amphibious Training Command
- Were on duty with scouts and raiders, naval combat demolition units, beach jumpers, joint assault signal companies, beach battalions, standard landing craft units
- Or were serving aboard the vessels: Tank Landing Ship (LST), Medium Landing Ship (LSM), Support Landing Craft (LCS), Attack Cargo Ship (AKA), High Speed Transport (APD), Large Infantry Landing Ship [LCI(L)], Tank Landing Craft (LCT), Amphibious Command Ship (LCC), Attack Transport (APA), Large Support Landing Ship [LCS(L)(3)], Vehicle Landing Ship (LSV), Dock Landing Ship (LSD), Amphibious Force Flagship (AGC).

By the end of 1944, three more shoulder patches for other important units received official approval for display on naval uniforms. These were:

- Motor Torpedo Boat Personnel
- Minecraft Personnel
- Naval Construction Battalion Personnel (Seabees)

In January 1947, following the war and return to a peacetime Navy, the Sea Service revoked the authorization to wear the shoulder patches.

AMPHIBIOUS WARFARE IN THE PACIFIC

Because of the need to invade Europe and Africa by sea and the requirement to capture many islands and extend the war across many island groups in the Pacific, amphibious warfare came of age during World War II. Following the Battle of Midway and Guadalcanal Campaign, in which U.S. military commanders had to rapidly plan and execute combat operations to counter and push back the threat Japanese forces posed, the enemy was put on the strategic defensive. The lull provided by these victories enabled planners to utilize a deliberate and streamlined process for amphibious assault operations. Referred to by the acronym PERMA, the process involved sequential Planning, Embarkation, Rehearsal, Movement, and Assault.[2]

Following necessary planning for a particular operation, came the embarkation of combat troops in amphibious and transport ships, as well as the vehicles, ammunition, food, fuel, and other supplies necessary to support them ashore. The rehearsal phase was not always possible for the entire assault force before Assault Day because components of the force typically came together from different geographic locations. The final two components of PERMA were movement to the objective and the amphibious assault. The focus of this book is amphibious assaults late in the war when LSMs (medium landing craft) were involved. The first of these was the invasion of Leyte in December 1944 and the last one, the invasion of Borneo which began in May 1945.[3]

At the highest levels of command, Admiral Chester Nimitz and General Douglas MacArthur provided unity of command in their respective Pacific Ocean Areas and South West Pacific theaters, while their staffs focused on the details of amphibious planning efforts directed toward designated objectives.[4]

Photo Preface-3

General Douglas MacArthur, Supreme Commander, Allied Forces, Southwest Pacific Area (left), and Admiral Chester W. Nimitz, Commander in Chief, Pacific, and Pacific Ocean Areas (right), discuss Pacific war strategy at MacArthur's headquarters, Brisbane, Australia, 27 March 1944.
U.S. National Archives photograph #SC 190409

Specific amphibious landings were put in motion by the receipt by the designated commander of an Amphibious Task Force (CATF)—a Navy Admiral—of an initiating directive that tasked him to conduct an amphibious operation to seize an area, and provided him with the assets, command/control, and authority to carry out his responsibilities. Assets were often scarce and in direct competition between each theater, but normally they were sufficient to achieve a relative combat power advantage over the Japanese.[5]

The Commander of the Landing Force (CLF)—a Marine or Army General—determined his own concept of operations ashore and the associated requirement for shipping (vessels, troops, and cargos) that supported his scheme of maneuver ashore. Once the load plan was developed, forces were embarked in such a manner as to best support the planned landing ashore. The load plan was tested during the rehearsal phase to ensure that the ship-to-shore movement placed forces ashore in the proper sequence, at the correct time, and under the protective umbrella of supporting air/naval gunfire. A practice landing in a friendly area was followed by movement to the objective area and the actual assault.[6]

Amphibious planners using the PERMA process, and the forces carrying out and supporting the actual landings, built an ever-increasing reservoir of expertise. In association with and as a result of U.S. shipbuilding efforts as the war progressed, the landings became larger and more complex. During the Guadalcanal campaign in late 1942, the amphibious task force had 51 ships, a figure that was dwarfed by the 495 committed to Iwo Jima in early 1945.[7]

PREPARATORY ACTIONS / CONSIDERATIONS

Preliminary operations prior to an amphibious landing against serious opposition would likely include the following:

- Reconnaissance
- Seizure of a supporting base
- Operations against defending aircraft
- Operations against naval defense forces[8]

The selection of a particular date for an assault (D-Day or other letter designation), and the hour that day that landings were to commence (H-Hour), involved careful consideration of the probable effect of light and darkness, as modified by the expected meteorological conditions, and navigational considerations. The following conditions might influence the hour of landing:

- Prevailing winds
- Surf conditions
- Prevalence of fogs or mists
- Direction of the sun
- Phase of the moon
- Tides[9]

Night attacks were extremely difficult to execute and thus rarely attempted in amphibious warfare except under special conditions. Even if a night landing was contemplated, the bulk of the force would likely be landed shortly before or at daybreak so that the troops would have the benefit of light in conducting the operations on shore. For the more prevalent day landings, it was desirable to fix H-Hour early enough to allow sufficient daylight for the operations planned for the first day.[10]

Selection of the day and hour of landing involved consideration of a number of conflicting factors including the meteorological conditions, availability of own forces, and current enemy activities and/or suspected intentions. The weight given each of these factors varied widely according to the type of operation and the conditions existing in the theater of operations.[11]

PROTECTION AND DEFENSE OF THE AMPHIBIOUS TASK FORCE

Protective measures taken during movement of the amphibious task force to the objective, and during ship-to-shore movements to put the landing force ashore and support it, usually included the following:

- Minesweeping of the approaches to the landing beaches, naval gunfire support areas, transport ship areas, and other areas as directed
- UDT (Underwater Demolition Team) reconnaissance of landing beaches and offshore surf zone, and neutralization/ destruction of obstacles and explosives found
- Air Warfare
- Surface Warfare
- Anti-submarine Warfare

Allied offensive air, surface, and anti-submarine operations were conducted wherever possible to degrade enemy combat strength/ capabilities in the theater. Separately, combatant ships and aircraft off landing beaches or in the vicinity were charged with screening/

protecting the amphibious task force from enemy ship, submarine, and aircraft attacks.   In late 1944 through war's end, owing to the continued high attrition of Japanese forces and increased desperation of military leaders, piloted suicide aircraft, suicide swimmers, and human-steered suicide torpedoes, small boats, and bombs also posed threats.   The most widely employed were the famous Kamikaze aircraft.

ASSAULT LANDINGS (SCENARIOS)

Unless surprise was the prime consideration, following any necessary minesweeping and work by UDT teams, naval gunfire ships, rocket ships, and aircraft would conduct pre-landing naval bombardment of landing beach areas to destroy enemy defenses before the first wave of assault craft beached. The delivery of accurate, timely, and effective naval gunfire/air bombardment was essential for assaults against island defenses. Synchronizing and concentrating the delivery of this combat power required detailed coordination and extensive communication.[12]

Photo Preface-4

Destroyer USS *Monssen* (DD-798) firing her 5"/38 guns during support of an amphibious landing operation.
Naval History and Heritage Command photograph #S-090.03

Photo Preface-5

Painting by James Turnbull, 1945, of troops going down landing nets as they embark in landing craft from an APA (attack transport) preparatory to assault operations. Naval History and Heritage Command photograph #88-159-KJ

The landing boats were lowered from transport ships upon their arrival in the transport area. Boats which were rail-loaded (had everything aboard including troops) before launching and immediately departing for the rendezvous area where craft assembled in preparation for the run to the Line of Departure. A control boat, identified by the signal flag it flew, marked this position. LCVPs (personnel and vehicle landing craft) and LCMs (mechanized landing craft) which were lowered over the side of their AKA (attack cargo ship) or APA (attack transport) without assault personnel and cargo, hauled out to a designated assembly area near the transport area and formed assembly circles. From these positions they were summoned alongside other ships to embark troops (who descended ships' sides via landing nets to reach the boats), equipment, and supplies.[13]

ANDREW HIGGIN'S LANDING CRAFT

Andrew Higgins is the man who won the war for us. . . . If Higgins had not designed and built those LCVPs [Personnel and Vehicle Landing Craft], we never could have landed over an open beach. The whole strategy of the war would have been different.

—President Dwight D. Eisenhower, 1964 interview.

The famous Higgins LCVPs revolutionized military strategy. The boat's designer, Andrew Higgins—a fiery Irishman who drank whiskey like a fish and who had opined that the Navy "doesn't know one damn thing about small boats"—had attempted during the prewar years to convince the sea service of the need for small wooden boats. Once the war broke out, he was sure that the Navy would require thousands of small craft, and he also believed that steel would be in short supply. Accordingly, Higgins bought the entire 1939 crop of mahogany from the Philippines and stored it on his own. In 1941, he finally received a Navy contract to develop what would be the LCVP.[14]

The resultant 36-foot LCVP, commonly called "Higgin's boat," was designed to run through the surf to a beach, lower a ramp, unload men and cargo, back off, or retract, through the breakers and return to the transport or dock from which it started. The landing craft could hold a platoon of thirty-six fully equipped men or twelve men and a jeep, and its use allowed soldiers to storm open, less fortified beaches, instead of attacking well-defended ports. Waves of the boats could withstand punishing sea conditions, and still safely and rapidly deliver huge numbers of troops to the shoreline due to the numerous innovations that Higgins had incorporated in the design of the landing craft.[15]

Photo Preface-6

Loaded LCVPs heading for the beach at Zamboanga, Mindanao, 10 March 1945.
Naval History and Heritage Command photograph #80-G-308949

These included the use of durable veneer marine mahogany plywood—enabling the boats to absorb the stresses of pitching and rolling—and a solid pine log in the bow to allow collisions with objects without sustaining hull damage. A single 225-horsepower Gray diesel marine engine propelled the boat at speeds up to 12 knots, and a steel bow ramp protected passengers from gunfire and facilitated discharge of troops. In addition to being fitted with a rudder for normal movement, there was a second one forward of the propeller for backing, allowing the craft to quickly retract off hostile beaches and head for open water. The boats also had two .30-caliber machine guns, providing embarked troops a more robust means of self-defense than the personal weapons they carried.[16]

LARGER STEEL-HULLED LCM(3) LANDING CRAFT

Higgins Industries also built 50-foot, steel-hulled LCM(3) mechanized landing craft that were bigger and chunkier than the LCVPs. The LCM(3)—which other American manufacturers also produced— carried more troops and cargo, and had more power, but was more difficult to operate. Like the LCVP, it boasted speed, lightness, power, toughness, long cruising range, sizeable cargo capacity, maneuverability, armament, and simplicity.[17]

Diagram Preface-1

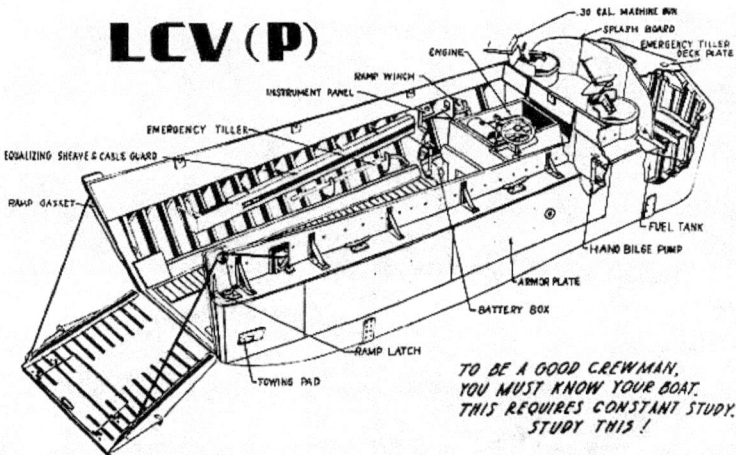

Diagram of an LCVP.
"Skill in the Surf A Landing Boat Manual February 1945."

Diagram Preface-2

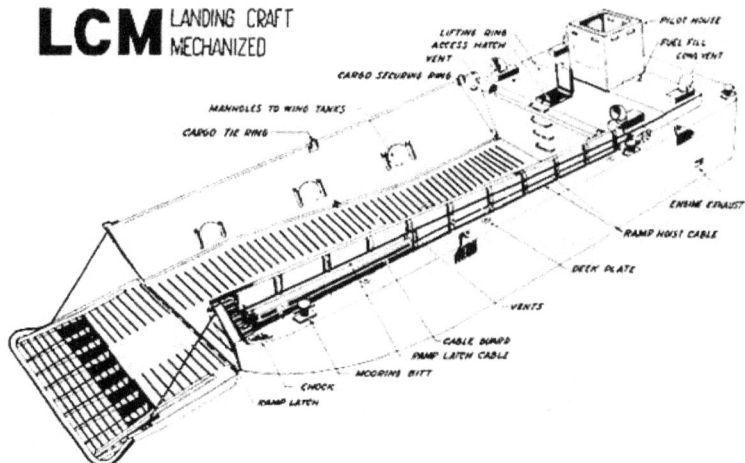

LCM LANDING CRAFT
MECHANIZED

Diagram of an LCM(3) (Landing Craft Mechanized).
"Skill in the Surf A Landing Boat Manual February 1945"

The two types of early landing craft described were joined later in the war by additional craft including:

- LCI(L) (large infantry landing craft)
- LVTs (tracked amphibious vehicles commonly referred to as "amtraks," "alligators" or "gators" for short)
- DUKWs (amphibious trucks also called ducks).

Photo Preface-7

USS *LCI(L)-191* under way in a harbor, probably on the U.S. East Coast, circa February-March 1943.
National Archives photograph #26-G-1605

The 158-foot LCI(L) was a large beaching craft intended to transport and deliver troops, typically a company of infantry or Marines, to a hostile shore once a beachhead was secured. These landing craft carried personnel, but could not transport vehicles. They typically had a crew of 24-60 sailors, and carried 200 troops, who descended from ramps on each side of the craft during landings. LCI(L)s were not originally designed for cross-ocean voyages, but did so out of necessity, sailing from shipyards in the United States to the European and Pacific Theaters propelled by two sets of quad General Motors 6-cylinder diesel engines (8 engines total).[18]

LCI(L)s, like other amphibious ships and craft, did not share the limelight with more glamorous aircraft carriers, battleships and destroyers. In fact, they earned the name "Waterbug Navy," when an admiral looking down from the bridgewing of his battleship and seeing the LCI(L)'s down below scurrying back and forth, commented that they looked like a bunch of waterbugs.[19]

Photo Preface-8

Echelons of LVTs (amtraks) carrying Marines churn their way ashore off Iwo Jima before crawling up the invasion beaches.
Naval History and Heritage Command photograph #NH 104223

A DUKW was a 2.5-ton six-wheel amphibious truck used by the U.S. Army and Marine Corps primarily to ferry ammunition, supplies, and equipment from supply ships in transport areas offshore to supply dumps and fighting units at the beach. DUKW was a manufacturer's code, with D indicating the model year, 1942; U referring to the body style, utility (amphibious); K for all-wheel drive; and W for dual rear axles. The vehicle was shaped like a boat. with a hollow airtight body for buoyancy and used a single propeller for forward momentum. At sea the vehicle could make a speed of 5 knots, and on land it could go 50 miles per hour.[20]

Photo Preface-9

A U.S. Army DUKW amphibious truck bringing supplies ashore on a Normandy beach, 11 June 1944.
National Archives photograph #80-G-252737

SHIP TO SHORE MOVEMENT

The assault schedule prescribed the formation, composition, and timing of boat waves landing over each beach. The times of landings were carefully coordinated within and between waves and with supporting naval gunfire because of the concentration of forces in limited space.[21]

Once loaded, the craft would rendezvous several miles off the landing beaches and form up into assault waves. When the control craft gave the appropriate signal, the assault waves would head for the beach and land their troops. After retracting, the craft would then return to their ship to pick up another load of personnel and equipment.[22]

Assault coxswains and their landing craft had to pound in through breakers crashing down on shore, then beach, unload, retract, and return successfully for another load. The embarked assault troops had to first make the beach without drowning or expiring under enemy fire, then hold their swath of sand against determined Japanese defense forces.

Photo Preface-10

Painting "Philippine Foreclosure" by James Turnbull, 1945. Following a pre-landing Navy aerial and gunfire barrage, infantrymen prepare to storm ashore at Luzon from Navy amtraks in Lingayen Gulf, Philippine Islands. Naval History and Heritage Command photograph #88-159-KT

Photo Preface-11

Drawing "The Wave Breaks on the Reef" by Kerr Eby, 1944, of an assault boat jarred to a halt by a hidden reef. The Marines embarked must abandon it, and wade ashore under a storm of fire from an enemy well-trained on this objective. Naval History and Heritage Command photograph #88-159-CL

Photo Preface-12

Drawing "Marine Fall Forward" by Kerr Eby, 1944. The road to victory in the Pacific was littered with the bodies of gallant fighting men, like this Marine (right center) who fell in the assault on a Tarawa pillbox (type of blockhouse, normally equipped with loopholes through which defenders can fire weapons).
Naval History and Heritage Command photograph #88-159-CM

On the heels of boat waves carrying the assault troops, came LSM and LST landings to discharge tanks, gasoline, ammunition, and other matériel required by the troops ashore trying to establish a beachhead. The medium landing ships usually landed before the tank landing ships, owing to their smaller size and shallower drafts (only six feet at the bow), which resulted in greater flexibility regarding where and when they beached. The highly maneuverable LSMs were adept at finding their way onto crowded shores amid wreckage and reefs. Their flat bottoms slipping across sand bars and beaches, yielded them the moniker "Sandscrapers." In two of the operations described in this book, LSMs were a part of the sixth wave in the first operation, along with LCI(L)s (large infantry landing craft), and comprised the entirety of the sixth wave in the second one.[23]

Of course, LSMs and LSTs carrying armored vehicles and troops were prime targets for enemy attack, yielding the previously mentioned nickname "large, slow targets" for LSTs. This reality provided plenty of motivation for the gun crews of landing ships to gain and maintain proficiency in the use of their anti-aircraft weapons.

Photo Preface-13

Drawing by Kerr Eby of a tank landing ship (LST) discharging tanks in World War II.
Naval History and Heritage Command photograph #88-159-CS

Photo Preface-14

Painting "Dry Run" Target Drill by Reginald Marsh, 1944, of the gun crew of
a 40mm mount aboard an LST conducting a drill involving no actual firing.
Naval History and Heritage Command photograph #88-159-HP

Photo Preface-15

Painting "Suicide in Pairs" by James Turnbull, 1945. Streaking down from a sullen flak-pocked sky, a Japanese Kamikaze suicide plane heads toward its target, a tank landing ship, already smoking and in wreckage from another enemy plane that crashed on its deck a few seconds before. This action occurred during the Philippines campaign. Naval History and Heritage Command photograph #88-159-KI

LSM MEDIUM LANDING SHIPS

Following the preceding several-page overview of the planning and execution of assault landings, and backdrop against which the LSMs operated in the Pacific in 1944-1945, greater detail is now provided about medium landing ships, the subject of *Sandscrapers*.

One of the challenges facing amphibious planners in the Pacific Theater was finding the optimum way to maximize the movement of men and machines onto sandy beaches. Each type of landing vessel— from small boats such as the LCVP, to larger LCI(L) (infantry landing craft) and LCT (tank landing craft), and much larger LSTs—had advantages and disadvantages. There remained in the Asia-Pacific campaign a need for a well-armed ship larger than a tank landing craft and smaller than a tank landing ship, specifically designed for operations in those waters, where beaches were shallower and distances greater than in the European theater.[24]

The result designers came up with, was a type of cross between the LST and the LCT, combining the seakeeping qualities of the former with the carrying capacity of the latter. The addition of LSMs to an amphibious force afforded greater flexibility by allowing the force (troops and mechanized equipment) to be pre-loaded at a port at a considerable distance from the objective.[25]

Photo Preface-16

Port and starboard sides of an LSM, and views from off the ship's starboard bow, and nearly dead ahead, of her doors open to discharge cargo down a ramp.
ONI 226 Allied Landing Crafts and Ships, 7 April 1944

The loading capacity of an LSM roughly corresponded to the requirements of a mechanized platoon. The ship's high bow housed doors similar to those on the LST, which opened to reveal a loading ramp on which jeeps, trucks, and tanks could drive directly from the ship's welldeck onto the beach. The ship's hull had nine athwartship bulkheads for added survivability and watertight integrity. When an LSM approached a beach, the stern anchor was dropped and its chain played out, helping her go straight into the beach. When she was ready to withdraw, the stern anchor was brought in, effectively retracting the ship from the beach without assistance.[26]

Diagram Preface-3

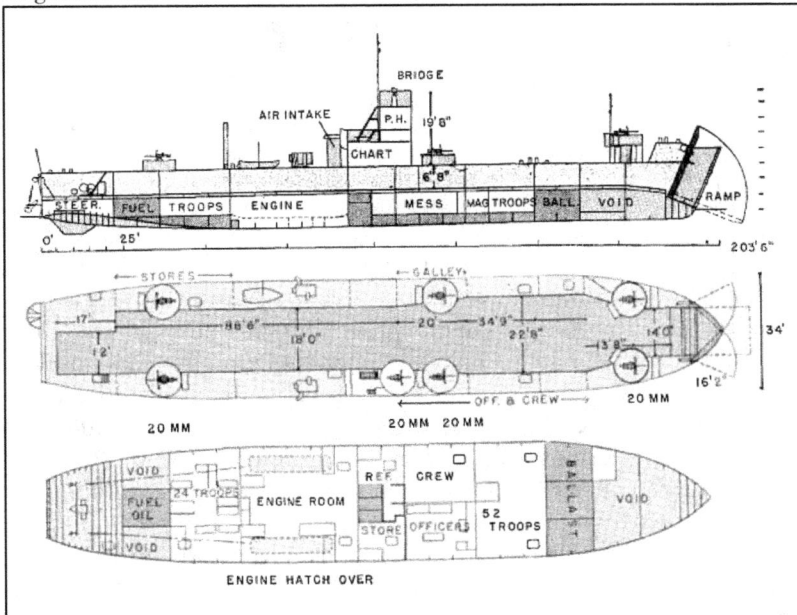

U.S. Navy Medium Landing Ship (LSM) drawings.
ONI 226 Allied Landing Crafts and Ships, 7 April 1944

LSMs, stretching 203 feet in length with a 35-foot beam, could carry five medium or three heavy tanks, or six tracked landing vehicles. Their open well deck made them suitable for loading by hand or derrick, and they offered a few bunks for landing force personnel. They were powered by two economical Fairbanks-Morse or General Motors diesel engines producing 2,800 hp, which yielded a top speed of more than 12 knots and a range of 4,900 miles.[27]

Photo Preface-17

Painting "Stern Anchor" by Reginald Marsh, 1944. The large anchor shown on the stern of an LST is dropped just before the ship lands on a beach to hold it in position while discharging its cargo, and to aid the ship in retracting from the shore. Naval History and Heritage Command photograph #88-159-HV

The first LSMs were armed with six 20mm guns. "Top brass" quickly determined that the ship's bow needed more firepower, and the forward 20mm mount was replaced by a 40mm one. A few ships, including *LSM-42*, had a single 40mm at the bow, but most boasted twin 40mms. The large gun barrels, housed in a gun tub, couldn't be trained down to repel small craft, so some crews added .50-caliber machine guns. Armor against small arms fire consisted of 10-lb STS (special treatment steel) splinter shields for gun mounts, with the same material installed on pilot house and conning station.[28]

Twelve LSMs modified to serve as rocket-launching platforms, and designated LSM(R)s saw combat in World War II. With a deck full of continuous-loading 5-inch (127mm) rocket launchers, as well as guns, they brought awesome firepower to later invasions, including Iwo Jima. Having so much explosive munitions topside also made them attractive targets to Kamikaze suicide aircraft.[29]

The first LSM was completed in April 1944 and soon, six shipyards were churning them out. About 528 were produced through to the end of the war. They were crewed by 50 enlisted men and 5 officers who were quickly but rigorously trained. Despite the large numbers of these ships, they were relatively unknown in the Fleet. Frequently, when entering a new port, they received a flashing light signal, querying, "what kind of ship is that?"[30]

Photo Preface-18

An LSM(R) fires a salvo of 5-inch rockets, during 1944-1945.
Naval History and Heritage Command photograph #NH 51436

Photo Preface-19

USS *LSM-132* unloading a road grader at Tsurimi, Japan, September 1945.
Courtesy of NavSource and the USS LSM / LSMR Association

Before leaving this introduction in our wake, delving into the text, and (vicariously) standing out to sea aboard an LSM/LSM(R), it is appropriate to provide an overview of Army structure in World War II.

U.S. FIELD ARMY STRUCTURE

Photo Preface-20

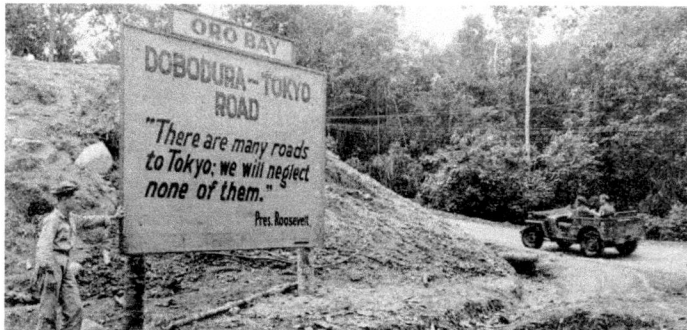

An engineer of the 116th Engineers surveys with pride the Army road consructed by his unit on the Oro Bay-Dobodura road at Oro Bay. William F. McCartney, *The Jungleers A History of the 41st Infantry Division* (Washington, D.C.: Infantry Journal Press, 1948).

Field Army
- U.S. Army's largest unit structure (50,000 and more soldiers)

Corps
- Operational unit of employment; comprised of 20,000-45,000 soldiers
- At least two divisions, maybe more
- One division is usually armored
- Divisions are attached (e.g., not permanently assigned)

Division
- The number of modular units is flexible; number of soldiers is 10,000-15,000
- Composition
  - Usually, three brigades or regiments
  - Three battalions of light artillery & one battalion of medium artillery
  - Division troops
    - HQ company
    - Engineer combat battalion
    - Medical battalion
    - Cavalry Reconnaissance troop

- Ordnance company
- Quartermaster company
- Signal company
- Military Police platoon

Regiment
- 2,000-5,000 soldiers, normally split among three to five battalions
- Armored cavalry and ranger forces are grouped into regiments, but are most often deployed in battalion size (rangers) or squadron size (armored cavalry) or smaller units

Infantry Regiment
- Authorized strength 3,118
  - Three infantry battalions
  - HQ & HQ company (regimental troops)
  - Anti-tank company
  - Cannon company
  - Service Company
  - Regimental medical detachment

Battalion
- Normally three companies (300-1,000 soldiers), but can have up to five companies
- Infantry: Authorized strength 860
  - Three rifle companies
  - HQ & HQ company (HHC)
  - Heavy weapons company
- Armored cavalry units are called squadrons rather than battalions

Company, Battery or Troop
- Normally three platoons (60-200 soldiers), but can have more. An artillery unit is called a battery and armored cavalry units are called troops
- Infantry: Authorized strength 193
  - Three rifle platoons

Platoon
- Three to four squads (18-50 soldiers)
- Infantry: Authorized strength 41
  - Three squads with small HQ

Squad
- Smallest unit, consisting of six to ten soldiers
- Infantry: Authorized strength twelve[31]

Photo Preface-21

Painting "The Navy's Happy Medium" by Reginald Marsh, 1944.
Naval History and Heritage Command photograph #88-159-HN

1

USS *LSM(R)-193* Unscathed by Waves of Kamikaze Attacks

Radar Picket duty on isolated stations 350 miles from the coast of JAPAN is decidedly hazardous duty.

These pickets are natural targets for enemy planes, both because they are isolated and because the enemy knows they are performing the vital function of fighter direction and early air warning. They have undoubtedly saved shipping and combatant types off the assault beaches from more severe air attack than has thus far been experienced. The picket stations have been maintained, but at considerable loss and damage to destroyer types.

—United States Fleet Headquarters of the Commander in Chief,
Battle Experience, Radar Pickets and Methods of Combating Suicide Attacks Off Okinawa March-May 1945 (Washington, D.C.: Navy Department), 10 July 1945.

Diagram 1-1

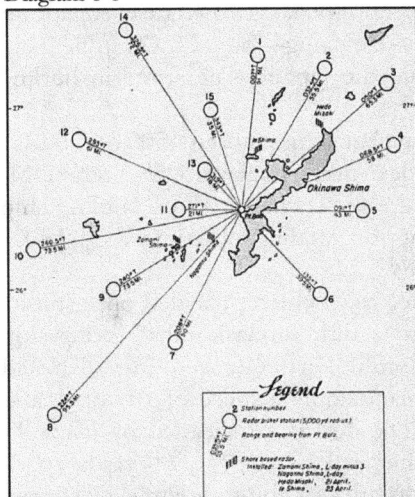

Radar Picket Stations at Okinawa
ComPhibsPac Op Plan A1-45

Photo 1-1

View of the Hagushi anchorage and Yontan airfield on Okinawa, on 3 April 1945, looking southeast from Zampa Misaki.
U.S. Navy photograph 80-G-339242

In early afternoon on 10 May 1945, the destroyers USS *Hugh W. Hadley* (DD-774) and USS *Evans* (DD-552) left the Hagushi anchorage on the west side of Okinawa, bound for Radar Picket Station #15 located to the north-northwest of Okinawa. The invasion of Okinawa on 1 April (the largest amphibious assault in the Pacific Theater of World War II), had launched the prolonged battle for its control then in progress, which would last until 22 June 1945. The last remnants of Japanese resistance on the island would end on the 21st, and the last two Kikusui suicide air attacks—small and relatively undamaging—on 21-22 June but meanwhile the battle continued and the Japanese persisted in hurling aerial attacks against the Allies.[1]

The destroyers arrived on the picket station about 1500 on 10 May and took over the duties from the destroyer minelayer USS *Smith* (DM-23). In support on that station were the rocket medium landing ship USS *LSM(R)-193*, and the large support landing craft USS *LCS(L)-82*, USS *LCS(L)-83*, and USS *LCS(L)-84*.

It being much safer to be under way, which provided opportunity to maneuver against attacking aircraft and "unmask guns" (bring ship weapons to bear on targets), the amphibious craft were in a diamond formation, 1,000 yards on a side, maintaining a speed of 10 knots, and reversing course every half hour. The destroyers, headed by *Hugh W. Hadley* and followed by *Evans* in her wake spaced 1,500 yards apart, circled the support formation at a distance of about one mile at a speed of 15 knots. *Hadley* was the picket station Fighter Director Ship and controlled a small Combat Air Patrol of fighter aircraft, and *Evans* the Fire Support Ship (tasked with naval gunfire support of *Hadley* and the other vessels).[2]

Some readers might now be asking themselves, "If the two DDs were assigned to protect the amphibious craft, how is it that these craft were considered supporting vessels?" If so, an explanation is in order, as well as greater detail about the importance of the radar picket stations off Okinawa, and the grave danger associated with assignment to one.

PICKET STATION VALUE / DEARTH OF IDEAL SHIPS

Facilities for early information of approaching enemy planes, and their interception by Combat Air Patrol (CAP) aircraft controlled by fighter direction ships, was critical to naval operations in Japanese waters and land operations on the islands under attack. To operate over a dozen advanced radar pickets off Okinawa required a sufficiency of properly equipped ships, adequately supported by other surface craft and covered by CAP for as much of the time as possible.[3]

During the Battle for Okinawa, it was necessary to station pickets at considerable distances (75 miles) from the center of the area in order to cover the most probable directions of approach of aircraft from enemy bases and at the same time to prevent approaching enemy planes from taking advantage of "land masking" (using adjacent smaller islands to hide their movements from radar detection).[4]

If only one or two picket stations had to be maintained, it might have been possible to provide the ship acting as radar picket and fighter director with a substantial number of other warships for mutual support—such as a division of destroyers with perhaps a light cruiser with anti-aircraft capability. However, the multitude of picket stations required and unavailability of sufficient ships precluded adoption of these ideal measures. Even with seemingly ideal support, substantial losses of destroyer types remained a distinct possibility.[5]

The alternative approach forced on the commanders was greater use of smaller vessels as pickets—the loss or damage of which could be more readily accepted than "higher value" destroyers. To provide an intense volume of fire against suicide planes, it was decided that the greatest possible number of 40mm gun mounts, controlled by latest types of directors, should be installed in these craft. This decision proved sound. During operations off Okinawa, many enemy aircraft were reported shot down by various kinds of small craft, particularly LCS(L)s and LCIs (large support landing craft and infantry landing craft), owing to the high rate of fire of their 40mm mounts against large number of enemy planes attacking in force.[6]

These considerations accounted for the assignment of the three LCS(L)s to Radar Picket Station #15, to add their fire power to that of the two destroyers.

USS LSM(R)-193 was a different story. Armed to the teeth, she could discharge a barrage of combined rocket/gun fire equal to that of several destroyers. An LSM(R) (landing ship, medium, rocket) was not actually a landing ship, because they did not land on the beach. Equipped with a bristling armament of guns and rockets, the function of these modified, landing craft was to lay off hostile shores and support amphibious operations with a pre-landing heavy barrage of fire against enemy troops/fortifications before the first assault wave hit the beach.[7]

However, these rockets, which could not be trained nor elevated rapidly enough, were ineffective against fast moving aircraft. Her rocket armament included six Mk 30 rocket launchers, swung inboard for loading, outboard for firing, which could be elevated manually at 5-degree intervals. At 17 degrees, 5-inch finned rockets had a range of 5,550 yards. Mounted inboard were four Mk 36 (modified Mk 4 aircraft rocket) launchers at a fixed 45-degree angle of elevation that also fired 5-inch rockets. It was *LSM(R)-193*'s naval guns that were desired on the radar picket station.

Photo 1-2

USS *LSM(R)-193* under way, location and date unknown.
U.S. Navy photograph

The LSM(R) was developed late in the war as a result of the Navy's search for a shallow-draft vessel capable of operating close inshore and providing heavy gunfire support and for shore bombardment with barrage rockets. At that time, there was a plentiful supply of 558 LSMs which could easily be converted for this purpose. During 1944 the Navy converted twelve LSMs into LSM(R)s by covering the well deck, sealing the bow doors, increasing the number of guns and adding rocket launchers. The following year, 1945, forty-eight additional LSMs were transformed into this class of rocket fire support ships.[8]

LSM(R)s were fitted with 10 rocket launchers, continuously fed and automatically fired, and aimed by remote control, each capable of firing 30 spin-stabilized rockets per minute, or 300 rockets per minute per ship. In addition, the rocket ships boasted one 5-inch 38-caliber dual-purpose gun, two twin 40mm AA guns, four twin 20mm AA guns, and four 4.2-inch mortars. They were equipped with directors for the 5-inch and anti-aircraft guns and the launchers, and fire control radar for the 5-inch guns.[9]

Photo 1-3

First Loader Robert A. Studley and Gun Trainer William D. Erwin pose with twin 40mm gun mount on board an unidentified ship during relaxed time at sea, early 1944. National Archives photograph #80-G-K-13850

The crew complement of an LSM(R) was 7 officers and 133 men. As is related in the following account, despite her impressive armament those assigned to USS *LSM(R)-193* were in harm's way at Okinawa—like every other Allied ship and craft in the battle. Two LSM(R)s were sunk during World War II, both in the Okinawa campaign. *LSM(R)-195* was lost a week earlier on 3 May to air attack, and the following day *LSM(R)-194* went down under the impact of an exploding suicide plane.[10]

INITIAL ENEMY ACTION ENCOUNTERED

Returning to the narrative of the action, that evening, 10 May, the crews of the ships on Radar Picket Station #15 went to General Quarters (battle stations) at sunset; this and sunrise being prime times to expect enemy air attacks. Vanishing sunlight at dusk and its scarcity at the crack of dawn, made it difficult for lookouts to visually detect attacking planes until very close at hand; but conversely often provided enemy pilots advantage by adequate, though dim views of ships silhouetted against the horizon. Thus, at these times, gun crews were "closed up" (at their battle stations), and repair parties, medical facilities, and other watch stations optimally manned in preparation to combat any fires and flooding, or personnel casualties, suffered as a result of enemy action. Thus, the ships were prepared at 1926, when a "Kate" attacked the formation. Both destroyers took it under fire, and the *Evans* reported seeing it destroyed.[11]

Photo 1-4

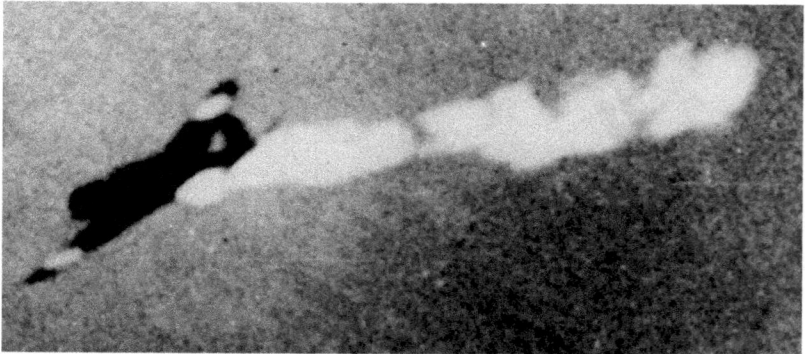

Japanese Kate (Nakajima B5N Navy Type 97 carrier attack bomber) hit by anti-aircraft fire during earlier action, late in the morning of 8 May 1942.
National Archives photograph #80-G-16638

Enemy action that night was light and spasmodic with very few alerts in the area and no planes sighted by the picket station ships since the previous evening. The following morning, 11 May, brought fair weather with low, scattered clouds, sunshine, and limited visibility. The sea was calm—almost a flat calm—with light and variable winds.[12]

At 0605, the Combat Air Patrol of twelve planes assigned to Picket #15 reported on station. Previously, after a picket reported a contact with enemy planes, control of all or part of those sections of CAP orbiting at a point nearest the contact was often shifted by the force fighter director to that picket for control of the planes. The picket then vectored planes to intercept. Interceptions were often made many miles distant of picket stations with the result that planes which evaded friendly fighters were able to attack the picket without further air opposition.   Subsequently, special protective CAPs operating much closer were assigned to cover pickets in particularly exposed stations.[13]

At 0755, *Hadley* and *Evans* opened fire at two low flying "bogies" (unknown aircraft) which had made an undetected approach from the north. *Hadley* "splashed" (shot down) one Jake (Aichi E13A Navy Type 0 reconnaissance seaplane), apparently scouting the location of Allied ships; the other enemy plane retired.[14]

Photo 1-5

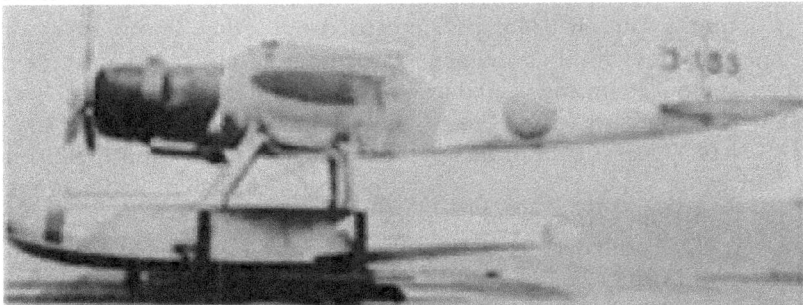

Japanese Jake II Navy reconnaissance aircraft.
Japanese Operational Aircraft "Know Your Enemy!"
CinCPac - CinCPOA Bulletin 105-45

SUCCEEDING WAVES OF ATTACKING PLANES

At 0832 the *Hadley* again began firing and reported bogies in the area. Two Bettys (Mitsubishi G4M Navy Type 1 land-based attack aircraft) were sighted by *LSM(R)-193* off each quarter of the ship (total four), at a distance of about 6,000 yards flying parallel to the formation. One made a low-level bomb run from the port quarter of *Evans*; but it was shot down and settled into the water. *LSM(R)-193* fired 5-inch anti-aircraft rounds, but observed no hits. The two planes to starboard retired without making a serious attack when taken under fire by the rocket ship's 5-inch and the 40mm guns of the LCS(L)s.[15]

Photo 1-6

Japanese Betty II Navy land attack plane.
Japanese Operational Aircraft "Know Your Enemy!"
CinCPac - CinCPOA Bulletin 105-45

Minutes later at 0845, a Kate carried out a dive bomb attack on *Evans*, missing with its ordnance. The plane did not try to crash dive. It instead pulled up and veered toward *LSM(R)-193*, which shot it down with 40mm and/or 5-inch fire.[16]

At 0847, two F4U Corsairs of the Combat Air Patrol appeared from cloud cover on the starboard bow of the rocket ship, and received friendly fire until recognized.[17]

At 0858, both destroyers began firing at two low flying planes from astern. *LSM(R)-193* also opened fire with 5-inch, but at 0859 shifted targets to a Kate attempting to gain altitude for a dive from starboard. Several 40mm and one 5-inch hit were observed before the damaged plane did a wing-over and spun into the water, barely missing *LCS(L)-84*. Lt. Donald E. Boynton, USNR, commanding officer of the rocket ship, believed that the pilot had intended crashing her in a suicide dive. *LCS(L)-83* then splashed a Hamp (Mitsubishi A6M Navy Type Zero carrier fighter) which was making an attack on her from dead astern.[18]

Photo 1-7

A Japanese Navy Zero fighter launching from the aircraft carrier *Akagi*, on its way to attack Pearl Harbor during the morning of 7 December 1941.
National Archives photograph #80-G-182252

ACTION TOO RAPID TO DOCUMENT ACCURATELY

At 0907 two bogies approached the DD's from their port side (Northeast), and one was sighted attacking this ship [LSM(R)-193] almost overhead. At this point so many enemy planes were in view that an accurate chronological narrative would be impossible. Several planes were driven off this ship by gunfire. The EVANS was hit by one suicide plane and began to slow down. One plane (HAMP) was blown to pieces by 5" and 40mm fire while diving on this ship from starboard at 0912. Shortly after this, three planes appeared to starboard. One was splashed by this ship at 0914 and the other two were splashed by LCS's, this ship assisting. During this melee one plane dived on the HADLEY apparently missing, but later information proved that this plane did considerable damage.

—Commanding Officer, USS *LSM(R) 193*, Action Report –
Battle of Okinawa 11 May 1945.

At 0914, an enemy plane followed by two F4Us was taken under fire by *LSM(R)-193* to port. This plane crashed into *Hadley*'s No. 4 40mm mount, causing fire and knocking her main engine out of commission.[19]

Photo 1-8

Damage to midship deckhouse of the destroyer USS *Hugh W. Hadley* following a third Kamikaze crash on her off Okinawa, and ensuing fire. This plane struck the base of her director tower (left center) and its bomb the No. 4 40mm mount (lower right). Destroyer Report: Gunfire, Bomb and Kamikaze Damage Including Losses in Action 17 October, 1941 to 15 August, 1945

RESCUE OF *HADLEY* SURVIVORS AND ASSISTANCE RENDERED TO ASSIST IN SAVING THE DESTROYER

Comdr. Baron J. Mullaney, USN, ordered *Hugh W. Hadley* abandoned, where upon *LSM(R)-193* and *LCS(L)-83* stood by to pick-up survivors, and subsequently rescued about eighty men. Since many of her crew, including wounded, were still aboard, the rocket ship then went alongside the destroyer to port at 0933. Lieutenant Boynton described subsequent actions undertaken to provide assistance:

> At this time *HADLEY* had a fire below decks apparently in the Engine Room and had lost all propulsion and electrical power except for the auxiliary diesel generators. Many minor explosions, apparently of 40mm ammunition were occurring. Transfer of wounded men and ship's records as well as intense fire fighting measures were undertaken immediately. Eleven hoses were put on the fire, the first at 0935. The wherry was put over to gather survivors. Also foam, fire axes, two handy billies [portable pumps], and three submersible pumps as well as several working parties to handle lines and help control damage. At 0944 *LCS 83* came alongside to starboard assisting in a similar manner.[20]

At 1024, with the fire aboard *Hadley* being put out and pumping operations to dewater the destroyer well underway, the rocket ship cast off and picked up approximately ninety-five additional survivors still in the water. Survivors were given dry clothing, and casualties cared for by *LSM(R)-193* and *Hadley*'s Pharmacist's Mates, and *Hadley*'s Medical Officer. Owing to the numbers of injured, it was necessary to organize medical treatment on a mass production basis, through the use of several additional crew members as well.[21]

HADLEY TAKEN UNDER TOW

At 1125, no survivors remained in the water and *LSM(R)-193* again went alongside *Hadley*, and made up to her in preparation for towing. All uninjured and slightly injured survivors were transferred back to the destroyer. Towing commenced at 1146 with the rocket ship made up to port and *LCS(L)-83* to starboard.[22]

LSM(R)-193 cast off at 1339, and prepared to take *Hadley* in tow astern. The rescue tug USS *ATR-14* came alongside *Hadley* to port to continue pumping operations. At 1401, the rocket ship commenced towing the destroyer astern with *ATR-14* and *LCS(L)-83* alongside *Hadley*. Upon receipt of instructions from *Hadley*, course was set for Kerama Retto. At 1652, *LCS(L)-83* cast off and *ATR-23* came alongside *Hadley* in her place. The transit continued at a towing speed of about six knots. At 1841, the *Hadley* arrived in the anchorage at Ie Shima. *LSM(R)-193* cast off the tow, leaving the tugs in charge, and proceeded to the Hagushi anchorage.[23]

Map 1-2

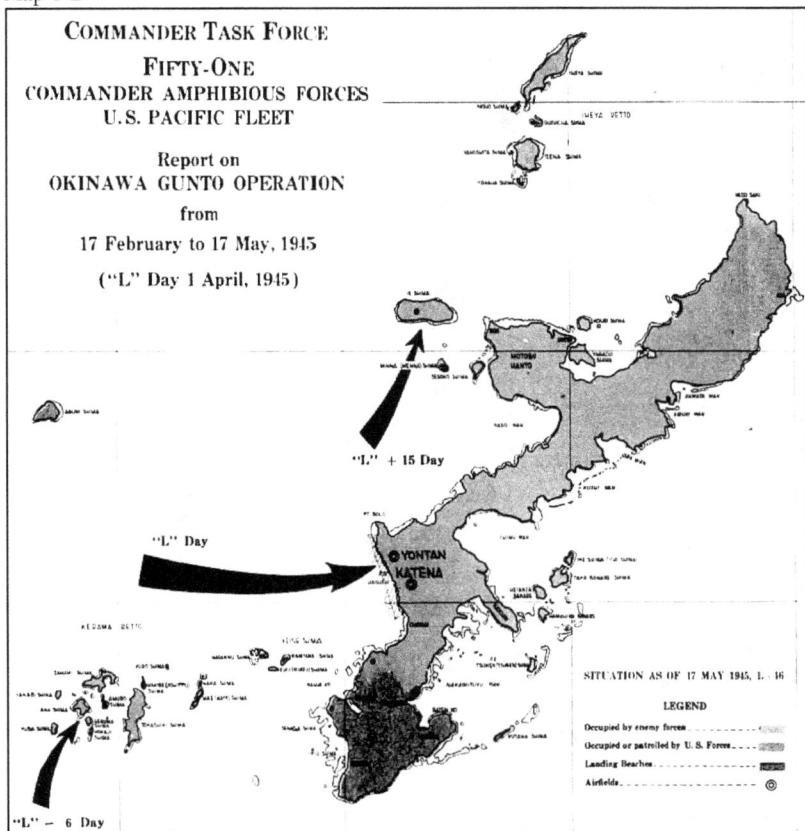

Amphibious landings at Kerama Retto (lower left of map) on 26 March 1945 preceded those at Okinawa to the northeast
Commander Amphibious Forces, U.S. Pacific Fleet, General Action Report, Capture of Okinawa Gunto, Phases I and II, 17 February 1945 to 17 May 1945 – Submission of, 25 July 1945

SHIPS / INDIVIDUALS ON PICKET STATION LAUDED

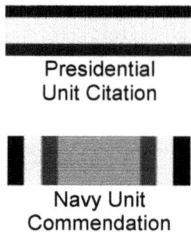

Presidential
Unit Citation

Navy Unit
Commendation

Navy Cross

Silver Star

Bronze Star

As summarized in the table, three of the six ships assigned to Picket Station #15 were awarded the Presidential Unit Citation (PUC) for the action on 11 May 1945. (The PUC is the highest award for heroism by a military unit, and the equivalent of the Navy Cross for an individual.) The other three ships received the Navy Unit Commendation.

Five of the ships' commanding officers were awarded the Navy Cross, Silver Star, or Bronze Star for heroism. The other commanding officer, Lt.(jg) John A. Naye, likely also received a personal award, but the author was unable to find any record of this action.

President Unit Citation	Navy Unit Commendation
USS *Evans* (DD-552)	USS *LCS(L)-82*
Cdr. Robert John Archer, USN	Lt. Peter G. Beierl, USN
Navy Cross (later Rear Adm.)	Bronze Star
USS *Hugh W. Hadley* (DD-774)	USS *LCS(L)-83*
Cdr. Baron Joseph Mullaney, USN	Lt. James Morris Faddis, USN
Navy Cross (later Rear Adm.)	Silver Star
USS *LSM(R)-193*	USS *LCS(L)-84*
Lt. Donald E. Boynton, USNR	Lt.(jg) John A. Naye, USNR
Silver Star	

USS *LCS(L)-82* previously received a Navy Unit Commendation for an action on 3 May 1945 off Okinawa, Ryukyu Islands.

HUGH W. HADLEY'S PRESIDENTIAL UNIT CITATION

The grave and prolonged danger the six ships faced on 11 May 1945, associated with multiple attacks made against them by groups of Japanese Kamikaze and conventional aircraft, is succinctly described in the citation for the PUC awarded to the destroyer USS *Hugh W. Hadley*.

> The President of the United States takes pleasure in presenting the PRESIDENTIAL UNIT CITATION to the UNITED STATES SHIP USS *HUGH W. HADLEY* (DD-774) for service as set forth in the following CITATION:

For extraordinary heroism in action as Fighter Direction Ship on Radar Picket Station Number 15 during an attack by approximately 100 enemy Japanese planes, forty miles northwest of the Okinawa Transport Area, May 11, 1945. Fighting valiantly against waves of hostile suicide and dive-bombing planes plunging toward her from all directions, the U.S.S. *HUGH HADLEY* sent up relentless barrages of antiaircraft fire during one of the most furious air-sea battles of the war. Repeatedly finding her targets, she destroyed twenty enemy planes, skillfully directed her Combat Air Patrol in shooting down at least forty others and, by her vigilance and superb battle readiness, avoided damage to herself until subjected to a coordinated attack by ten Japanese planes. Assisting in the destruction of all ten of these, she was crashed by one bomb and three suicide planes with devastating effect. With all engineering spaces flooded and with a fire raging amidships, the gallant officers and men of the *HUGH W. HADLEY* fought desperately against almost insurmountable odds and, by their indomitable determination, fortitude and skill, brought the damage under control, enabling their ship to be towed to port and saved. Her brilliant performance in this action reflects the highest credit upon the *HUGH W. HADLEY* and the United States Naval Service.

The citation for Lt. Donald Boynton's, USNR, Silver Star similarly describes the actions of his rocket-equipped medium landing ship, and her crew, in the combat action that day:

The President of the United States of America takes pleasure in presenting the Silver Star to Lieutenant Donald E. Boynton, United States Naval Reserve, for conspicuous gallantry and intrepidity in action on 11 May 1945, as Commanding officer of the U.S.S. *LSM-193*, a close-in fire support ship, during the assault on Okinawa Shima. During an extended air attack by a large force of enemy suicide planes, he, with exceptional skill and courage caused his ship to deliver such accurate and effective anti-aircraft fire that three of the attacking planes were shot down and five others were damaged. After a friendly ship had been hit by a suicide plane and raging fires ensued, he demonstrated outstanding seamanship and valor, in the face of exploding ammunition, by coming alongside the stricken vessel, extinguishing the fires and towing it to a place of safety. By his exceptional coolness under fire and devotion to duty, he contributed materially in saving the stricken ship and the rescuing of numerous survivors. His courage and conduct throughout were in keeping with the highest traditions of the United States Naval Service.

LSM Commissioning, Shakedown, Movement Forward to the Pacific

Photo 2-1

USS *LSM-126* and *LSM-127* ready for launching, at the Charleston Navy Yard, South Carolina, 15 March 1944.
National Archives photograph #80-G-K-14465

In 1944, as construction of Medium Landing Ships (LSMs) was completed at the six American shipyards listed below, they were commissioned, outfitted, fueled, and supplied before leaving for a "shake down" period to identify any construction or equipment deficiencies. Shake downs also provided necessary and valuable training for their newly formed, relatively inexperienced crews.

- Brown Shipbuilding, Houston, Texas
- Charleston Naval Shipyard, Charleston, South Carolina
- Dravo Corporation, Wilmington, Delaware
- Western Pipe, San Pedro, California
- Federal Shipbuilding, Newark, New Jersey
- Pullman Std. Car, Chicago, Illinois

The experience/schedules of USS *LSMs 138* and *139*, commanded by Lt. Merle Prinkey and Lt. James H. Decker, respectively, were representative of that of sister ships. *LSM-138* was commissioned at the Charleston Navy Yard in the early afternoon on 10 June 1944. She, joined by *LSM-139*, passed out of Charleston Harbor six days later on the evening of 16 June, bound for Little Creek, Virginia.[1]

Arriving at the Amphibious Training Center, Little Creek, on the 18th, *LSM-138* undertook a thirteen-day shakedown period. Following completion of this assessment and training on 1 July, the medium landing ship reported to the Norfolk Navy Yard, St. Helena Branch, at Norfolk, Virginia, for repairs and alterations.[2]

Photo 2-2

Painting by Reginald Marsh, 1944, of LSTs (tank landing ships) and their smaller sisters, LSMs (medium landing ships) maneuvering off Amphibious Training Base, Little Creek, Virginia, as their officers and crews learn the ropes of landing operations. Navy History and Heritage Command photograph #88-159-HU

The preceding period had consisted of independent shakedown operations, followed by group shakedown operations. During the latter portion, *LSM-138* conducted anti-aircraft firing practice in the Chesapeake area in company with LSMs *139*, *144*, *145*, *257*, and *258*, using an aircraft-towed sleeve target. The following day, the same ships participated in surface firing practice, with the same guns they had used for the anti-aircraft practice.[3]

On 1 July, *LSM-139* was conducting power runs at sea; first two hours at full speed (720 rpm), followed by two hours at flank speed (795 rpm). *LSM-139* moored at Pier Two, St. Helena, the next day to undergo various Navy Yard work orders. On 8 July, she left the yard and moored at Imperial Docks, Berkeley, Virginia, for two days before getting under way on the 10th for Craney Island flats, where her magnetic compasses were compensated (adjusted). Craney Island is a point of land in the city of Portsmouth, near Norfolk in the South Hampton Roads region of eastern Virginia. She also received fuel oil before returning to Imperial Docks to obtain lubricating oil and fog oil for smoke generators that were used to shield ships from view during enemy aircraft attacks.[4]

On 12 July, *LSM-139* returned to St. Helena, Pier Three, for armament alterations. This work involved removing No. 1 and No. 2 20mm guns forward, and replacing them with one 40mm gun, and its associated mount and magazine. Other work orders in progress included a recirculating system for the ship's generators. Upon completion of all work, the medium landing ship returned to Imperial Docks on 20 July, to onload ammunition.[5]

BOUND FOR DUTY WITH PACIFIC FLEET

On 29 July, *LSM-138* left the Norfolk Navy Yard at 1235, her repairs and alterations completed. In company with *LSM-259*, she proceeded out Hampton Roads, then down the eastern seaboard of the United States for Key West, Florida. Key West, the westernmost island in the Florida Keys connected by highway to the Florida mainland, has a total land area of 4.2 square miles. It and most of the rest of the Keys are on the defined dividing line between the Atlantic and Gulf of Mexico.[6]

Map 2-1

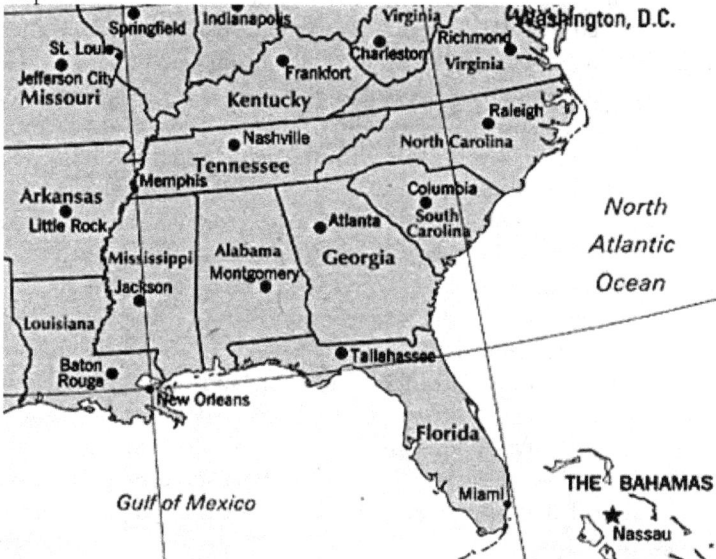

The Florida Keys (curved line in sea below Miami), extending southwest from the Florida mainland, form the northern boundary of the Florida Straits which separate Florida and the island nation of Cuba.

Photo 2-3

Aerial view of Key West, Florida, circa May 1960, showing the Naval Air Station in the right distance. The Naval Station is in the lower center.
Naval History and Heritage Command photograph #NH 93210

The two LSMs arrived at Key West on 2 August. Per orders from Port Director, Key West, *LSM-138* left the harbor on 4 August, setting course for Coco Solo, on the Atlantic (northwest) side of the Panama Canal Zone. They arrived there four days later on the 8th.[7]

Photo 2-4

View of the U.S. Naval Station Coco Solo, Panama, in 1941.
Naval Aviation News July 1964

Photo 2-5

Group of American sailors at a bar in Coco Solo on "Bottle Alley," circa 1946-1948.
Naval History and Heritage Command photograph #2017.38

On 13 August, after receiving voyage repairs, fuel, and stores, *LSM-138* departed Coco Solo for the long voyage via the Panama Canal to Bora Bora in the Society Islands. Five days later after exiting the canal on the evening of 18 August, she crossed the equator heading south. Having but a single shellback aboard, the burden of carrying out the time-honored initiation fell to him alone.   However, the proper ceremony was conducted and all of the ship's company was accepted into the "Solemn Mysteries of the Ancient Order of the Deep."[8]

Photo 2-6

Neptune party held on board the aircraft carrier USS *Enterprise* (CV-6) in 1938. A few of the Royal Bears are at work trying to get as much salt water as possible into the "Pollywogs" systems before they emerge to run a gauntlet of Royal Cops and Royal Detectives, equipped with various forms of blackjacks and paddles to leave one last imprint on the thoroughly miserable Pollywogs before they emerge with the title "Shellback."
Naval History and Heritage Command photograph #NH 54240

Photo 2-7

Shellback Certificate of Raymond Stone earned on board USS *Solace*, September 1908.
Naval History and Heritage Command photograph #NH 115398

Following the Shellback Initiation, *LSM-138* continued her voyage westward across the Pacific.   In the early morning on 28 August, landfall was sighted on the Society Islands.   That afternoon, the medium landing ship entered the harbor at Bora Bora.[9]

Photo 2-8

U.S. Navy ships in Teavanui Harbor, Bora Bora, in February 1942.
National Archives photograph #80-G-K-1117

The following day, after fueling and loading 100 tons of Quonset huts, *LSM-138* left Bora Bora on 29 August with orders to proceed to Noumea, capital city of the French colony of New Caledonia. Bora Bora was the midway point for shipping destined for Australia. Leaving there, vessels passed through or close to a number of the South Pacific Island groups in which the Allies had established bases. First came the Cook Islands, then the Samoa, Tonga, and Fiji groups. Finally, a thousand miles or so from the Australian coast, she entered the New Hebrides group and New Caledonia that formed the eastern rim of the Coral Sea.[10]

Map 2-2

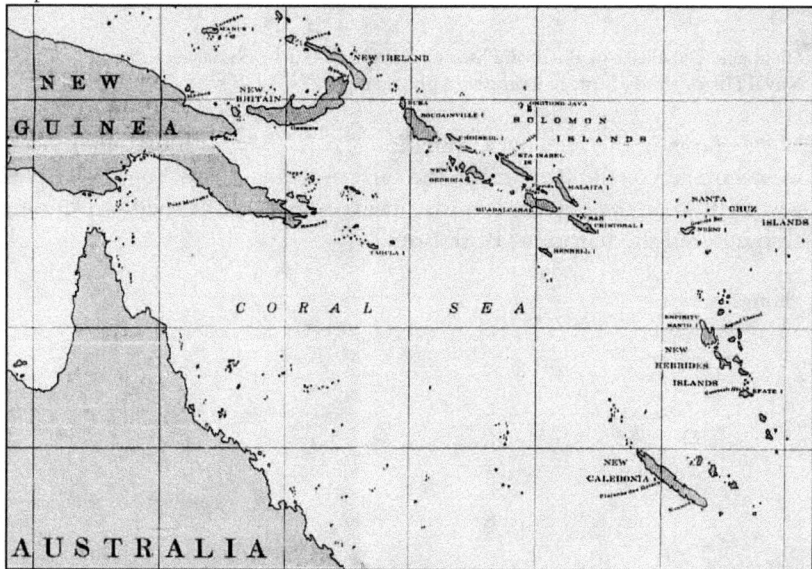

Southwest Pacific
Combat Narratives, Solomon Islands Campaign: I, The Landing in the Solomons 7-8 August 1942 (Washington DC: Office of Naval Intelligence, 1943)

New Caledonia marked the end of the island-protected portion of the Australian shipping lane across the Pacific; from the French colony westward to Australia there was nothing but the open Coral Sea.

On the evening of 7 September, *LSM-138* arrived at Noumea, the capital city of New Caledonia, anchoring offshore. Voyage repairs were completed the following day. After unloading the ship, which took until 14 September, a cargo of Army vehicles was taken aboard. On the 16th, after three officers and thirty-nine men of the 13th Air Depot Group, U.S. Army, embarked as passengers, *LSM-138* stood out of Noumea

Harbor. She, and *LSM-311* sailing in company, were not bound for
Australia. They set a north-northwest course for Manus Island in the
Admiralties.[11]

Photo 2-9

Shipping in the harbor at Noumea, New Caledonia, 1942.
National Archives photograph #80-G-K-948

Allied forces control of the Admiralty Islands, which are located off
the northeast coast of New Guinea and were a crucial staging point on
Gen. Douglas MacArthur's "road back to the Philippines," had come at
a high cost. Earlier in the war after defending Port Moresby, Papua,
from a Japanese invasion, and establishing a base at Milne Bay,
MacArthur's Australian and American forces advanced northwestward
up the east coast of Papua and New Guinea against Japanese opposition,
while concurrently Adm. William Halsey's forces moved northwestward
up the Solomons to Green Island (on the northwest edge of the
Solomon Island chain, not shown on the following map) and Emirau
Island in the Bismarck Archipelago (upper right of map).

Map 2-3

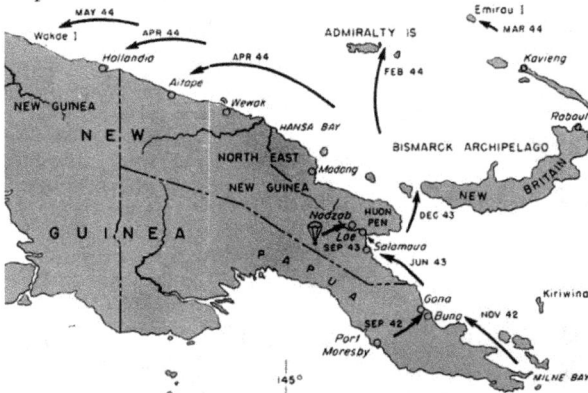

General MacArthur and Admiral Halsey's advancement

Photo 2-10

Escort carriers and other ships of the U.S. Pacific Fleet lying in the huge
anchorage of Manus Island of the Admiralty Islands, circa September 1944.
Naval History and Heritage Command photograph #NH 58404

In mid-afternoon on 23 September, *LSM-138* entered Seeadler
Harbor on the northeast coast of Manus Island, reporting for duty with
LSM Group Four under Lt. Comdr. Reginald C. Johnson, USN. Later
she unloaded her Army cargo on Red Beach, Los Negros, Admiralties
on the 29th. On 8 October, *LSM-138* took aboard mobile cargo and
personnel of the 1st Cavalry Division, U.S. Army for transport to White
Beach, Leyte, Philippine Islands. Three days later, she sailed on 11
October 1944, as a member of Task Group 78.1 under the command of
Rear Adm. Daniel E. Barbey, USN, bound for Leyte to participate in
the initial assault on that island.[12]

3

Leyte Landings

The suffering, humiliation and mental torture that you have endured since the barbarous, unprovoked and treacherous attack upon the Philippines nearly three long years ago have aroused in the hearts of the American people a righteous anger, a stern determination to punish the guilty and a fixed resolve to restore peace and order and decency to an outraged world...

On this occasion of the return of General MacArthur to Philippine soil with our airmen, our soldiers and our sailors, we renew our pledge. We and our Philippine brothers in arms – with the help of Almighty God – will drive out the invader; we will destroy his power to wage war again, and we will restore a world of dignity and freedom – a world of confidence and honesty and peace.

—Excepts from a message by President Franklin D. Roosevelt to President Osmena for the Philippine people, October 20, 1944.

Photo 3-1

Gen. Douglas MacArthur and Philippine president Sergio Osmena in a landing craft on their way to ceremonies proclaiming the liberation of Leyte, 23 October 1944. National Archives photograph #80-G-289537

Newcomers in the amphibious set-up were the Landing Ship, Medium (LSM), 203 feet long, 900 tons, which had the vehicle capability of an LCT [tank landing craft] but was faster, more seaworthy and comfortable. They had bow ramps like the LSTs, and were distinguished by conning towers resembling the turret of a medieval castle.

—Samuel Eliot Morison in *Leyte June 1944-January 1945*, describing the use of medium landing ships (LSMs) during the Leyte landings that initiated the Allied Invasion of the Philippines.[1]

Photo 3-2

USS *LSM-311* and other LSMs prepare to land on the beach at Leyte, 20 October 1944. National Archives photograph #80-G-59511

The landing of the American invasion forces on Leyte on 20 October 1944 brought to fruition the long-cherished desire of Gen. Douglas MacArthur to return to the Philippine Islands and avenge their humiliating conquest by the Japanese in the early days of World War II.

General MacArthur, Supreme Commander Southwest Pacific Area since 1942, commanded all ground forces, some air forces and the U.S. Seventh Fleet for the operation. Under him were Vice Adm. Thomas C. Kinkaid (commander, U.S. Seventh Fleet), commander, Philippines Attack Force; and Lt. Gen. Walter Krueger (commanding general, U.S. Sixth Army), commander, Expeditionary Force. Under Vice Admiral

Kinkaid were two attack forces: the Northern, to land at Tacloban; and the Southern, to land at Dulag—both on the western shore of Leyte Gulf (center on the map).[2]

Map 3-1

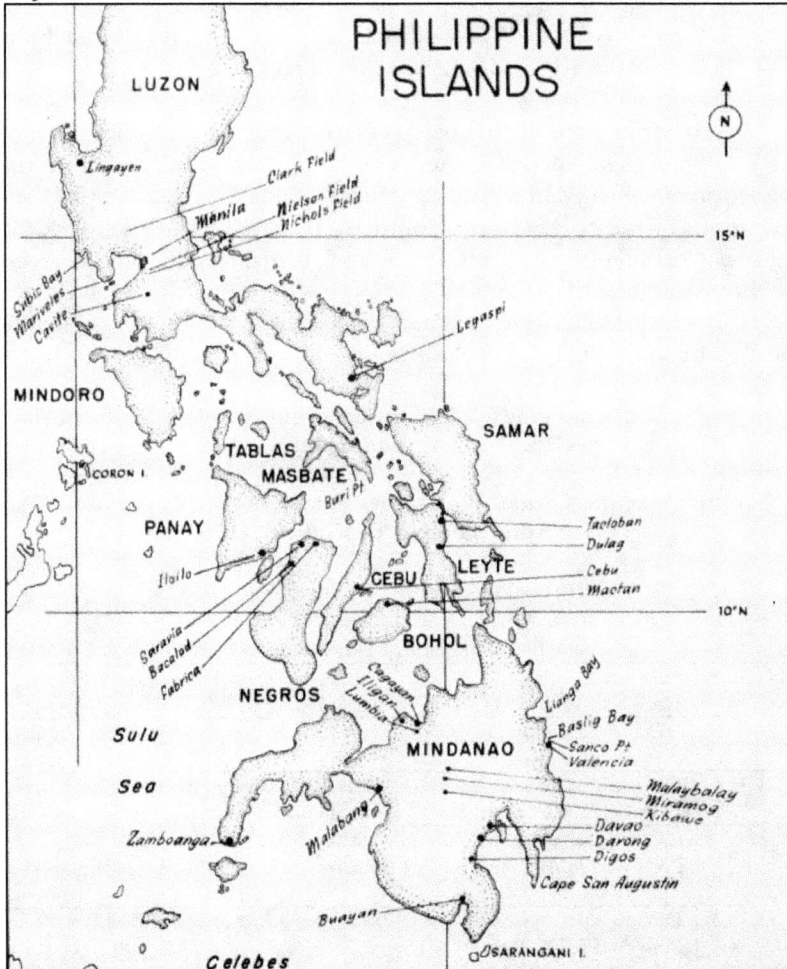

Philippine Islands
Commander in Chief, U.S. Pacific Fleet and Pacific Ocean Areas,
Operations in the Pacific Ocean Areas - September 1944, 7 March 1945

As a result of the magnitude of the Leyte operation, three other "top" commands, in addition to MacArthur's Southwest Pacific Area, were involved. These were:

- Adm. Chester W. Nimitz's Pacific Fleet and Pacific Ocean Areas—which provided Adm. William Halsey's U.S. Third Fleet and the U.S. VII Army Air Force
- Gen. Henry H. (Hap) Arnold's U.S. XX Army Air Force, through his deputy, Maj. Gen. Curtis E. LeMay
- Gen. Joseph W. Stillwell of the China-Burma-India Command's U.S. XIV Army Air Force[3]

Many books have already been written about the Allied invasion of the Philippines launched at Leyte. This short chapter is devoted to the role/actions of medium landing ships (LSMs) during amphibious operations by the Northern and Southern Attack Forces. The following abbreviated Philippines Attack Force Task Organization with its levels of command, identifies the attack groups within the Northern Attack Force to which LSMs were assigned. There were no LSMs assigned to the Panaon and Dinagat Attack Groups.

Supreme Commander, Allied Forces, Southwest Pacific Area
Gen. Douglas MacArthur, USA

Seventh Fleet and Central Philippines Attack Force (Task Force 77)
Vice Adm. Thomas C. Kinkaid, USN

Northern Attack Force (Task Force 78)
Rear Adm. Daniel E. Barbey, USN
X Corps: Maj. Gen. Franklin C. Sibert

TG 78.1	Palo Attack Group/	Rear Adm. Daniel E. Barbey, USN
	USA 24th Infantry Division	Maj. Gen. Frederick A. Irving
	LSM-19 (flagship), *LSM-21*, *LSM-257* (Lt. Edward L. McComb, USNR)	

TG 78.2	San Ricardo Attack Group/	Rear Adm. William M. Fechteler, USN
	USA 1st Cavalry Division	Maj. Gen. Verne D. Mudge
	LSM-18 (flagship), *LSM-20*, *LSM-22*, *LSM-23*, *LSM-34*, *LSM-138*, *LSM-139*, *LSM-258*, *LSM-311* (Lt. Comdr. Reginald C. Johnson, USN)	

TG 78.3	Panaon Attack Group/	Rear Adm. Arthur D. Struble, USN
	USA 21st RCT, 24th Infantry Division	

TG 78.4	Dinagat Attack Group	Rear Adm. Arthur D. Struble, USN
	USA 6th Ranger Battalion	

The components of the Northern and Southern Attack Forces began departing from Manus in the Admiralty Islands on 10 October, and Hollandia, New Guinea, on the 12th, all bound for a position designated "Point Fin" located off the entrance to Leyte Gulf through which all of the Expeditionary Force must pass.[4]

Task Unit 78.1.3 (Transport Division 24) got under way from Hollandia, New Guinea, in mid-afternoon on 13 October, joined by the Royal Australian Navy landing ships HMAS *Manoora*, HMAS *Kanimbla*, and HMAS *Westralia*. Transiting with the Americans, the Australians were a part of the Panaon Attack Group (TG 78.3) under Rear Adm. Arthur D. Struble that came ashore some seventy miles south of the main landing beaches to secure the strait between Leyte and Panaon Islands. Details about the Panaon operation, which is not taken up here, may be found in my book *Ready to Haul, Ready to Fight: U.S. Navy, Royal Australian Navy, and British Merchant Navy Cargo Ships in the Pacific in World War II*.[5]

The disposition of which Transport Division 24 was the centerpiece consisted of transport ships formed up in four columns; with LCIs, LSMs, and LSTs to be used to effect landings on the beaches astern of the transport unit; with cruisers and patrol craft positioned on the forward flanks of the transports; and destroyers in inner and outer screening stations. At 0300, in early morning darkness on 20 October, HMAS *Manoora*, *Kanimbla*, and *Westralia* were detached to join the Panaon Attack Group (Task Group 78.3).[6]

PALO ATTACK GROUP (TG 78.1)

At 0645, upon the signal "Deploy" by Rear Admiral Barbey, Capt. Thomas B. Brittain, USN (commander, Transport Division 24, and commander, Task Unit 78.1.3) took command of the transports, LSTs, LSMs, and sub-chasers of the associated Control Unit which would guide the landing craft of the transports to the beach. H-hour, the time at which the first troops were to land, was 1000. The troops landed on schedule, no boat waves up to the thirteenth were late, and the sixteenth and final one was only 21 minutes late. As part of this operation, LSMs *19*, *21*, and *257* landed abreast on their designated beaches, Red 1 and Red 2 near the town of Palo in that order from left to right.[7]

As shown in the following snippets (extracted from Annex A of ComTransDiv 24 Attack Landing Order No. 18-44), the LSMs and LCVP landing craft from the attack transport USS *Fayette* (APA-43), comprised the sixth wave of the attack at that location. Their mission was landing the 24th Infantry Division on Red Beaches 1 and 2. The landing schedule called for the LSMs to be at the LOD (Line of Departure) at H Hour plus 5 minutes (1005), depart for their respective beaches at 1008, and land at 1025.[8]

Diagram 3-2

Landing schedule for LSMs *19*, *21*, and *257* at Red Beaches 1 and 2

Map 3-3

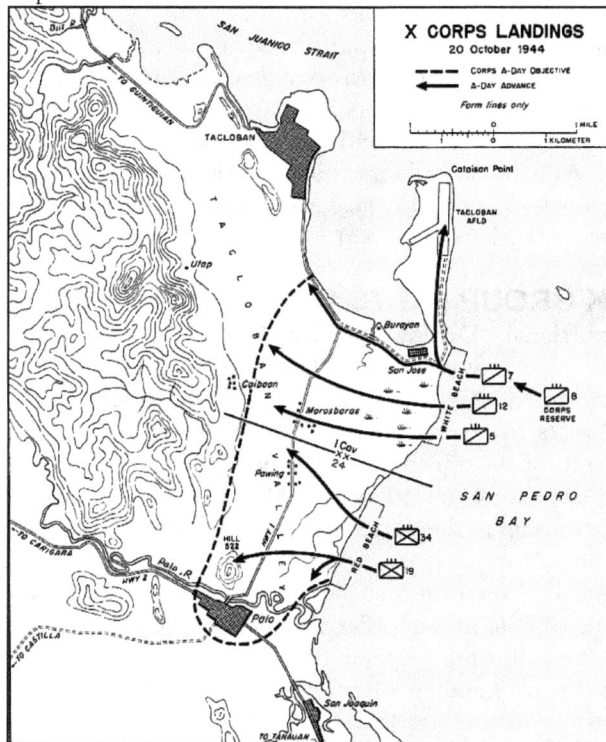

Northern Attack Force landing beaches in Leyte Gulf
https://www.gutenberg.org/files/48991/48991-h/images/m05.png

At 0945, the three LSMs proceeded toward Red Beach. They beached at 1025 and commenced offloading tanks. First contact with the enemy came while the medium landing ships were a short distance offshore, in the form of a sniper bullet. Lt. Edward L. McComb, USNR, commanding officer of *LSM-19*, described this and subsequent events:

> 1020 Shell in 40MM gun hit by sniper bullet. Shell exploded but no casualties resulted. 1025 Hit beach and commenced unloading vehicles. Our tanks pinned down by enemy 25's. Unable to get all tanks off ship. Heavy sniper and mortar fire from beach. 1130 Completed unloading and retracted under enemy fire from mortar and 75's. Several hits scored on LST's on our port hand. 1334 Moored alongside [the attack transport USS *Leedstown*] APA 56 to take on load of ammunition. 1537 Beached at Red Beach to unload. 1722 Retracted and awaiting orders to go alongside [the cargo ship] USS *Hercules* [AK-41]. 1845 Fired on enemy aircraft. 1940 Anchored.[9]

Photo 3-3

Troops aboard an LSM cleaning the gun of a Sherman tank just before landing at Leyte. National Archives photograph #80-G-258314

The three LSMs received no damage to ship or personnel, even though the Japanese were firing mortar rounds from a pillbox in the center section of the beach. The closest round landed 50 yards astern of the LSMs when, after having discharged their cargo and retracted, they were 1,000 yards off the beach steering a zig-zag course seaward.[10]

Some of the larger tank landing ships in succeeding waves were not so fortunate. At 1045, LSTs were directed to proceed to Red Beach. A half hour later at 1115, some received mortar fire off the beach. Within three minutes, *LST-452*, *LST-171*, and *LST-181* were hit while beaching, and the *181* was on fire. Two LCIs (infantry landing craft) equipped as firefighting vessels assisted in bringing the blaze under control. But when Admiral Barbey directed all LSTs to retract at 1125, the *181* was unable to do so. (In the other two LSTs, twenty-six sailors and soldiers were killed.)[11]

At 1201, LSTs *452* and *181* were the only tank landing ships on the beach unloading, when mortar fire was resumed. *LST-171*, which was offshore, reported sick bay hit with a number of casualties, and no electrical power for lights. At 1418, LST unloading conditions were greatly enhanced when the White Beach commander advised they were ready to receive Red Beach tank landing ships.[12]

SAN RICARDO ATTACK GROUP (TG 78.2)

Photo 3-4

USS *LSM-311* and other sister ships landing cargo at Leyte, 20 October 1944. National Archives photograph #80-G-59504

Rear Admiral Barbey's Northern Attack Force was divided into three components; one, the Panaon Attack Group, landed on Panaon Island off the southernmost point of Leyte. The other two, the Palo and San

Ricardo Attack Groups were assigned Red and White Beaches near Tacloban. Rear Adm. William M. Fechteler, commanding the San Ricardo Group, was responsible for landing the 1st Cavalry Division on White Beach, a mile-long sandy stretch extending southwest from the base of the Cataisan Peninsula. Red Beach, on which the 24th Infantry Division landed, lay south of White Beach separated by 1,500 yards of swampy bush, and some eleven miles north of Liberanan Head where the Southern Attack Force beaches began.[13]

The San Ricardo Group enjoyed good fortune that day. The LSTs were able to beach on the northern half of White Beach, and the landings were virtually unopposed. An enemy battery which fired on shoreward bound craft at 1122 was quickly silenced by the light cruiser USS *Boise* (CL-47). By midday on 20 October, transports and cargo ships were unloading rapidly, and of the servicemen present, none could have been more pleased than General MacArthur.[14]

Earlier that day, Task Unit 78.2.5 (LSM Group)—LSMs *18, 20, 22, 23, 34, 138, 139, 258,* and *311*—crossed the line of departure at 1008 on their way to White Beach to land as the sixth wave. They beached at 1030 and discharged all mobile cargo. Representative of the other LSMs, flagship *LSM-18* (which had loaded six tanks, twenty tons of ammunition, sixty-five barrels of gasoline, and thirty troops at Aitope, New Guinea, on 10 October), unloaded tanks and gasoline. At 1050, LSMs *18, 20,* and *22* retracted from the beach to undertake unloading transports for Red Beach. The remaining LSMs—*23, 34, 138, 139, 258,* and *311*—retracted at the same time, and proceeded to the transport area to take on cargo for White Beach.[15]

SUBSEQUENT OPERATIONS / EVENTS

Through 21-23 October, the LSMs were busy engaged in unloading transports at Red and White Beaches. During this period, there were several enemy aircraft warnings (Red alerts): during the day and night of the 21st, twice during day and night on the 22nd, and once during the day and night on the 23rd.[16]

On 24 October, LSMs *18, 19, 20, 21, 22, 23, 34, 138, 139, 257, 258,* and *311* anchored in Leyte Harbor, to provide opportunity for the performance of minor repairs and equipment overhaul. Red alerts were given many times that day and night. During air raids, four Japanese planes were shot down. The 25th was much the same, with a Val shot down. Enemy air raids increased on 26 October; two Bettys, one Val, and four Zeroes went down in flames; and *LSM-311* reported one casualty: Fireman Second Class Carrell R. Powers, gun captain of the ship's No. 5 20mm gun, who died as a result of an explosion of a 20mm projectile from the No. 4 gun.[17]

Amid air raids the following two days (27-28 October):

- *LSM-138* was dispatched to Violet Beach in the Southern Attack Force Area
- *LSM-34* was directed to take urgently needed rations from a Liberty ship into White Beach
- *LSM-139* reported three men injured from falling shrapnel[18]

Photo 3-5

A Japanese Kamikaze pilot taxies his bomb-laden Mitsubishi "Zero" fighter on a Philippine air field in preparation for take-off during the Leyte Operation. Naval History and Heritage Command photograph #NH 73098

The early morning of 29 October brought a radio message warning of heavy enemy air attack expected at dawn, which did not materialize. At 0700, LSMs *19, 20, 22, 23*, and *139* were ordered to Yellow Beach (Southern Attack Force Area) to unload Liberty ships. That evening, commander Task Group 78.2 warned ships to be prepared for strong easterly wind from 40 to 50 knots. An hour later, all LSMs were instructed to use their stern anchor to provide additional holding power at their anchorages. Subsequently, at 2000, a typhoon struck with maximum winds of 71 knots.[19]

Presumably the knowledge of the expected typhoon by the enemy had negated the strong air attack expected that morning. However, some enemy planes flew missions, and a Betty bomber was shot down on the beach. At 0600 the following morning, 30 October, the winds subsided and the typhoon ended. The month ended amid the resumption of Red alerts, some LSMs unloading Liberty ships at Yellow Beach, and the others at anchor.[20]

SOUTHERN ATTACK FORCE – GROUP BAKER

The remaining six medium landing ships involved in the invasion of Leyte on 20 October were assigned to Rear Adm. Forrest B. Royal's Attack Group Baker, a part of the Southern Attack Force. Group Baker stood out of Seeadler Harbor in the Admiralties on 11 October, en route to the Philippines. The medium landing ships of Task Unit 79.6.14—LSMs *24, 29, 136,* and *233*—under Lt. Comdr. J. G. Blanche Jr., USN, were joined by LSMs *134* and *135* during passage to Leyte.[21]

Southern Attack Force (Task Force 79)
Rear Adm. Thomas S. Wilkinson, USN
XXIV Corps: Maj. Gen. John R. Hodge

TG 79.1	Attack Group Able/ USA 7th Infantry Division	Rear Adm. Richard L. Conolly, USN Maj. Gen. Archibald V. Arnold

TG 79.2	Attack Group Baker/ USA 96th Infantry Division	Rear Adm. Forrest B. Royal, USN Maj. Gen. James L. Bradley

Task Unit 79.6.13 (Reserve Unit One): *LSM-134, LSM-135, LST-269, LST-270* (flagship), *LST-615, LST-704* (Lt. Barber)
Task Unit 79.6.14 (Reserve Unit Two): *LSM-24, LSM-29, LSM-136, LSM-233, LCI(A)-755, LCI(A)-974* (Lt. Comdr. J. G. Blanche Jr., USN)[22]

Nearing the Southern Attack Force landing beaches on the morning of 20 October, General Quarters were sounded at 0413 aboard the LSMs, all guns were manned, and lookouts posted. At 0530, crewmembers observed anti-aircraft (AA) firing from ships of the screen on both port and starboard bows of Attack Group Baker. A few minutes later, an enemy plane was sighted astern beyond the range of LSM guns. There was also heavy AA seen put up by ships astern, presumably the Transport Group and escorts.[23]

Upon deployment (release from the Attack Group), LSMs *134* and *135* left Task Unit 79.6.14 and joined 79.6.13 LSMs *24, 29, 136,* and *233*—after maneuvering to keep clear of transports approaching from astern and passing shoreward through their assigned anchorage area— anchored in their assigned berths awaiting orders.[24]

During the period the LSMs were off the beach (20-24 October), the weather was generally fair in Leyte Gulf with occasional periods of overcast, and a few scattered showers. Visibility was average except toward the shore where mists and frequently employed screening smoke created a continuous haze of varying density.[25]

Map 3-4

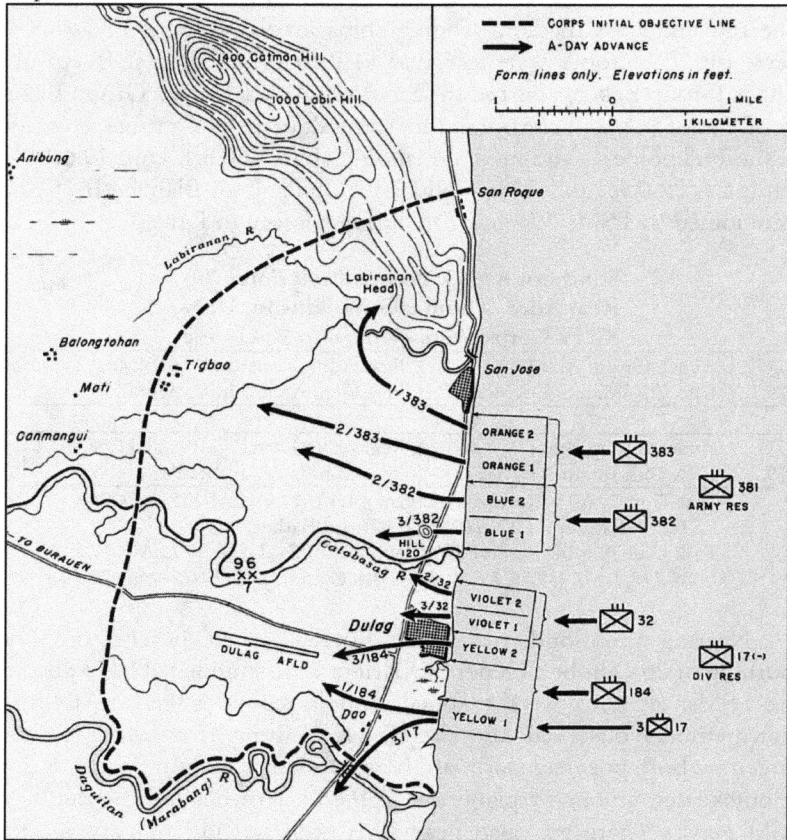

Southern Attack Force (XXIV Corps) landing beaches in Leyte Gulf
https://www.ibiblio.org/hyperwar/USA/USA-P-Return/maps/USA-P-Return-4.jpg

Enemy air attacks by small units and single planes occurred regularly each dawn and twilight without apparently causing any significant damage, as general alerts were regularly held and smoke used very extensively for screening with good results.[26]

One Japanese twin-engine bomber came within range of the LSMs and was shot down at 0620 on 21 October, as described by Lt. Comdr. J. G. Blanche Jr., USN:

> 0620: An enemy aircraft, identified as a Mitsubishi Type 01 bomber, emerged from smoke screen on starboard bow of *LSM 24*, flying at a height of about 800 feet, and rather slowly. LSMs *24* and *136* immediately opened fire with 40 MM and 20 MM guns, getting repeat hits with both caliber guns. *LSM 29* also opened fire with 40

MM and 20 MM guns but it could not be determined whether hits were scored. A fire appeared in the plane's port engine and it went into a dive toward the water. The tracers from the LSMs *24* and *136* appeared to have scored several hits in front of fuselage and motor nacelles. The plane nosed over and crashed into the sea and sank immediately about 800 yards on port bow of *LSM 24*.... An LST and APD were also firing at this plane when it was shot down.[27]

Later that morning, 21 October, *LSM-136* beached at 0930 and commenced unloading her cargo. She completed unloading at 1835 that evening and retracted, then returned to area Yoke and anchored.[28]

LSM-24 landed at Violet 1 beach at 1022 on 21 October, and assisted by Army personnel aboard (1 officer and 13 men) began discharging her cargo. She also completed unloading at 1835, retracted, and returned to area Yoke and anchored.[29]

LSM-29 and *LSM-233* did not unload their cargoes which consisted of explosives for possible use by Underwater Demolition Teams to clear obstacles; conditions found did not warrant their use.[30]

SUBSEQUENT DUTIES AND DEPARTURE

At 1000 on 23 October, LSMs *24*, *134* and *135* reported to the commander of Transport Division Ten for use in unloading AKAs (amphibious cargo ships), then landing their cargos ashore. That evening, *LSM-24* beached at Orange 2 to deliver, principally, small heavy units of ammunition. Normally the responsibility of unloading was with army personnel but there being inadequate numbers available to unload, "all hands" aboard the *24* turned to and worked continuously to transfer the ammo into army vehicles.[31]

After this marathon, in late morning on 24 October, LSMs *24* and *136*, being completely unloaded, attempted to retract from the beach but were unable to do so. *LSM-135* pulled *LSM-136* off the beach, but efforts to do the same for *LSM-24* were unsuccessful until the fleet tug USS *Menominee* (ATF-73) lent a hand. That afternoon, Blanche's Task Unit 79.6.14 joined Task Unit 79.14.5 (Control Unit and Landing Craft Unit) for passage to Hollandia. *LSM-233* was not in company, having left with an earlier convoy at the regular sailing time; *LSM-135*, having been delayed assisting *LSM-136*, sailed with this group escorted by the *Menominee*, sub-chaser USS *PC-1603*, and minesweeper USS *YMS-176*.[32]

MEDIUM LANDING SHIPS' FIRST BATTLE STARS

The twenty LSMs that participated in the Leyte Landings earned a battle star to affix to the Asiatic–Pacific Campaign Ribbon displayed topside on ribbon boards.

The ships' officers and men proudly sported the same bronze star on the ribbon that adorned their uniform blouses.

The Asiatic–Pacific Campaign Medal was initially issued as a service ribbon in 1942. A full medal was authorized in 1947, the first of which was presented to General of the Army Douglas MacArthur.

Asiatic–Pacific Campaign Medal and associated ribbon with two battle stars

Ship	Award Date(s)	Ship	Award Date(s)
LSM-18	13 Oct-29 Nov 44	LSM-134	13 Oct-29 Nov 44
LSM-19	13 Oct-29 Nov 44	LSM-135	20 Oct 44
LSM-20	13 Oct-29 Nov 44	LSM-136	20 Oct 44
LSM-21	13 Oct-29 Nov 44	LSM-138	11 Oct-29 Nov 44
LSM-22	13 Oct-29 Nov 44	LSM-139	11 Oct-29 Nov 44
LSM-23	13 Oct-29 Nov 44	LSM-233	20 Oct 44
LSM-24	20 Oct 44	LSM-257	13 Oct-29 Nov 44
LSM-29	20 Oct 44	LSM-258	11 Oct-29 Nov 44
LSM-34	13 Oct-29 Nov 44	LSM-311	11 Oct-29 Nov 44
LSM-51	19-29 Nov 44	LSM-318	19-29 Nov 44

SUMMARY

Samuel Eliot Morrison aptly characterized in *The Two-Ocean War*, the great success of the Allied Leyte Gulf assault landings, which were executed smoothly and relatively uncontested by enemy forces:

> The Leyte Gulf landings were easy, compared with most amphibious operations in World War II—perfect weather, no surf, no mines or underwater obstacles, slight enemy reaction, mostly mortar fire. Admiral Wilkinson's Southern Attack Force landed XXIV Corps on a 5000-yard stretch of beach which began about eleven miles south of the Northern Force left flank. A welcome addition to the amphibious fleet was the Landing Ship, Medium (LSM), 203 feet long, 900 tons, which had the vehicle capability of an LCT [tank landing craft] but was faster, more seaworthy, and more comfortable.[33]

4

USS *LSM-20* Sunk, USS *LSM-23* Damaged by Kamikaze Aircraft

1110 [5 December 1944] Fifteen Jap[anese] planes attacked convoy in suicide attacks. DD's and LSM 20 and 23 hit by suicide planes. 1120 Jap plane crash-dived at us but our gun fire damaged wing enough to cause him to miss so that he passed over us and crashed into water 35 feet on port beam. 1140 LSM 20 seen to be sinking. We continued with undamaged ships. 1631 Anchored off White Beach [east coast of Leyte].

—USS *LSM-19* War Diary, December 1944.

Photo 4-1

USS *LSM-20* sinking in Surigao Straits, 5 December 1944, after being struck by a Kamikaze plane amidships, killing 8 and wounding 9 of those aboard.
Naval History and Heritage Command photograph #NH 68792

Map 4-1

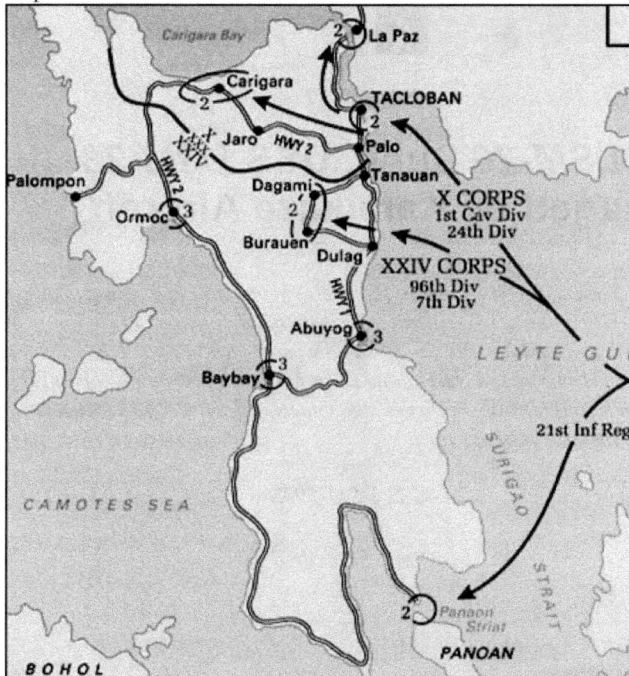

Baybay is located on Leyte's central west coast, SSW of the landing beaches
where U.S. Sixth Army invasion forces stormed ashore on 20 October 1944.
https://ibiblio.org/hyperwar/USA/USA-C-Leyte/maps/USA-C-Leyte-3.jpg

TASK UNIT 78.3.10 DISPATCHED TO BAYBAY, LEYTE

On 4 December 1944, Task Unit 78.3.10—a modest group of four
destroyers, eight medium landing ships, and three large infantry landing
craft under Capt. William M. Cole, USN—took departure from Leyte
Gulf, just off Dulag, bound for Baybay, Leyte Island.

- Destroyers: USS *Flusser* (DD-368), *Drayton* (DD-366), *Lamson*
  (DD-367), *Shaw* (DD-373)
- Medium landing ships: USS LSMs *18, 19, 20, 21, 22, 23, 34, 318*
- Large infantry landing craft: USS LCI(L)s *1014, 1017, 1018*[1]

Heavy rains had damaged the dirt roads of Leyte, and Sixth Army
found it difficult to move men and materiel from the gulf beachhead to
the west coast. In order to alleviate this problem and strengthen the
American position south of Ormoc Bay, prior to a planned amphibious
assault there, Cole was charged with transporting army troops, vehicles
and ammunition from Leyte Gulf to a beach one mile north of Baybay.

Transit there required passage down Leyte Gulf and through the Surigao Straits, round the southern tip of Panaon Island (not shown on the map), and northward up Leyte's west coast to Baybay.[2]

During passage, the weather was clear, except for occasional light showers, and the sea smooth. The amphibious ships were formed in two columns with the LSMs leading. The four screening destroyers were stationed in four quadrants, at a distance of about 3,000 yards off the port and starboard bows and quarters of the formation.[3]

At 1600 that afternoon, the task unit rounded Panaon Island and by sunset was off Maasin Village. From that point onward, the ships proceeded up the coast approximately one mile off the beach, while following the convolutions of the shoreline to take advantage of land masking and reduce the chances of detection by Japanese forces. The destroyers were then stationed: one ahead of the amphibious formation, one astern, and two on the offshore flank. To minimize electronic emissions, and associated possible disclosure of the task unit's position to the enemy, all air search radars except that of the *Lamson* were secured.[4]

That evening at 2000, the ships passed through the channel between Canigao Island and Leyte. From then on, enemy search planes were detected over the Camotes Sea, approaching at times to within ten miles of the unit which, it was believed, remained undetected. At 2248 the task group arrived off the designated beach one mile north of Baybay. After efforts to establish communications with army shore parties, as previously arranged, failed, Captain Cole directed the LSMs and LCI(L)s to beach and unload.[5]

During unloading operations, the destroyers patrolled slowly about two miles off the beach. After 0034 on 5 December, when the last of the LCI(L)s had been emptied of their troops and equipment and had retracted from the beach, they laid off the beach with the other LCI(L)s which had already cleared.[6]

The LSM landings were successful and unloading proceeded well with two exceptions. *LSM-20*'s first attempt was on a "too shelving" (unsuitable) area of beach from which she had difficulty retracting. After moving to a more suitable location, she succeeded in discharging most of her cargo before her ordered departure. *LSM-22* was heavily loaded with combat equipment and unable to beach even in locations where others had done so (presumably owing to excessive draft). She tried to land five times, unsuccessfully, and was finally forced to proceed independently to Abuyog, Leyte, to discharge her cargo there. After doing so, she continued on to San Pedro Bay, and anchored there at 1805 on 5 December.[7]

At 0100 on 5 December, a single enemy plane closed the task unit undetected until heard and seen passing overhead. It dropped one bomb near the *Lamson* which did no damage.[8]

An hour later, Captain Cole directed Lt. Comdr. Reginald C. Johnson (commander, LSM Group Four embarked in flagship *LSM-18*) to have all ships clear of the beach for departure at 0300. About this time, 0200, another enemy plane appeared overhead and made several strafing runs on the destroyers, apparently attempting to draw AA fire to determine in the dark, their exact locations. Neither this plane, nor the earlier one, was fired on by any ships.[9]

DEPARTURE FROM BAYBAY, AND RETURN TRANSIT

As ordered, at 0300 all LSMs retracted, formed in two columns, and with LCIs and destroyers proceeded on the return transit toward San Pedro Harbor, Leyte, with at 12 knots, once again via a route close inshore. At 0550, radar contact was made with enemy planes. The first plane dropped a bomb close aboard the starboard side of the destroyer *Drayton*, killing two men and wounding five, and causing minor damage. A second plane strafed the destroyer to port of the left column of the landing vessels. A third plane strafed the righthand column from the rear, attacking first the *LCI(L)-1017* at the rear of the column. [Note: some LSI(L)s were converted to LSI(G)s in late 1944 and 1945, but little information exists on the exact dates. *LCI(L)-1017* referred to above is identified as *LCI(G)-1017* in the following photograph.][10]

Twenty-millimeter projectiles from the plane passed a few feet over the bridge of the *1017*, and some struck the water about ten feet from the starboard side of the ship.[11]

Photo 4-2

Eight LCIs nested together, location unknown, circa 1945. From right to left: USS *LCI(G)-1060*, USS *LCI(G)-1018*, USS *LCI(G)-964*, USS *LCI(G)-1016*, USS *LCI(G)-1017*, USS *LCI(G)-961*, USS *LCI(L)-982*, and USS *LCI(G)-1015*.
Naval History and Heritage Command photograph #NH 74313

Another plane dropped a bomb on Canigao Island, apparently mistaking it for a ship of the task unit. At least one other bomb was dropped in the vicinity without causing any resultant damage.[12]

Most of the ships fired on these planes retiring shoreward. Being dark, it made accurate engagement of the aircraft against the even gloomier background of the shoreline very difficult. Following this attack, the task unit rounded the southwest tip of Leyte at 0600 and proceeded eastward. Friendly fighter cover arrived in the area and at 0615, P38 Lightning aircraft shot down an enemy plane in the vicinity of the convoy.[13]

Diagram 4-2

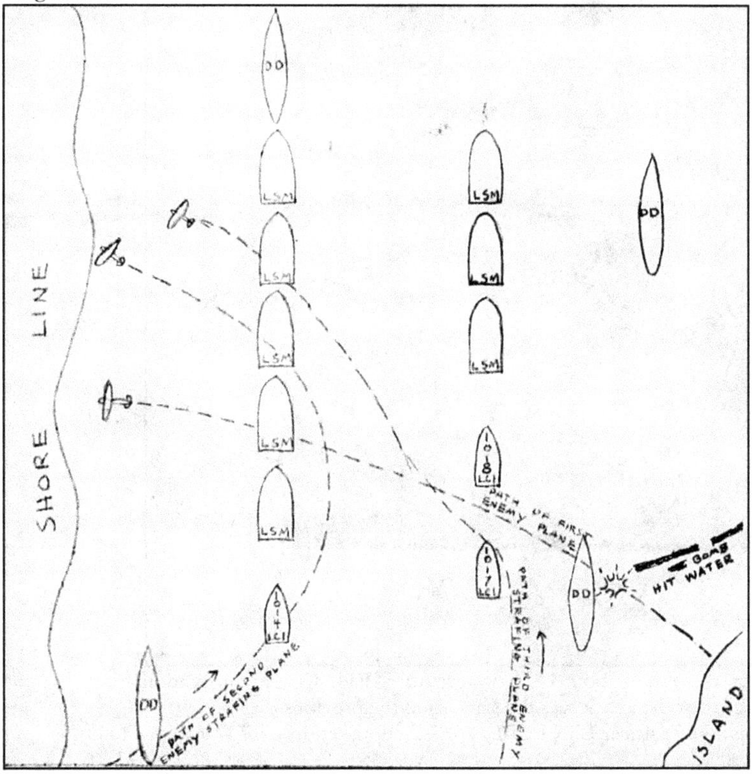

Position of ships and action during 0550 enemy aircraft attack, 5 December 1944. (This diagram is apparently not entirely correct. It shows eight LSMs but, per her war diary, *LSM-22* was then proceeding independently to Abuyog, Leyte.) Commanding Officer USS *LCI(L) 1017*, Action, report of, 7 December 1944

KAMIKAZE ATTACKS ON CONVOY

At 1100 on 5 December while continuing their return transit to San Pedro Bay, the task unit was attacked by suicide planes at a point just east of Cabalian Bay and south of Amaguaan Point, on the east coast of Leyte. These Kamikaze aircraft appeared out of the clouds without having been previously detected on radar. The first warning of an attack to the convoy was when one plane crashed astern of the formation, having evidently been shot down by fighter cover. During the next ten minutes, the remaining planes overhead made attacks in succession.[14]

Diagram 4-3

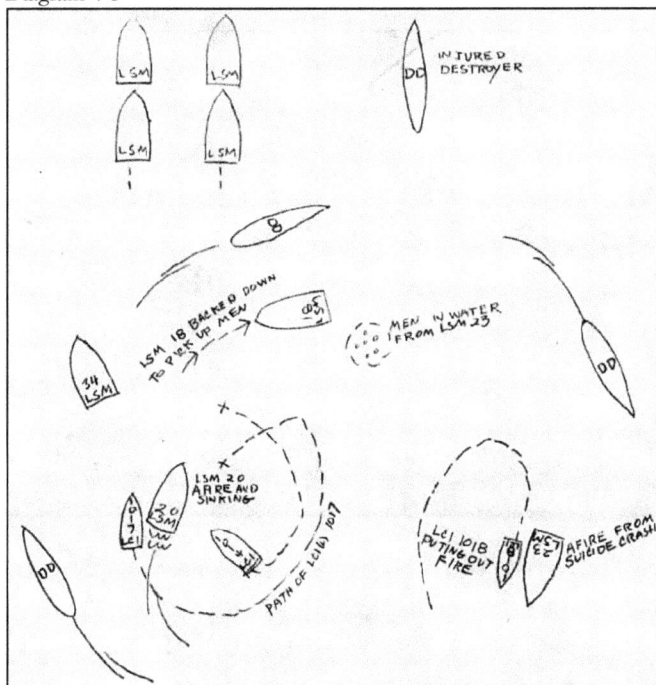

Position of ships at about 1125, 5 December 1944. Cruising formation at the time of the attack was the same as in the previous diagram.
Commanding Officer *USS LCI(L) 1017*, Action, report of, 7 December 1944

The commanding officer of *LCI(L)-1017* (Richard G. Jacob) described how the attacks unfolded as witnessed from the vantage point of his ship's bridge:

> An enemy plane dove out of the sky and strafed the destroyer off our port quarter.... At 1112 an enemy plane was shot down by one of the destroyers which was then a few hundred yards off this ship's

starboard bow. A third enemy plane approached from astern of this ship and passed close overhead to port. This plane was hit in the cross-fire of this ship's No. 1, 2, and 4 guns; the plane was out of control but managed to crash into the destroyer ahead to the starboard. A fourth plane approached from this ship's starboard quarter, passed low over the bow where it was hit by the No. 1 and 3 guns. It crashed in flames about 500 yards to port. A fifth plane made a dive and very nearly crashed into USS *LCI(L) 1018*. This plane was shot down by the USS *LCI(L) 1018* and was out of control when it crashed into the water. Two other planes made suicide dives for *LSM 23* and *LSM 20* crashing just aft of midships on each of the vessels.[15]

Commander, LSM Group Four, cited in his action report that one plane was shot down by the destroyer *La Vallette* (DD-448), which was patrolling with *Mugford* (DD-389) in the vicinity. A third plane was shot down by the *Flusser* while attempting a suicide dive on the destroyers. A fourth was shot down by an LSM and crashed close aboard the stern of the *LSM-34*.[16]

LSM-20 SUNK BY KAMIKAZE; *LSM-23* DAMAGED

The ship commenced to settle down stern first. I ordered the ship abandoned and saw that all wounded were put over the side into the water. The ship was in a vertical position, bow up when I dove into the water; the ship sank in approximately twenty (20) minutes in three hundred (300) fathoms of water at Latitude 10-11-7 North, Longitude 125-19 East.... A total of eight enlisted men were lost, two officers and seven enlisted men wounded.

—Lt. John R. Bradley, USN, commanding officer, USS *LSM-20*.[17]

The Kamikaze that crashed squarely into the *LSM-20*, breeched her hull, allowing water to surge into the ship, and set her on fire. Another, attempting to crash dive the *LSM-23*, fell short but ricocheted on the water's surface into the ship causing extensive damage, killing seven men and wounding another seven. One plane, apparently shot down by fighter coverage, made an attempt to crash down on the *LSM-34*. It missed, but impacting the water, propelled parts of the plane and the pilot aboard her. Several bombs also hit near the *34*, shaking her badly and causing minor damage. The last of the planes dove on the destroyer *Drayton*, striking a glancing blow near her No. 1 gun.[18]

The *LSM-20* was hit by an Oscar army fighter, believed to be carrying two 100-lb bombs. The aircraft dove into the ship from an altitude of about 3,000 feet, and at a very low angle of dive. Striking the ship starboard side, just aft of the conning tower and about three feet above the water line, the plane breeched the hull and passed into the engine room, where its bombs exploded. The force buckled the forward bulkhead to the after troop-compartment and the port side of the engine room. In addition to this structural damage, the main port engine and auxiliary engines, and the fire main and flushing system were knocked out of commission; rudder control froze with the rudder over hard left. The starboard main engine continued running.[19]

Photo 4-3

Japanese Oscar (Nakajima Ki-43 Hayabusa Army Type 1 fighter).
Japanese Operational Aircraft "Know Your Enemy!"
CinCPac - CinCPOA Bulletin 105-45

LCI(L)s RAPIDLY UNDERTAKE RESCUE WORK

Before the Kamikaze attacks ended, the three infantry landing craft had begun rescue efforts to assist *LSM-23* and *LSM-20*. The commanding officer of *LCI(L)-1017* described events as they unfolded:

> A number of men had been thrown clear of *LSM 23* when the enemy plane crashed into it and were directly ahead in the water about 1000 yards from this ship. This ship proceeded in the direction of these men to pick them up, but *LSM 18* backed down and performed this operation. As *LSM 20* had subsequently been hit by suicide plane this vessel turned around and at the same time fired on an enemy plane overhead....
>
> The LSM was covered with smoke and listing to starboard. Her engines were still running and steering was out of control.... This

ship made an approach and came alongside *LSM 20*'s port side at 1126. It was difficult to stay alongside because of the circular motion of the ship's headway. Water was put on the fire by this ship, but as the LSM was taking water in the stern badly it practically extinguished itself.

This ship moved ahead as it was evident the ship would soon sink. A bow line was passed to the bow of the LSM to hold the bow of this ship to the bow of the LSM. Passowski, J.R., S1c, on a stretcher was passed to this ship and was the first [rescued] man aboard. Many of the men jumped to this vessel's starboard ramp. As the bow began to rise quickly some made a desperate effort to jump, and some made leaps of at least 20 feet.

The stern settled very fast, and as the bow rose the bow line was cut. In order to prevent casualty to this ship which was being endangered by the stern of the LSM, the order of full speed ahead had to be given. Several men fell between the two ships. They fell clear however as the bow of the LSM rose upward and to the right, and the bow of this vessel swung to the left when the line was cut. This ship cleared very quickly. The bow of the sinking ship remained a moment above the water, but by 1131 it had disappeared. (Lt. John R. Bradley, USN, in his report on the loss of *LSM-20*, indicated that she sank at 1120.) Twenty-three men managed to get aboard before this ship pulled away.[20]

LCI(L)-1014 was close by the starboard side of the burning and sinking *LSM-20*, and immediately began picking up the men that fell in the water, about sixteen in total. *LCI(L)-1017* picked up four including the *20*'s commanding officer. An officer and enlisted man from the *LSM-18* in a wherry aiding in the rescue work were also picked up by the *1017*, because they were unable to row back to their ship due to the current.[21]

DAMAGE TO / CASUALTIES ON BOARD *LSM-23*

At 1110 sounded General Quarters as enemy plane observed. This vessel's SCR [search radar] was inoperative and [we] received no advance warning of the attack. A VAL was observed diving on the escort on right flank and plunged across her forecastle [foc's'le]. Another VAL dove directly into LSM 20 *causing her to sink. Another VAL dove at* LSM 34 *directly astern of this vessel. At first the plane was thought headed for this ship and all engines were put ahead flank and the rudder full right to turn into the plane.*

—Lt. Kark K. Hickman, USNR, commanding officer, USS *LSM-23*,
describing in a war diary entry, suicide attacks by a group of VALs
(Aichi D3A Navy Type 99 carrier bombers) against task unit
ships, which included a deadly one against his own ship.[22]

As previously noted, *LSM-23* suffered damage and men killed and
wounded in the same Kamikaze attack by a group that sank *LSM-20*.
Believing that one of the Vals was making an attack run on her, *LSM-23* turned toward a plane in order to present the smallest cross-section
of the vessel as possible as a target. Once it was determined that she
was not the plane's objective, the medium landing ship began to
maneuver to resume her position in the convoy.[23]

The attacker crashed into the water near the bow of *LSM-34*, but
another plane following the previous one, dove directly at *LSM-23* from
off her starboard beam. Avoidance maneuvering was successful but, as
described by her commanding officer, the downed plane skipping across
the water's surface, impacted the ship:

> All engines were put ahead flank and rudder was put full right to
> turn toward the attacker. The plane, VAL, first hit the water about
> fifty yards from the ship and bounced into the hull on a level with
> the superstructure deck and into the chart house and radio room.
> Other parts of the plane struck the ship in various places inflicting
> considerable damage.
>
> A bomb (500 lb.) penetrated the hull on the starboard side at the
> waterline and plunged all the way through the ship and out through
> the port side about three-and-one-half feet above the waterline.
> Personnel casualties were as follows: one officer and six enlisted
> men killed: One enlisted man missing: One officer and six enlisted
> men wounded (third degree burns).
>
> The entire chart house and radio room and equipment were
> destroyed by the crash and by the ensuing fire. Moderate damage
> was sustained on the signal bridge and in the pilot house.[24]

Prompt and substantial assistance from the *LCI(L)-1018* was given
the *LSM-23* in combating the fire, and also the services of one of her
Pharmacist's Mates. Wounded personnel were transferred by small boat
to the destroyer *Lamson* (DD-367). At 1215, *LSM-18* took the *23* in
tow; repeated efforts to start her diesel engines had failed owing to
insufficient starting air pressure.[25]

TASK UNIT 78.3.10 SPLIT INTO TWO GROUPS

Following the loss of *LSM-20*, Lt. Comdr. Reginald Johnson (commander LSM Group Four) ordered LSMs *19*, *21*, and *318* to proceed to San Pedro Harbor at best speed. Captain Cole directed destroyers *Drayton* and *Shaw* to accompany them as escorts.[26]

The remainder of the task unit proceeded separately, formed around *LSM-18* with damaged *LSM-23* in tow. The other ships were *LSM-34* and LCI(L)s *1014*, *1017*, and *1018*; screened by the destroyers *Flusser*, *Sampson*, *La Vallette*, and *Mugford*. (*La Vallette* and *Mugford* had earlier at 1130, joined the destroyer screen. At 1645, *La Vallette* was released to return to her patrol duties.)[27]

Diagram 4-4

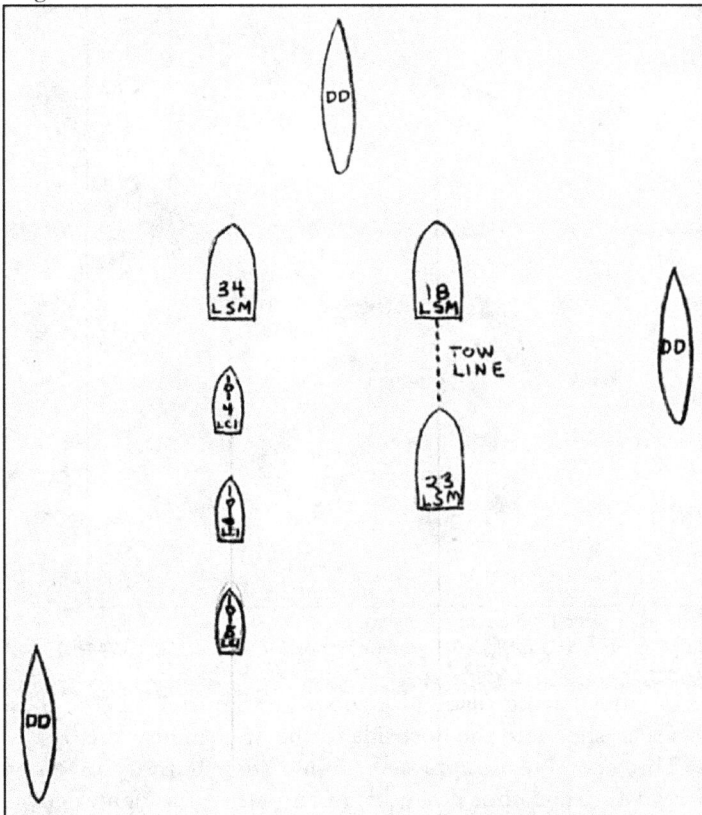

Cruising disposition before 1705 enemy attack, screened by destroyers *Flusser*, *Sampson*, and *Mugford*
Commanding Officer *USS LCI(L) 1017*, Action, report of, 7 December 1944

FINAL JAPANESE AIR ATTACK ON TASK UNIT

The remainder of this narrative is devoted to the second, larger sub-unit of Task Unit 78.3.10, which included the damaged *LSM-23* under tow. At 1707 off Hingatungan Point, two enemy planes approached from the east where they had been under the fire of Cruiser Division Fifteen (Task Group 77.3). Many expended gun rounds from this action landed in the vicinity of the group. The enemy planes were taken under fire by *Flusser, Lamson,* and *Mugford* as they came into range.[28]

Diagram 4-5

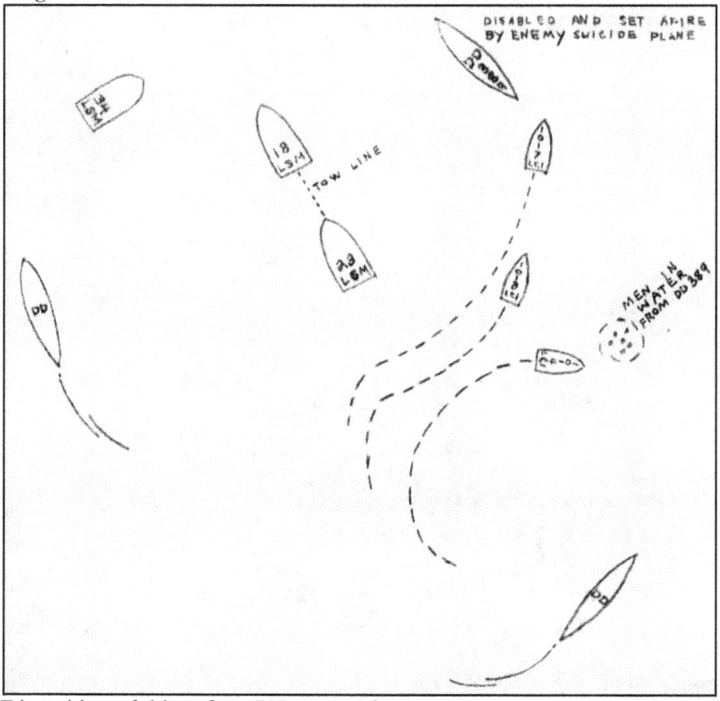

Disposition of ships after 1705 enemy plane attack
Commanding Officer *USS LCI(L) 1017,* Action, report of, 7 December 1944

At 1715, after having made a previous strafing run, one of these suicide planes crashed into the port side of the *Mugford* near the base of her stack. The second plane approached the *Flusser,* but was driven off by anti-aircraft fire, and shot down by an aircraft of the fighter cover. At 1744, *Mugford* reported the resultant fire under control and *LSM-34* took her in tow. The ships (originally constituted Task Unit 78.3.10) arrived at San Pedro Harbor that night.[29]

5

Landing Ship Lost, Others Damaged at Ormoc Bay

Embark at Leyte, transport, escort, protect and land the landing force together with its supplies and equipment in the Ormoc Bay Area and support the landing by naval gunfire, in order to assist the Army in destroying Japanese forces opposing our advance on Leyte Island.

—Adm. Arthur Struble's attack order to Task Group 78.3, as a prelude to its amphibious landing at Ormoc, Leyte, on 6 December 1944.[1]

Photo 5-1

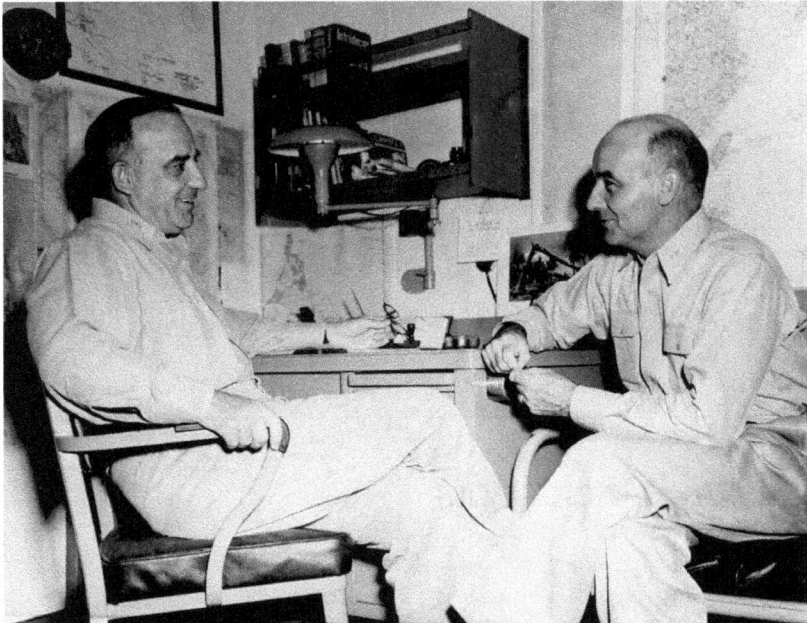

Rear Adm. Arthur D. Struble (right) and Rear Adm. Daniel E. Barbey (left) aboard Barbey's flagship, USS *Blue Ridge* (AGC-2), circa October 1944. National Archives photograph #80-G-301530

As December 1944 opened, Allied ground forces had cleared the Japanese from most of eastern Leyte, and were moving westward through the central range of mountains.   Three American Army divisions—the 1st Cavalry, and 24th and 32nd Infantry—were pressing Japanese ground forces from the north and east, while two divisions— the 7th and 96th Infantry—were pushing from the south and the east. The Japanese still held the western portion of the island, including nearly all of the Ormoc corridor, which extends from Pinamopoan on the north coast to Ormoc Bay on the south.[2]

On 7 December, the veteran U.S. 77th Division of the 24th Corps was landed in Ormoc Bay, a few miles southeast of the port of Ormoc through which the Japanese were being supplied and reinforced. This insertion of troops, on a new front by amphibious operation, was undertaken to threaten the Japanese troops fighting from their well-prepared positions to defend the Ormoc corridor, and cut off their principal supply routes.[3]

Map 5-1

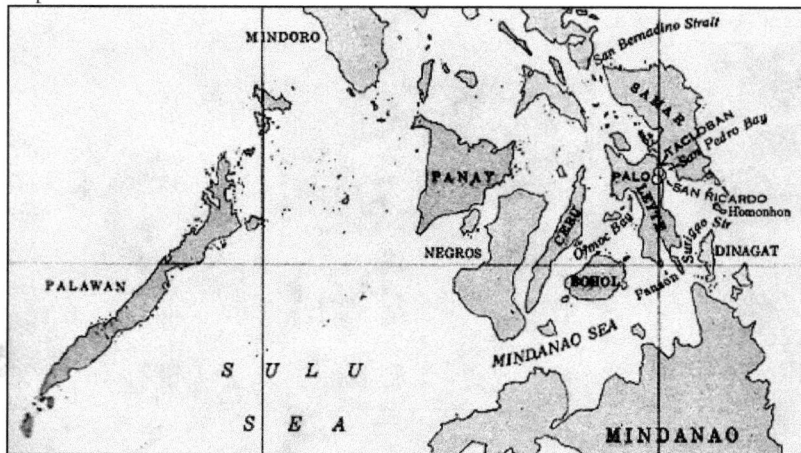

Central Philippine Islands

ORMOC ATTACK GROUP

The Ormoc Attack Group assembled to land the 77th Infantry Division (commanded by Maj. Gen. Andrew D. Bruce, USA) at Ormoc—which had no combatant ship larger than a destroyer, nor troop-lift ship larger than a destroyer transport (APD)—was organized as follows:

Ormoc Attack Group (Task Group 78.3)

Task Unit	Composition	Commander
Fast Transport Unit	8 APD	Comdr. W. S. Parsons
Light Transport Unit	27 LCI, 12 LSM	Comdr. W. V. Deutermann
Heavy Transport Unit	4 LST	Comdr. J. C. Schivley
Escort	12 DD	Capt. W. L. Freseman
Minesweeping Unit	9 AM, 1 APD	Comdr. E. D. McEathron
Control and Inshore Support	1 SC, 4 LCI(R), 1 ATR	Lt. Comdr. P. C. Holt, USNR

AM: minesweeper	DD: destroyer	LSM: medium landing ship
APD: high-speed transport	LCI: infantry landing craft	LST: tank landing ship
ATR: rescue tug	LCI(R): rocket LCI	SC: sub-chaser[4]

Comdr. William V. Deutermann, USN (who would retire as a rear admiral) commanded the Light Transport Unit. Directly under him and responsible for the LSMs was Lt. Comdr. Reginald C. Johnson, USN, commander, LSM Group Four. As shown in the preceding table, 27 infantry landing craft and the 12 medium landing ships identified below, constituted the Light Transport Unit (Task Unit 78.3.3):

- *LSM-18* (flagship), *LSM-19, LSM-22, LSM-34, LSM-51, LSM-138, LSM-139, LSM-257, LSM-258, LSM-310, LSM-311, LSM-318*[5]

In mid-afternoon on 6 December, the Attack Group convoy left Leyte Gulf at 1400, and proceeded without incident to Ormoc. All the LSMs were in one unit formed-up within the convoy as diagrammatically shown below:

LSM-19	*LSM-311*		*LSM-18*
LSM-139	*LSM-310*	*LSM-51*	*LSM-257*
LSM-138	*LSM-34*	*LSM-318*	*LSM-258*[6]

LSM-22, which was to have led the third column of medium landing ships, had suffered the failure of her engines earlier that day. Thus, she did not sail with the Assault Group, nor participate in the landing at Ormoc.[7]

The minesweepers—*Saunter* (AM-295), *Pursuit* (AM-108), *Requisite* (AM-109), *Sage* (AM-111), *Salute* (AM-294), *Scout* (AM-296), *Scrimmage* (AM-297), *Sentry* (AM-299), and *Triumph* (AM-323)—under Comdr. Ellsworth D. McEathron, preceded the rest of the group. They swept a 5,000-yard-wide channel for the assault group in Canigao West Pass on the 6th without finding any mines.[8]

ORMOC LANDING ON 7 DECEMBER

Photo 5-2

A *Mahan*-class destroyer conducting shore bombardment
at Ormoc Bay, Leyte Island, Philippines, 7 December 1944.
National Archives photograph #80-G-47406

Beginning at 0707 on 7 December, following a 20-minute bombardment
of the Ormoc assault beach by destroyers and rocket craft, the U.S. 77th
Infantry troops landed on schedule. By 0900, all ships were unloaded
with the exception of one LSM and one LCI caught on a reef.[9]

Photo 5-3

The second wave of assault craft heads for the beach at Ormoc Bay, Leyte.
National Archives photograph #80-G-321978

Upon arrival at Ormoc Bay at approximately 0615, the LSMs had formed column on signal, and proceeded toward the line of departure. As they approached the line, the group commander (Lt. Comdr. Reginald C. Johnson) formed the ships in a line abreast 270 degrees relative to his flagship, *LSM-18*, and they continued shoreward to the beach at two-thirds speed.[10]

LOSS OF *LSM-318* TO SUICIDE AIRCRAFT ATTACK

It is the commanding officer's belief that the LSM 318 *could have been saved if repeated enemy air attacks had not interfered. Due to the damage to our fire fighting gear, we would have needed another ship alongside to take care of the fire, and have required a vessel to tow us. Under the circumstances, this was not possible.*

—Report by Lt. Percy W. Rairden Jr., USN, on the loss of his ship.[11]

Photo 5-4

LSM-318 afire in Ormoc Bay, Leyte, after she was hit by a Kamikaze, 7 December 1944. Naval History and Heritage Command photograph #NH 102682

The subsequent information about *LSM-38* is from a report by her commanding officer, Lt. Percy W. Rairden Jr., USN, which he prefaces with a caution that, owing to the loss of the Quartermaster's Notebook, and Signal and Radio Logs, the times given were approximate. Additionally, the chronology of action might be slightly inaccurate as the report was constructed purely from his memory and he had been unable to consult with commander, LSM Group Four, or the commanding officers of other LSMs involved.[12]

As *LSM-318* approached the beach, Rairden observed *LCI(L)-970* grounded offshore, only a few yards to port of his ship's "slot." He altered course to starboard as much as the close interval between ships would permit, but the *318* still grounded about 80 yards off the beach.[13]

Several attempts to retract and re-beach more effectively were unsuccessful. The Army was finally prevailed upon to unload with the aid of a bulldozer and, when nearly all vehicles had been discharged, retraction was possible on a favorable tide at about 1440. *LSM-318* then immediately re-beached in a more favorable spot to continue discharging vehicles. Speaking of *LSM-318*, other units of the Task Group had departed the area with the exception of LSMs *18*, *19*, *318*, and the stranded large infantry landing craft.[14]

While *LSM-318* was retracting—heaving in on the stern anchor and backing down on the engines—the first of a series of air attacks occurred. (The wind and seas were calm at the time of the action, the sky 30 percent overcast with cumulus clouds between 6,000-8,000 feet, and bearing of the sun from the southwest.) Seven enemy aircraft, four identified as Oscars and three tentatively as Bettys (Mitsubishi G4M Navy Type 1 land-based attack aircraft), came in from the northeast, flying over the Army units landed on the beach.[15]

Photo 5-5

Japanese Betty (Mitsubishi G4M Navy Type 1 land-based attack aircraft).

These planes were taken under fire by Army .50-caliber guns while still about 6,000 yards from the *LSM-318*. One Betty "peeled off" (separated from the others) and made a bombing run on her, dropping a 500-lb bomb which hit the water about 150 yards on the ship's port quarter. This plane did not then attempt to strafe the *318*. It instead joined the other aircraft in attacking the LSMs *18* and *19*, and the *LCI(L)-970*. By this time, the infantry landing craft had been freed of the hard rock formation or reef upon which she had been grounded, allowing all three of these vessels to be clear of the beach and able to maneuver. Rairden wryly noted about the circumstances:

> The Japs misjudged in failing to concentrate on us. We could not maneuver at the time, as there were still about forty fathoms of stern anchor cable out. We were almost a "sitting duck" target.[16]

After bringing in her anchor, *LSM-318* cleared the beach at flank speed, heading seaward to join the other three ships. Upon reaching them, they formed a column, in the following order: LSMs *18, 318, 19*, and *LCI(L)-970*. The ships had a brief reprieve from air attack during this time because P38 Lightning fighter cover was engaging enemy planes.[17]

Photo 5-6

Lockheed P38 Lightning fighter aircraft.

A short time later, at approximately 1524, four Oscars were sighted approaching the formation, again from over land. One of these aircraft veered off to its starboard, apparently to attack the *LSM-19* and *LCI(L)-970* which had fallen behind at that point. The focus of Rairden was on the remaining three planes, closing the *LSM-318*, and the *LSM-18* positioned ahead of her which was leading the column:

> I lost sight of the other plane that went for them, and concentrated my attention on the other three. They were taken under fire by our 40MM gun at about 2500 yards range, and the Portside 20MMs commenced firing at about 1500 yards. One of the planes was attacking the *LSM 18*, and the other two made for us. Our 40MM

was seen to explode one of the OSCARS in the air when it was about 75 yards from us. A piece of its wing struck the forward part of the ship and small fragments were raining all over us. Almost simultaneously a second OSCAR (the one attacking the *LSM 18*) was taken under fire by our Port forward 20MM and the portside and after 20s of the *18*. Our 40MM switched to this target as well – and he too was blown apart.[18]

Meanwhile, the third Oscar passed overhead and continued out over the water, flying low on a course that took him out on *LSM-318*'s starboard bow to a distance of about 8,000 yards. He then went into a climbing turn to port, apparently to gain altitude for an attack. The Oscar was engaged by a P38, which Rairden believed failed to hit the enemy plane with gunfire. He explained:

> The OSCAR turned sharply inside the 38 and came in to attack us flying very low over the water. The P38 was following him in, but at such an angle that he bore well forward of the enemy plane from our ship. We took the enemy plane under fire with the 40MM and the starboard side 20s. Using full right rudder in an attempt to turn toward him proved to be an ineffective maneuver – he merely slipped to his Port enough to continue making his approach on the same bearing. Despite the fact that he was under the combined fire of our guns and those of the *LSM 18*, he came right in and crashed into the Starboard Side of the ship at the water line directly below the flagbag [located by the mast aft of the bridge]. He carried on through the ship and into the engine room, his bomb exploding in the vicinity of the Port main engine.[19]

The plane and the bomb (or bombs) it had aboard passed through the lube oil settling tank, lube oil storage tank, one fuel oil settling tank, and the refrigeration space on the port side. Some wreckage (at least the engine) emerged from the port side of the ship below No. 2 and 4 life rafts, making a hole about six feet in diameter.[20]

The bomb(s) blast knocked out the port main engine, both generators, and both fire and flushing pumps, and starting a blazing fire. The ship also suffered the loss of steering and because the rudder had jammed right full, the ship was circling slowly to starboard. An attempt by the engineering officer to secure the starboard engine using the remote-control shutoff valve was only particular successful, and it continued running though at somewhat reduced speed. Damage control measures were undertaken without success. When the *LSM-18* was sighted steaming slowly toward the *318*, Rairden reluctantly had the word passed, ordering his crew to abandon ship.[21]

The men left the ship in an orderly fashion, with the wounded put overboard into the water first. The *LSM-18* stood in and lay to nearby, carrying out highly effective rescue work. In his report, Lieutenant Rairden praised the actions of the LSM Group Four commander aboard the *18*, for his planning and execution of this operation:

> It was discovered later by the originator [Rairden] that the Group Commander [Lt. Comdr. Reginald C. Johnson], who knew of the presence of enemy aircraft in the immediate area, had cooly and accurately calculated the risks involved and executed his plan superbly. Accurate ship-handling was needed, as the stricken ship still had way on for about 15 or 20 minutes and was spewing burning oil out onto the water both to Port and Starboard. It is very strongly felt by the originator that the rescue work was outstanding. It was persistently carried out until the ships were again taken under intensive air attack, and even then the Group Commander pulled his ships away only when he had seen Army-manned LCMs [landing craft] approaching from the direction of the 77th [Infantry] Division beach. The planes, of course, followed the larger vessels and ignored the LCM's and the few remaining survivors who were in the water.[22]

REMAINING THREE SHIPS BEACH TO AVOID LOSS

Following the abandonment of *LSM-318*, and in view of continuing attacks by groups of Japanese aircraft, Lt. Comdr. Reginald C. Johnson ordered *LCI(L)-970* to beach, and subsequently LSMs *18* and *19* after they had retrieved nearly all *LSM-318* survivors. Johnson (embarked aboard *LSM-18*) described, in his war diary, the aircraft attacks that caused the loss of the *318*, and follow-on attacks that induced him to order the remaining ships to beach and their crews to seek shelter ashore. This action may have prevented the sinking of one or more of the remaining two LSMs or LCI(L) offshore, and associated loss of life:

> While retracting, which was advisable because of Jap mortar shells hitting very close, four Jap planes made a bombing attack. At least five salvos of bombs landed close aboard LSMs. A few minutes later, four or more dive bombers attacked. One plane was shot down by the *LSM 18*. After dropping bombs, all near misses, a suicide plane struck the *LSM 318* amidships, passing completely through her, and set her on fire. It was found necessary to abandon the *318*. *LCI 970* was ordered to beach and LSMs *18* and *19* to pick up survivors.

While picking up survivors, six Jap bombers attacked. LSMs *18* and *19* successfully avoided all bombs, but both were badly shaken up, and considerable minor damage was incurred. Another plane was shot down by *LSM 18*, just as the bombs were released. LSMs *18* and *19* then beached, having first arranged with the Army to pick up the remaining survivors with LCMs.

Upon beaching at 1650, Commander LSM Group FOUR ordered the ships abandoned when another Jap attack of 12 planes came in. The bombing attack resulted in several near misses and the destruction of several LCMs. During all attacks, air cover was giving a brilliant performance, shooting down several planes. All personnel were kept under cover on the beach until darkness, when the ships were manned and under cover of darkness proceeded to San Pedro Harbor, arriving there about 1000 on 8 December.[23]

SUMMARY

The conquest of LEYTE was greatly facilitated by an amphibious landing at ORMOC Bay, which brought our ground forces into position to attack the enemy rear, and at the same time to cut off his major port of supply.

—Admiral Chester Nimitz, in Commander in Chief, U.S. Pacific Fleet and Pacific Ocean Areas, Operations in Pacific Ocean Areas – December 1944, 25 June 1945.

The cost to Rear Adm. Arthur Struble's Task Group 78.3 of successfully landing the 77th Infantry Division at Ormoc was three sunken ships—the destroyer *Mahan* (DD-364) high-speed transport *Ward* (APD-16), and medium landing ship *LSM-318*—and five damaged ones. The latter ships were the destroyer *Lamson* (DD-367), high-speed transport *Liddle* (APD-60), tank landing craft *LST-737*, and LSMs *18* and *19*.[24]

General Walter Krueger, commander, U.S. Sixth Army, later commented about the operation, "The landing of the 77th Division near Ormoc, serving to split the enemy forces and to separate them from their supply base, proved to be the decisive action of the Leyte Operation."[25]

6

Luzon Operation: Mindoro Landings

The mission of the Task Group was to embark at LEYTE, transport, protect, and land the landing force, together with its supplies and equipment, in the SAN JOSE Area of Southwest MINDORO, and support the landings by close gunfire, in order to establish air forces in Southwest MINDORO for direct support of further operations in the PHILIPPINE Area.

—Rear Adm. Arthur Struble, commander, Amphibious Group 9 and Task Group 78.3, in his Action Report on the Mindoro Landings.[1]

Map 6-1

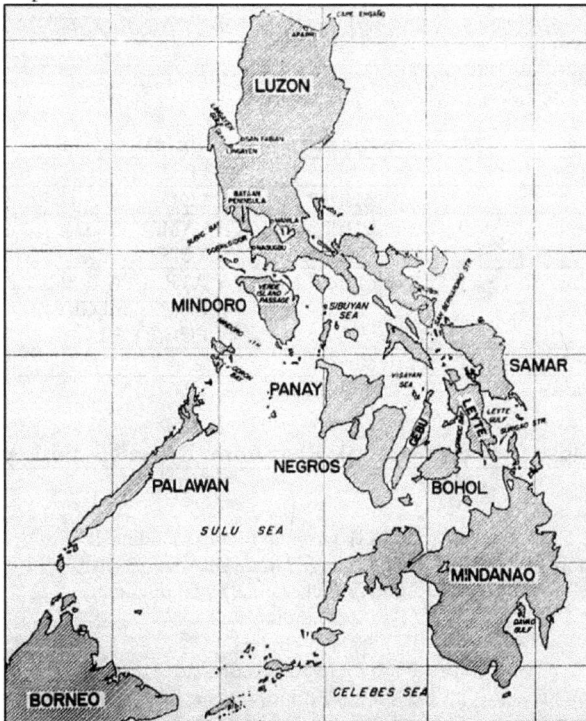

Philippine Islands

In mid-afternoon on 12 December 1944, Rear Admiral Struble's Task Group 78.3 sortied from the Dulag area of the Leyte Gulf, bound for waters off southwest Mindoro Island. Aboard the ships were elements of the 503rd Parachute Regiment and the 19th Regimental Combat Team of the 24th Infantry (reinforced), and equipment and supplies, loaded at Leyte. The numbers and types of ships assigned to each subordinate task unit of the task group are identified in the table. The Light Transport Unit's (78.3.3) unnamed LCI(L)s and LSMs are further identified by their hull numbers. The numbers and type of ships of supporting Task Group 77.3 (Close Covering Group) are also included in the table.

Task Group 78.3: Rear Adm. Arthur Struble, USN

TU	Title	Commander	Ship(s)
78.3.1	Group Flagship	Capt. Coney	1 CL
78.3.2	Assault Unit	Comdr. W. S. Parsons	8 APD

78.3.3 (Light Transport Unit): Comdr. William V. Deutermann

LCI(L)s 972 (flagship), 578, 579, 607, 609, 611, 612, 613, 685, 686, 687, 758, 759, 962, 963, 964, 965, 966, 970, 976, 977, 978, 980, 981, 983, 1014, 1017, 1018, 1021, 1022, 1065

LSMs 258 (flagship), 21, 22, 34, 37, 40, 138, 139, 148, 150, 310, 311

TU	Title	Commander	Ship(s)
78.3.4	Heavy Transport Unit	Capt. Webb	30 LST
78.3.5	Escort Unit	Capt. Martin	12 DD
78.3.6	Minesweeping Unit	Comdr. Ellsworth E. D. McEathron	10 AM, 1 APD, 7 YMS
78.3.7	Control and Inshore Support Unit	Comdr. Linthicum	1 ATR, 1 PC, 1 SC, 4 LCI(G), 5 LCI(R), 1 PCE(R), 1 LCI(D)
78.3.8	Beach Parties No. 1 and 7	Lt. Walter	
70.1.4	PT Boat Squadron	Lt. Comdr. Davis	23 PT

Task Group 77.3 (Close Covering Group): Rear Adm. Russell S. Berkey

1 CA, 2 CL, 8 DD

AM: minesweeper
APD: high-speed transport
ATR: rescue tug
CA: heavy cruiser
CL: light cruiser
DD: destroyer
LCI(D): underwater demolition
        infantry landing craft[1]

LCI(G): gunboat infantry landing craft
LCI(L): large infantry landing craft
LCI(R): rocket infantry landing craft
LST: tank landing ship
PC/SC: sub-chasers
PCE(R): rocket escort patrol craft
YMS: yard minesweeper

At around dawn the following morning, 13 December, the task group shifted from a cruising disposition to an anti-aircraft formation in anticipation of encounters with Japanese aircraft.[2]

Also on this date, which was two days in advance of the planned assault date, the U.S. Army Fifth Air Force on Leyte began furnishing air cover for the task group. That afternoon, one single-engine plane was able to sneak in low about 1500, unobserved by lookouts with deadly consequences to USS *Nashville* (CL-43), Admiral Struble's flagship. The aircraft approached just above the water from starboard to port astern, then banked sharply to the right and crashed into the light cruiser's port side, aft of the admiral's cabin.[3]

Photo 6-1

Crewmen cleaning up the port side 5"/25 gun battery of USS *Nashville* (CL-43) after the ship was hit in that area by a Kamikaze on 13 December 1944, while en route to the Mindoro invasion.
National Archives photograph #80-G-K-6886

A tremendous explosion shook the cruiser from stem to stern. The blast wrecked the flag bridge, CIC (combat information center), and communication office—and caused secondary explosions of ready ammunition for the 5-inch and 40mm mounts on both the port and starboard sides. Tragically, approximately 131 men were killed and about 158 wounded. The deceased including flagstaff personnel consisting of the chief of staff, communications officer, medical officer, and two enlisted men.[4]

At 1600, the destroyer *Dashiell* (DD-659) came alongside the *Nashville* to take Admiral Struble and members of his staff aboard, clearing the side of the cruiser about 1700. After dark, the *Nashville*, escorted by the destroyer *Stanly* (DD-478), returned to Leyte.[5]

Shortly after the first suicide attack, that on the *Nashville*, others against the group developed and continued intermittently until about 1900. These were successfully countered by naval gunfire from ships in the screen, and by the Combat Air Patrol.[6]

At about 0200 on the morning of the pending amphibious assault, on 15 December, the "Black Cat" PBY Catalina aircraft on night patrol reported several surface objects ahead of the convoy. The plane was ordered to investigate and, if enemy were encountered, to attack. Several minutes later, the Black Cat reported: "Bombed enemy target, one bomb seen to hit amidships." Just before dawn, the destroyers *Ingraham* (DD-694) and *Barton* (DD-722) investigated the reported contact and found a Japanese 500-ton inter-island freighter of the SC type, which they immediately took under fire and left in a flaming and sinking condition.[7]

Photo 6-2

A "Black Cat," PBY Catalina, skims the waters of San Pedro Bay off Samar Island, in the Philippines, circa 1945. The Black Cat Squadron to which it belonged, VPB-34, was awarded the Presidential Unit Citation. They were painted black for camouflage at night. Naval History and Heritage Command photograph #L01-11.04.02

ASSAULT LANDINGS ON MINDORO

Arrived at Blue and White Beaches, Mindoro, P.I., at about 0630. 0800 Seven LSMs beached at Blue Beach and five at White Beach. All LSMs unloaded and retracted by 1000. While on the beach, Jap planes attacked, suicide planes hitting two LSTs. LSM 258 and 34 assisted in picking up survivors. All LSMs rendezvoused by 1100 for the return trip to San Pedro Harbor, Leyte, P.I. The return trip was uneventful...

—Commander LSM Group Four War Diary, December 1944.

All LCI and LSM waves beached at the appointed time or very close thereto. The beaches in the main were good and most of the units had dry landings. No difficulties were experienced in unloading or retracting and no shore opposition was encountered while ships of this Task Unit were at the Beach.

—Commander Task Unit 78.3.3, Action Report – Mindoro Operation, 30 December 1944.

At 0603 on 15 December, Task Group 78.3 passed the southern tip of Ilin Island abeam to starboard, and approached the transport area off the Mindoro assault beaches. In preparation for H-Hour set for 0730, naval bombardment of the beach commenced at 0705, while assault craft and landing ships formed in waves in preparation for the approach. Rocket bombardment began at 0725 immediately prior to the landings.[8]

Of the twelve medium landing ships assigned to the task group; seven—LSMs *258* (flagship), *21*, *22*, *34*, *37*, *40*, and *310*—landed on "Blue Beach" while the remaining five—LSMs *138*, *139*, *148*, *150*, and *311*—beached on "White Beach."

BLUE BEACH

At Blue Beach, the first wave, consisting of troops in small landing boats, hit the beach at 0730. The next two waves were comprised of troops in LSI(L)s. At 0735, in preparation for their landing as the fourth wave, seven LSMs formed a line abreast. The flagship *LSM-258* was at the extreme right with the others to her left, spaced 150 yards apart, in the order shown below:

Fourth Assault Wave

LSM-40   LSM-310   LSM-37   LSM-34   LSM-22   LSM-21   LSM-258[9]

At 0739, with the second wave (LCIs) at the beach, and the third wave on their way, the order "beaching" was sounded. Aboard the LSMs, Army vehicles were started and their personnel made preparations to land. At 0750, more LCIs hit the beach as wave three.[10]

At 0755, the LSMs approached the line of departure, preparing to make the beach as wave four. They arrived there at 0759, and headed for Blue Beach, San Agustin, Mindoro, on course 040°T, speed 2/3 ahead.[11]

The flagship *LSM-258* landed at 0813, with stern anchor dropped behind her on heading 356°T, with 575 feet of cable payed out stopped. The depth of water at her ramp was four feet, too great for unloading. She backed off the beach 200 feet by heaving in on her stern anchor, and with ballast tanks emptied, came in at full speed to get farther up on the beach. The water depth at the ramp was then 3½ feet, amidships 6½ feet, and aft 15½ feet. At 0825, a bulldozer left the ship and commenced building a sand ramp for the unloading of vehicles.[12]

At 0844, low flying Zeros appeared, bearing 180°T, course 010°T, from *LSM-258*, then disappeared on bearing 030°T. Heavy anti-aircraft fire was put up by escort warships with no hits observed. At 0856, three Zeros appeared bearing 185°T and prepared to crash-dive ships. Two struck LSTs and one went into the water. At 0858, *LSM-258* completed unloading and easily retracted from the beach. She and *LSM-34* were subsequently tasked with recovering survivors from the LSTs which suffered severe damage.[13]

Photo 6-3

USS *LST-738* burning after she was hit by a Kamikaze off the Mindoro landing beaches, 15 December 1944. The destroyer USS *Moale* (DD-693) is nearby.
Naval History and Heritage Command photograph #NH 97259

Photo 6-4

Navy ships fighting fires on USS *LST-742*, after she was hit by a Kamikaze off the Mindoro landing beaches, 15 December 1944. Photographed from on board USS *PCE-851*. The bow of USS *O'Brien* (DD-725) is at right, with firefighting parties spraying water on the burning ship. USS *Hopewell* (DD-681) is seen nearly bow-on in the center background, largely shrouded by smoke.
Naval History and Heritage Command photograph #NH 103030

LSM-34, part of the fourth wave, under the command of Lt. Howard J. Hicks, USNR, was attached to Group Five, within LSM Flotilla Two, but then operating with LSM Group Four. Embarked aboard her were fifty-three Army men and officers, and engineering vehicles and other equipment previously loaded at Red Beach, San Ricardo area, on 11 December.[14]

Like *LSM-258*, Hick's ship had to do some last-minute shifting to land successfully, based on conditions found off the assault beaches. He described his experience heading into Blue Beach One:

At 0720 we arrived near the line of departure, and prepared to form up for beaching. At 0750 seven (7) LSMs [abreast] started the run for Blue Beach No. 1. This vessel was in the center of the seven LSMs... As we neared the beach it became obvious to this command that we were headed directly for a reef. We edged over to the starboard gradually in order to clear the reef, and beached at 0809 at one-third speed with eighty (80) fathoms of cable out to the stern anchor. It appeared to this command that the four (4) LSMs to the right flank had beached at Blue Beach No. 2 instead of Blue Beach one. Whether this was caused by the line of departure being established incorrectly this command does not know. At any rate, if we had maintained our position as established at the line of departure we would have beached on the reefs.[15]

LSM-34 had a "dry door" landing—enabling army personnel going ashore to do so with dry feet. The vehicles aboard had no difficulty getting ashore via her bow ramp. They did have trouble traversing the beach sand with the customarily heavy loads put on the army trucks.[16]

Having discharged her cargo, *LSM-34* retracted from the beach at 0831. At this point enemy planes were over the area, attacking ships. Hicks reported ten enemy planes sighted from the vantage point of his ship, and witnessing two planes crash-dive into separate LSTs. Fires on both these vessels spread rapidly. An account of *LSM-34* and *LSM-258*'s rescue activities follow the next section.[17]

WHITE BEACH

Earlier that morning, following arrival of the task group off the objective area at 0640, the commanding officer of *LSM-311* had taken charge of the White Beach light transport unit (as officer in tactical command) of LSMs *311*, *34*, *138*, *139*, and *257*, and LCIs *609*, *1018*, and *1021*. Signal "Deploy" was hoisted at 0745, and the LSMs formed on a bearing 270 degrees relative from *LSM-311*. The ships reached the line of departure at 0753, and beached at 0800.[18]

No ground action was observed on the beach, and enemy air action was absent until about 0850, when several fighters attacked from the region of Ilin Island. However, the LSMs were able to retract independently after unloading without incident.[19]

The unloading of these ships and LSTs of the Heavy Transport Unit was accomplished before dark by the use of some 1,200 troops of the 77th Infantry Division, brought along for that sole purpose. These soldiers were returned to Leyte the following day.[20]

RETRIEVAL OF LST SURVIVORS

At 0950 a large ammunition explosion from LST 738 *was heard. At 1014 picked up 6 Naval survivors from a* PT *boat... At 1017 sent 2 stretchers over to LSM 34 which had picked up many survivors. At 1027 set course to rejoin convoy, engines ahead full. Passed* LST 472 *on our starboard hand, burning and abandoned. At 1137 joined convoy as lead ship in left column.... The convoy consisted of 11 LSMs (LSM 34 picking up survivors, was to rejoin convoy later), and 33 LCIs, with 8 APDs and 2 DDs acting as screen.*

—Commanding Officer, USS *LSM 258*, Action Report –
Mindoro Operation, 17 December 1944.

At 0918, *LSM-34* proceeded to the vicinity of *LST-738*, which had been hit by a plane, to rescue personnel. As she neared the ship's position a terrific explosion occurred which, it was learned later, was probably caused by the detonation of thousand-pound bombs which were part of her cargo.[21]

Lieutenant Hicks described subsequent actions by *LSM-34* to recover injured personnel, and of later rejoining the convoy of task force ships which had departed for Leyte:

> We took aboard approximately 225 personnel, Army and Navy, from PT boats, rafts, and other small craft. Eleven (11) stretcher cases were taken aboard.[20]

> We proceeded to join the convoy, and received instruction to place the army personnel ashore. This was done by transferring the army personnel to PT boats, for placing ashore. At this time, 1045, the first returning echelon had taken a lead of 11½ miles on us. We followed at flank speed, on an interception course, and caught up to the convoy at 1330.

> We took position astern of *LSM 40* on the starboard column, and requested a physician to take care of the 11 stretcher cases. A physician was placed aboard from *LCI 686*. We had aboard 11 casualties, 10 army and one navy, two army photographers, and 59 members of *LST 736* ship's company, including eight (8) officers.... The convoy arrived at Leyte Gulf without serious interference.[22]

MINDORO AND PRECEDING ORMOC OPERATIONS

The assault troops carried to Mindoro aboard Task Group 78.3 ships were landed on schedule, with no casualties. Since only about 200 enemy troops had been expected to be found in the objective area, and not more than 500 on the entire island, heavy forces of assault troops had not been considered necessary. The 19th Regimental Combat Team (Reinforced) of the 24th Infantry Division, and the 503rd Parachute Regiment, were successfully landed, plus service troops, to establish an airfield and other facilities.[23]

503rd Parachute Regiment: Formed on 2 March 1942 **24th Infantry Division:** Activated: 25 February 1921 in Hawaii as the Hawaiian Division Redesignated the 24th Infantry Division on 26 August 1941	

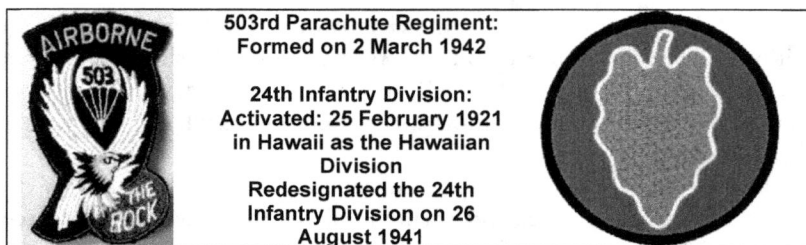

Although significant enemy ground opposition was not encountered on Mindoro beaches and in preceding Ormoc landings, Allied forces suffered heavy casualties in these operations as a result of Japanese Kamikaze attacks. In Seventh Amphibious Force Command History, Rear Adm. Daniel E. Barbey, commander, Seventh Amphibious Force, acknowledged these losses, and highlighted the importance of the associated assault landings:

> Ships of the SEVENTH Amphibious Force suffered high personnel casualties and heavy material losses from suicide air attacks during the ORMOC and MINDORO operations. However, these two landings contributed materially to the final capture of Leyte and to the success of the impending operations on Luzon.[24]

BATTLE STARS

All twelve medium landing ships that participated in the Mindoro landings earned a battle star for the period 12-18 December 1944.

Luzon Operation: Mindoro Landings

Ship	Award Period	Ship	Award Period
USS *LSM-21*	12-18 Dec 44	USS *LSM-139*	12-18 Dec 44
USS *LSM-22*	12-18 Dec 44	USS *LSM-148*	12-18 Dec 44
USS *LSM-34*	12-18 Dec 44	USS *LSM-150*	12-18 Dec 44
USS *LSM-37*	12-18 Dec 44	USS *LSM-258*	12-18 Dec 44
USS *LSM-40*	12-18 Dec 44	USS *LSM-310*	12-18 Dec 44
USS *LSM-138*	12-18 Dec 44	USS *LSM-311*	12-18 Dec 44

7

Lingayen Operation

The amphibious landing at LINGAYEN on 9 January 1945 followed the same general organization plan used at Leyte. Commander SEVENTH Fleet was in overall command of the landing; Commander SEVENTH Amphibious Force landed the I Corps on the northern beaches; and Commander THIRD Amphibious Force landed the XIV Corps on the southern beaches. Initial opposition to the landing was not strong but it stiffened as the troops moved from the beachhead to the hills just beyond, and naval gunfire support was used for several weeks. Fire support ships and minesweepers suffered substantial losses during the preliminary minesweeping and preassault bombardment. If the enemy had concentrated air attacks on transports with the same effectiveness achieved against supporting ships, the Lingayen operation might not have succeeded.

—Command History Seventh Amphibious Force.[1]

As 1945 broke, all of Leyte was firmly in control of Allied ground forces with only mopping up of isolated enemy remnants remaining, and its airfields were in condition to support major offensive action. Allied land-based air forces were firmly established in Mindoro, and Central Philippine waters had been largely cleared of all Japanese combatant ships, with the exception of some submarines.[2]

Lingayen Gulf, is a large inlet of the South China Sea that indents the western coast of central Luzon Island. It was there that the next incursion into the islands would occur. It was believed that the enemy's air power throughout the Philippines had been neutralized sufficiently that only small groups or single planes could be mustered from airfields to oppose continued Allied operations for the reconquest of the Philippines. However, the impending Lingayen Gulf operation would provide abundant difficulties, characterized by the greatly increased employment of suicide planes by the Japanese, made possible by the many airfields available in the close vicinity of that gulf.[3]

The impending significant enemy use of suicide (Kamikaze) aircraft and suicide (Shinyo) explosive boats was then unknown. From Allied leadership perspective, the stage was set for planned amphibious assault landings on 9 January 1945 in the Lingayen Gulf. The object of the Lingayen operation was the:

- Prompt seizure of the Central Luzon area
- Destruction of the principal defense forces
- Denial to the enemy of the northern entrance to the South China Sea
- Provision of bases for the support of further operations against the Japanese[4]

Lingayen Gulf is a generally rectangular area about 20 miles wide and 30 miles long, exposed to the northwest, with unlimited anchorage area at the inner end, shown in the map below. The inner end is bordered by sandy beaches with such a gradual slope in most places that it was believed the pontoon causeways would be necessary for LSTs to unload. However, some of the San Fabian beaches proved to be suitable for dry-ramp beaching of them, which contributed materially to the speed of unloading.[5]

The beaches selected for landing were distributed over most of the south and southeast shores of Lingayen Gulf; one group generally opposite the town of Lingayen, and the other extending beyond both sides of the town of San Fabian.[6]

Map 7-1

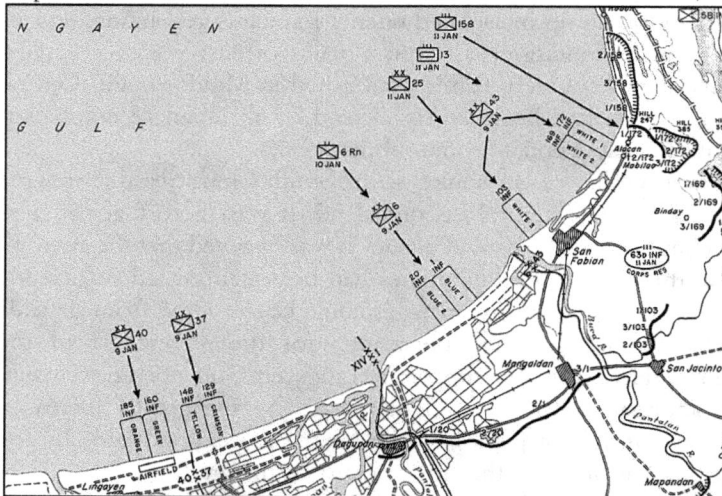

Landing beaches at Lingayen Gulf, from L–R: Orange (185th Inf.), Green (160th Inf.), Yellow (148th Inf.), Crimson (129th Inf.), Blue 2 (20th Inf.), Blue 1 (1st Inf.), White 3 (103rd Inf.), White 2 (169th Inf.), and White 1 (172nd Inf.)
https://ww2db.com/images/55f2482b5ad17.jpg

LUZON ATTACK FORCE

Task Force 77 assembled for the assault of Luzon was under the overall command of Vice Adm. Thomas C. Kinkaid, commander, Seventh Fleet, and organized into the following groups.

Task Force 77 (Luzon Attack Force)

TG	Title	Commander
77.1	Flag Group	
77.2	Bombardment and Fire Support Group	Vice Adm. Jesse B. Oldendorf
77.3	Close Covering Group	Rear Adm. Russell S. Berkey
77.4	Escort Carrier Group	Rear Adm. Calvin T. Durgin
77.5	CVE-DE Hunter-Killer Group	Capt. Joseph C. Cronin
77.6	Minesweeping and Hydrographic Group	Comdr. Wayne R. Loud
77.7	Screening Group	Capt. J. B. McLean
77.8	Salvage and Rescue Group	Comdr. Huie
77.9	Reinforcement Group	Rear Adm. Richard L. Conolly
77.10	Service Group	Rear Adm. Robert O. Glover
78	San Fabian Attack Force	Vice Adm. Daniel E. Barbey
79	Lingayen Attack Force	Vice Adm. T. S. Wilkinson[7]

CVE: Escort Carrier
DE: Destroyer Escort

U.S. ARMY ASSAULT TROOPS

San Fabian Attack Force (TF 78) ships transported troops of the I Corps, consisting of the 6th and 43rd Infantry Divisions (reinforced), to the beaches, while the Lingayen Attack Force (TF 79) carried troops of the XIV Corps, the 37th and 40th Infantry Divisions (reinforced). Aboard Reinforcement Group (TG 77.9) ships were the reserve troops of the Sixth Army, consisting of the 25th Infantry Division (reinforced) and the 158th Regimental Combat Team.[8]

MOVEMENT TO THE OBJECTIVE

The transits of assault forces to Leyte were generally uneventful. From Leyte Gulf, the route to the assault beaches passed through the Surigao Strait, Mindanao Sea, Sulu Sea, Mindoro Strait, and northward off the west coast of Luzon to Lingayen Gulf (see Map 7-2 on next page).[9]

On 8 January, the Australian heavy cruiser HMAS *Australia* and USS *LST-915* were hit by suicide planes at Lingayen and southwest of Luzon, respectively. *Australia* was crashed again the following day, sustaining a total of five hits by Japanese Kamikaze planes during 5, 6, 8, and 9 January. Suffering the loss of 44 crewmen and receiving extensive damage, she remained in action providing gunfire support for the Lingayen landings.[10]

Photo 7-1

Australian heavy cruiser HMAS *Australia* in Lingayen Gulf, Leyte, on 9 January 1945.
National Archives #80-G-273158

Map 7-2

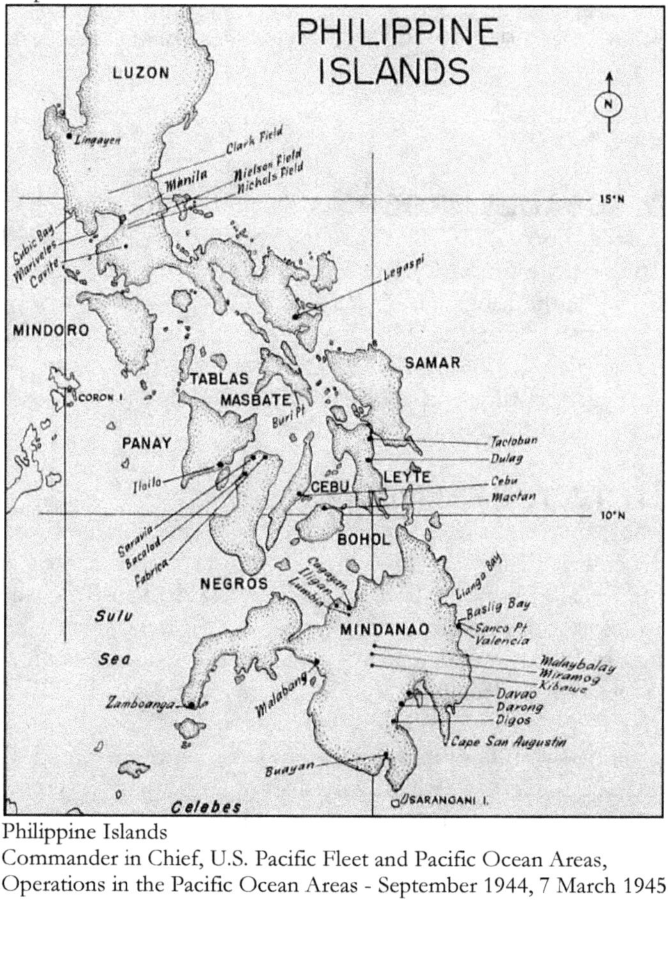

Philippine Islands
Commander in Chief, U.S. Pacific Fleet and Pacific Ocean Areas,
Operations in the Pacific Ocean Areas - September 1944, 7 March 1945

AMPHIBIOUS OPERATIONS

In early morning on 9 January, the ships of the attack forces arrived on schedule at the designated transport areas in lower Lingayen Gulf. Debarkation of troops in LVTs ("amtraks," also called "alligators") and other landing craft was begun about 0715. Under cover of very heavy bombardment by fire support groups and rocket infantry landing craft, and followed by strafing from aircraft ahead of them, the boats approached the beaches with the first waves landing at 0930. By 0940, only ten minutes later, many assault waves were ashore on all Lingayen and San Fabian beaches.[11]

There was negligible enemy opposition at the Lingayen beaches and the troops put ashore were able to advance inland in spite of very unfavorable terrain. Movement inland was hampered by two deep rivers in the immediate rear of the beaches and a terrain generally covered by rice paddies. Acknowledging that conditions could have been much worse, the commander of the Lingayen Attack Force thankfully stated "that a small force of determined men, properly armed and trained, could have inflicted very heavy casualties upon our troops, and held up their advance for several days, if not longer."[12]

At the San Fabian beaches, the troops already ashore and those landing encountered no opposition until about 1000 when Japanese mortar and artillery fire opened. Some of the beached landing ships and craft were forced to retract, while one LST, one LCI(L), and several LSMs suffered damage with casualties to army and navy personnel.[13]

The remainder of this chapter will focus on roles/actions of the LSMs assigned to the Lingayen and San Fabian Attack Forces.

LINGAYEN ATTACK FORCE

Within Vice Adm. Thomas S. Wilkinson's Lingayen Attack Force (Task Force 79) were two sub-ordinate Attack Groups designated Able and Baker, whose forces of attack transports, attack cargo ships, and other amphibious ships included thirty-one medium landing ships (LSMs):

TG 79.1 (Attack Group Able): Rear Adm. Ingolf N. Kiland, USN

LSM Flotilla 7: Comdr. William E. Verge, USN
LSM Group 7: Comdr. F. W. Morrison, USN
LSM-*54* (flagship), *12* (group flagship), *8*, *10*, *11*, *13*, *15*, *25*, *27*, *135* (total 10 LSM)
LSM Group 9: Comdr. J. A. Moss, USN
LSM-*313* (group flagship), *31*, *32*, *33*, *137*, *144*, *234*, *235* (total 8 LSM)

TG 79.2 (Attack Group Baker): Rear Adm. Forrest B. Royal, USN

LSM Flotilla 3: Capt. John P. B. Barrett, USN
LSM Group 8: Lt. Comdr. J. G. Blanche Jr., USN
LSM-312 (flagship), *24* (group flagship), *14, 28, 29, 30, 50, 52, 53, 65, 210, 233, 259* (total 13 LSM)[14]

ASSAULT LANDINGS BY ATTACK GROUP ABLE

The assault on CRIMSON AND YELLOW Beaches in the LINGAYEN Area was made at 0930 (J-Hour) on 9 January 1945, by the 37th Infantry Division (Re-enforced), landing two Regiments abreast, each with two battalions in assault, from left to right as follows: 1st Battalion, 129th Infantry on CRIMSON 1; 3rd Battalion, 129th Infantry on CRIMSON 2; 2nd Battalion 148th Infantry on YELLOW 1; 1st Battalion 148th Infantry on YELLOW 2.

—Rear Adm. Ingolf N. Kiland, USN, commander Task Group 79.1.[15]

Photo 7-2

Painting by James Turnbull, 1945. Following an intensive Navy aerial and surface barrage, infantrymen push ashore on 9 January 1945 from Navy LVT landing craft ("alligators") in Lingayen Gulf, Luzon Island, Philippines.
Naval History and Heritage Command photograph #88-159-KT

The assault companies that landed on Crimson and Yellow Beaches at Lingayen were embarked in three LSMs and eight LSTs and boated (transported ashore) in LVTs. Battalion and Regimental reserve troops were embarked in Transport Divisions 8 and 28, with Corps Reserve in Transport Division 38. After the landing of assault troops, regimental reserves were landed on schedule at 1011.[16]

On assault day, 9 January, Wave 1 consisted of 12 LVTs (alligators) guided by LCVP (Higgins boats). Waves 2 to 5 consisted of 94 alligators carrying assault troops, also guided by Higgins boats. The entire LVT (alligator) group was guided by sub-chasers and the yard minesweeper *YMS-311*. The remaining nine waves included the following identified types of ships and craft, which landed in the period from J-Hour (0930) plus 11 to plus 61 minutes:

- 165 LCVPs (Higgins boats)
- 12 LCMs (medium landing craft)
- 4 LSMs (medium landing ships)[17]

Fifteen DUKWs from the vehicle landing ship *Ozark* (LCV-2), carrying Engineer Boat and Shore Regimental personnel and equipment, landed at J-Hour plus 45 minutes. The landings were made in accordance with the plan, and all waves were very close to schedule. There was no enemy opposition encountered and no casualties to troops from enemy fire on the beaches. [18]

Photo 7-3

USS *Ozark* (LSV-2) under way near her builder's yard, Willamette Iron & Steel Corp., Portland, Oregon, 16 September 1944.
National Archives photograph #19-N-76631

Photo 7-4

Six months earlier in distant France, a U.S. Army DUKW amphibious truck
bringing supplies ashore on a Normandy beach, 11 June 1944.
National Archives photograph #80-G-252737

ATTACK GROUP BAKER (TASK GROUP 79.2)

On 27 December 1944, Task Group 79.6 (Tractor Group Baker) stood
out of Seeadler Harbor, Manus, bound for the Philippine Islands.
Under the command of Capt. Ronald D. Higgins, USN, the group was
comprised of 17 LSTs, 13 LSMs, and 20 LCI(L)s. The LSM component,
designated Task Unit 79.6.4 (LSM Reserve Unit) was under the
command of Capt. John P. B. Barrett, USN.[19]

Task Unit 79.6.4 (LSM Reserve Unit)
USS *LSM-312* (flagship)

USS *LSM-14*	USS *LSM-29*	USS *LSM-52*	USS *LSM-210*
USS *LSM-24*	USS *LSM-30*	USS *LSM-53*	USS *LSM-233*
USS *LSM-28*	USS *LSM-50*	USS *LSM-65*	USS *LSM-259*

En route to Lingayen Gulf, Task Group 79.6 steamed 1,500 yards
astern of Tractor Group Able (TG 79.5) assigned to Attack Group Able.
These two forces entered the gulf under cover of darkness in early
morning on 9 January, and at 0623 deployed in accordance with the
approach plans.[20]

Attack Group Baker transported and landed the U.S. Army 40th
Infantry Division at the objective. Troops of the 160th and 185th
Regimental Combat Teams (RCTs), comprising the first three waves to
land, beginning at 0930, via LVTs on Green and Orange beaches,
respectively, were embarked in LSTs. The remainder of the assault
waves of RCT 160 and RCT 185 soldiers were landed from ships of
Transport Group Baker by LCVPs (Higgins boats), LCM(6)s
(mechanized landing craft), and LCTs (tank landing craft).[21]

The LSMs initially laid to off Portuguese Point in the LSM Reserve Unit Anchorage, then later shifted to the LST area X-ray Anchorage at 0930.[22]

At 1110, orders were received from commander, Task Group 79.4 (Commodore Herbert B. Knowles, commanding Transport Group Bravo, carrying the 40th Infantry Division) for the LSMs to beach and discharge their assault cargo. *LSM-312* beached at 1159 and unloaded her 171 tons of cargo in twenty minutes. As a matter of interest, she disembarked/discharged:

- 1 officer and 26 men of Regimental Combat Team 185, 754th Tank Battalion, B Company, 2nd Platoon
- 5 M4A1 Sherman tanks
- 1 D-7 bulldozer[23]

Photo 7-5

A Sherman M4 tank wading ashore from USS *LSM-168* during the Invasion of Cebu Island, Philippines, 26 March 1945.
National Archives photograph #80-G-259238

The other LSMs of Task Unit 79.6.4 followed, beaching in order of landing priority, except for *LSM-14* which was held in reserve. Thereafter, all LSMs assisted in unloading APAs (assault transports) and

AKs (assault cargo ships) of Task Group 79.4 by lightering their cargo to beaches.[24]

The skies were clear and mostly cloudless that day, and wind slight for the most part. The sea was calm on 9 January; but on succeeding days heavy swells hampered beaching conditions. No LSMs of Task Unit 79.6.4 were attacked during the Lingayen operation.[25]

SAN FABIAN ATTACK FORCE

Vice Adm. Daniel E. Barbey's two attack groups within Task Force 78 were designated the White Beach (TG 78.1) and Blue Beach (TG 78.5) Attack Groups. These titles denoted the assault beaches (White 1, White 2, and White 3, and Blue 1 and Blue 2) on which his groups were to land Army troops. In addition to being the overall San Fabian Attack Force commander, Vice Admiral Barbey also directly commanded the subordinate White Beach Attack Group, while Rear Adm. William M. Fechteler, USN, the Blue Beach Attack Group.

TG 78.1 (White Beach Attack Group): Vice Adm. Daniel E. Barbey
TU 78.1.4 (LSM Group 19, temporary): Lt. Comdr. William A. Burgett
LSM-66 (flagship), *41, 63, 64, 67, 68, 127, 219, 268, 269* (total 10 LSMs)

TG 78.5 (Blue Beach Attack Group): Rear Adm. William M. Fechteler
TU 78.5.6 (LSM Group 5, temporary): Lt. Comdr. E. G. Smith
LSMs *36* (flagship), *35, 169, 203, 205, 217, 218, 223, 314,*
315 (total 10 LSMs)[26]

BLUE BEACH ATTACK GROUP

9 Jan. 1945: 1220 to 12 Jan. 1945: 1700 – LSM's unloaded transports, shuttling vehicles, bulk cargoes and troops to the beaches. A few enemy air attacks developed, drawing fire from 40's and 20's of LSM's. No LSM's were damaged and no damage inflicted on the enemy, excepting that LSM 314 claims hitting a Val and shooting away his landing gear. The action was not observed by this command. Several loads were discharged by LSM's of this unit over WHITE BEACH Three on 10 January. While unloading, the beach was taken under enemy fire (mortar or light artillery or both). No hits were sustained by LSM's of this unit.

—Summary by Lt. Comdr. E. G. Smith, commander Task Unit 78.5.6,
of the activities of the ten LSMs under his command from noon on
9 January (following their landing on Blue Beaches as the 12th
assault wave, and retraction after discharging their loads)
to early evening on 12 January 1945.[27]

As shown on preceding Map 7-1, the San Fabian Blue assault beaches lay nearest those at Lingayen to the southwest. Like the experience of LSMs landing on Lingayen beaches, there were no casualties as a result of enemy action aboard the ten LSMs landing at Blue Beaches. Such was not the case at San Fabian White Beaches further to the northeast, a subject taken up following this section.

At 0615 on 9 January, upon the order of Rear Admiral Fechteler, commander Task Group 78.5 (Blue Beach Attack Group), to deploy, all ships reached their assigned stations on schedule. At this time, a UDT (Underwater Demolition Team) member met with Fechteler to provide beach data, and informed him that surf conditions were favorable. It was then confirmed that assault landings at San Fabian were to commence at 0930 and they proceeded as planned.[28]

The first assault wave hit the beach at 0933, and succeeding waves landed as scheduled. The ten LSMs constituting the 12th wave, were split into two five-ship sections. Section One was led by *LSM-36* (flagship of Lieutenant Commander Smith) landing on Blue Beach 1, and Section Two led by *LSM-35* on Blue Beach 2.[29]

The LSM sections beached at 1100, without encountering enemy opposition. Six LSMs had to retract without discharging their assault loads (owing to depth of water greater than 4 feet forward) and re-beached in alternate, more favorable locations. By 1120, all LSMs had discharged their loads and retracted, except for two forced to retract and beach again to discharge a few remaining pieces of equipment.[30]

Succeeding waves following the LSMs also landed on time. LSTs reported beaching, but because of their distance from shore, owing to a shallow gradient and depth of water, they required pontoons for unloading.[31]

During an enemy air attack in early afternoon, HMAS *Australia* (as previously reported) and the battleship USS *Mississippi* (BB-41) were hit by suicide planes, and the attack transport USS *Banner* (APA-60) suffered a near bomb miss. At 1445, with troops landed, commanding general, 6th Infantry Division reported he had assumed command ashore. At 1716, commander, Transports reported that all assault day transports were unloaded and ready to sail. At 1830, this shipping departed, while unloading of LSTs, AKAs and AKs continued.[32]

There were no casualties to personnel of Task Unit 78.5.6 as a result of enemy action during the Lingayen operation.[33]

WHITE BEACH ATTACK GROUP

> *Entered Lingayen Gulf, Luzon, P.I. and about 0645 deployed for various beaches.... 0715 reported for duty to CTF 78.1.2 (Commander Transport Squadron 14, Commodore C. G. RICHARDSON). At 0830 directed task unit to divide into three units as planned and each unit proceed to own beach. LSM's 268 and 63 departed for Beach White 3; LSM's 127, 41 and 219 departed for Beach White 1; remainder of ships remained with me.*

> —Lt. Comdr. William A. Burgett, commander Task Unit 78.1.4, describing in a war diary entry, events preceding his ten LSMs landing on White Beaches at San Fabian on 9 January 1945.[34]

LVTs (alligators) comprised the first three waves carrying assault troops ashore on San Fabian White Beaches. Following them came LCVP (Higgins Boat) waves; then LCMs (mechanized landing craft), and LSM waves which landed at the times indicated on their designated beaches:

- 0958: 7th Wave (LSMs *63, 268*) at White Beach 3
- 1008: 8th Wave (LSMs *41, 127, 219*) at White Beach 1
- 1025: 11th Wave (LSMs *64, 66, 67, 68, 269*) at White Beach 2[35]

There was no initial opposition to the landing and the troops proceeded inland. The LCVPs and LCMs made dry ramp landings on all beaches but, as expected, difficulty was experienced in beaching LSTs and LSMs. White Beach 3 was found unsuitable for these type ships, and all equipment and supplies for White Beaches were unloaded over White Beach 1 and White Beach 2.[36]

LSMs HIT BY ENEMY MORTAR AND SHELL FIRE

> *While on the beach we sustained no hits from the heavy artillery fire which was falling on the LSM's 127 and 219. Apparently the enemy were concentrating on these two ships although it appeared that they were shifting to this ship as we retracted, the closest shell to us was about 25 yards away.*

> —Lt. Willard W. Williams, USNR, commanding officer, USS *LSM-41*.[37]

At 1000, LSMs on White Beach 1 came under enemy mortar fire, causing personnel casualties and minor damage. *LSM-127* suffered 1 crewman killed, 6 wounded, and 2 soldiers wounded, and hull damage which prevented further operation. Her commanding officer, Lt. H. R. Rodgers, USNR, described this action, and ensuing service following available battle repairs before departure for Leyte:

> Shell fire was encountered approximately 1000 yards from beach which became more rapid and extremely accurate as we closed the beach. 1015 – Beached. 1025 – Cargo and passengers having been disembarked, retracted and cleared beach. It is estimated that over twenty shells were fired at this ship while on the beach, seven were direct hits. It is believed that fire was from approximately 4" guns located in hills off our port bow. After retracting we took casualties to casualty ship, *LST 245*, then proceeded to [the landing craft repair ship USS *Egeria*] ARL 8 for battle damage repairs. Due to heavy swell we were unable to stay alongside ARL 8. As a result essential repairs were not completed until night of 11 January. 12 and 13 January – Unloaded miscellaneous cargo and troops from [the amphibious cargo ship USS *Arneb*] AKA 56. 14 January – Departed for Leyte for completion of battle damage repairs and further assignment.[38]

Photo 7-6

USS *LSM-127* beaching on Panay Island, Philippines, 8 September 1945. U.S. Navy photograph #350415

LSM-219 beached at White Beach on heading 111°T, in company with *LSM-41* and *LSM-127*, amid shell bursts from enemy shore installations, and immediately commenced discharging Army vehicles and personnel of the landing force.[39]

Photo 7-7

USS *LSM-219* offloading equipment, date and location unknown.
U.S. Navy photo from *All Hands* magazine, February 1947

The beach and surf at her location was ideal for landings and she had a dry ramp with no effort. At 1024, a shell struck the lower part of the conning tower, exploded in the radio room, killed the radio operator, wounded the gunner and talker on #1 20MM gun immediately forward of the conning tower and demolished the Mark 14 gun sight and the #1 life raft. It likewise disabled the TCS and SCR communications equipment.[40]

One minute later, a second shell hit about 2½ feet above the first impact exploding in void space A-0201-V. The impact buckled the deck in the pilot house, damaged spare parts stored in the void and sprayed shrapnel around the conning tower. At 1026, a third shell hit and exploded in one Mark 8 vehicle, exploding loaded ammunition and starting a fire.[41]

Although fewer shore battery rounds hit *LSM-219* than *LSM-127*, she suffered much higher casualties, most caused by the third and a fourth shell striking the ship. Lt. Harmon Burns Jr., USNR, her commanding officer, briefly described damage wrought, resulting in many casualties:

> This latter shell disabled the vehicle, killed the operator and shrapnel from it wounded three men on #2 20MM gun thus putting the gun out of operation. At 1027 a mortar shell hit the bow ramp causing relatively slight material damage but injured the ship's 1st Lt. and an unknown number of Army personnel. Simultaneously with these hits, shells could be heard passing and exploding around the ship and one near miss injured the Engineering Officer and three soldiers. It was apparent to me that the enemy had precise range on my ship and when it was reported that damaged vehicles were preventing further debarkation.[42]

Lieutenant Burns retracted at 1031, having discharged only part of the cargo aboard ship, explaining in a report the reasons for this action:

> Examination revealed that the operators of three of four vehicles obstructing further unloading were dead and that an Army officer was dead in the fourth one. To have remained beached under these circumstances and endeavored to debark the remainder of Army vehicles and personnel would have meant, I feel, loss of the ship.
>
> The decision, as I saw it, was whether to attempt to continue unloading and risk the ship or to retract, recoup and try again. In consideration of the rapidity and accuracy of the firing, it seemed to me the safety of the ship and her ability to further operate, dictated retracting. I did so.[43]

Burns believed that except for the one mortar shell (fourth hit), all the shells which hit were believed to have been from Japanese 77mm guns. *LSM-219* suffered 5 killed (1 Navy, 4 Army) and 23 wounded (6 Navy, 17 Army).[44]

OTHER LANDING RESULTS

Lt. Commander Burgett's flagship *LSM-66*, and *64*, *67*, *68*, and *269* landed on Beach White 2 at 1036 and were all clear by 1048 with no casualties. About 1055, enemy mortar fire fell on the beach and water area which these ships had just vacated. LSMs on Beach White 3 could not approach the beach close enough to land and required assistance of LCM landing craft to unload. It required about eight hours for them to discharge their cargo.[45]

When clear of the beach, all ships, except the damaged *LSM-127*, proceeded to the transport area for reloading. *LSM-219* transferred her casualties and had the vehicle blocking her unloading repaired, before proceeding to the beach and discharging her combat load.[46]

LSM CASUALTIES – LINGAYEN OPERATION

Enemy forces on the beach giving most trouble to LSM's were enemy mortars and artillery. One gun especially had the range on White Beach Two hitting this ship with three direct hits and approximately seven or eight near misses. This gun (or guns) did not fire continuously, but opened up in spurts. After the third day the enemy only opened up at night. Most of his shots that missed fell into the water just off the beach or just astern of ships beached. Fire on his part (the enemy) was most accurate and very disheartening to personnel caught under his barrage.

—Lt. H. T. Turner Jr., USNR, commanding officer, USS *LSM-269*.[47]

In early afternoon on 9 January, after loading vehicles and drivers from the amphibious attack transport *Bowie* (APA-137), *LSM-269* landed on White Beach 2. While unloading and retracting, an enemy shell burst close aboard, followed by a shell hit and two mortar hits. As a result, five crewmen were killed in action (KIA) and eight wounded in action (WIA).[48]

During the Lingayen operation, a total of 11 Navy crewmembers/ embarked Army personnel aboard LSMs were KIA, and 48 WIA. Among this total, five Navymen aboard *LSM-24* and three aboard *LSM-66* were wounded by "friendly fire," falling shrapnel from Allied ships' anti-aircraft fire.

Lingayen Operation LSM Army/Navy Casualties				
Ship	Cause	KIA	WIA	Total
LSM-24	falling shrapnel from Allied ships AA fire		5	5
LSM-66	falling shrapnel from Allied ships AA fire		3	3
LSM-127	mortar fire	1	8	9
LSM-137	near enemy plane bomb miss		1	1
LSM-219	shell fire	5	23	28
LSM-269	mortar fire	5	8	13
Total		11	48	59[49]

JAPANESE SUICIDE BOATS

At about 0350 a report was received by voice intercept that LST 925 was being attacked by three small boats and that she had been damaged by an explosion against the hull. Shortly thereafter and in rapid succession reports were received of damage to the transport WARHAWK *(AP 168), the destroyers* ROBINSON *and* PHILIP, LST 1028, LST 610, LST 548, LCI 365 *and* LCI 674. *Immediately all forces were alerted against attacks by small boats, midget submarines and swimmers. Within a few minutes the destroyer* EATON *was seen to be engaged in a machine gun fight with a small boat which she was seen to destroy.* RENSHAW *discovered a small craft near her and having illuminated it was unable to fire because of danger of hitting our own ships. It soon withdrew at high speed apparently undamaged. Another boat was sunk by gunfire from landing craft.*

—Vice Adm. Thomas S. Wilkinson commander, Task Force 79.[50]

Although there was a marked absence of enemy defense forces on Lingayen and San Fabian landing beaches, as evidenced by the above narrative, threats to Allied ships were not limited to Japanese suicide aircraft, and artillery and mortar fire from unseen hillside gun emplacements.

The Lingayen landings brought the first appearance of enemy suicide assault demolition boats of the war. They were about eighteen feet long, of wooden construction, and had a speed of about 20 knots. Owing to their small size, they could be used only in comparatively calm water. Depth charges were carried on either side of the cockpit and could be released either from the cockpit, or by ramming the bow of the boat into a ship.[51]

Photo 7-8

Japanese Shinyo explosive motorboat on the beach at Lingayen Gulf, Philippine Islands, circa early 1945.
Naval History and Heritage Command photograph #NH 44316

Vice Admiral Wilkinson's action report on the Lingayen Gulf Operation described the tactics employed by the boats, which often resulted in the loss of life of their operators:

> The primary purpose of these boats is to attack enemy convoys approaching a beach. Night attacks are contemplated, when the small size of the boats makes radar and visual detection difficult. Proposed procedure is to come alongside a ship abreast the engine compartments at high speed, drop the charges while executing a U turn and attempt a getaway. It is probable that the operator will be killed by the explosion in a majority of cases.

BATTLE STARS AWARDED LSMs

Forty-four LSMs earned battle stars for the Lingayen landings. Since the U.S. Navy only allowed a single battle star for any one operation—no matter how many qualifying actions—LSMs which had previously been awarded a battle star for "Luzon operation: Mindoro" did not receive one for the successive "Luzon operation: Lingayen Gulf landing."

Luzon Operation: Lingayen Gulf Landing

Ship	Date(s)	Ship	Date(s)	Ship	Date(s)
LSM-8	9 Jan 45	LSM-31	9 Jan 45	LSM-201	9 Jan 45
LSM-10	9 Jan 45	LSM-32	9 Jan 45	LSM-203	4-12 Jan 45
LSM-11	9 Jan 45	LSM-33	9 Jan 45	LSM-205	4-12 Jan 45
LSM-12	9 Jan 45	LSM-35	4-12 Jan 45	LSM-210	9 Jan 45
LSM-13	9 Jan 45	LSM-36	4-12 Jan 45	LSM-217	4-12 Jan 45
LSM-14	9 Jan 45	LSM-50	9 Jan 45	LSM-218	4-12 Jan 45
LSM-15	9 Jan 45	LSM-51	16-18 Jan 45	LSM-233	9 Jan 45
LSM-18	16-18 Jan 45	LSM-52	9 Jan 45	LSM-234	9 Jan 45
LSM-19	16-18 Jan 45	LSM-53	9 Jan 45	LSM-235	9 Jan 45
LSM-24	9 Jan 45	LSM-54	9 Jan 45	LSM-259	9 Jan 45
LSM-25	9 Jan 45	LSM-65	9 Jan 45	LSM-312	16-18 Jan 45
LSM-27	9 Jan 45	LSM-135	9 Jan 45	LSM-313	9 Jan 45
LSM-28	9 Jan 45	LSM-137	9 Jan 45	LSM-314	4-12 Jan 45
LSM-29	9 Jan 45	LSM-144	9 Jan 45	LSM-315	4-12 Jan 45
LSM-30	9 Jan 45	LSM-169	4-12 Jan 45		

8

Subsidiary Landings at Zambales, Grande Island, and Nasugbu

Photo 8-1

Members of the Philippine Army paddle out to meet U.S. forces landing at Nasugbu, just south of Manila Bay, on 31 January 1945. In the center of the boat is 1st Lt. Mario Vrrutia, with a United States flag preserved during the Japanese occupation. National Archives photograph #80-G-273128

Before dusk on 9 January 1945, the commanding generals of U.S. Army divisions that landed on San Fabian and Lingayen assault beaches that day assumed command of their forces ashore. Two days later, the commanding generals of parent Sixth Army I and XIV Corps, of which the divisions were a part, assumed command in their respective areas.[1]

The I Corps, which landed over San Fabian beaches, was responsible initially for operations on the eastern side of the Central Plains of Luzon; while the XIV Corps, landed over Lingayen beaches, conducted operations on the western side of the Central Plains. By month's end, southward advancing XIV Corps had seized Clark and Mabalacat airfields, and reached Calumpit thirty miles northwest of Manila. The I Corps to the north was pressuring strong enemy forces blocking their way into Baguio, headquarters of Gen. Tomoyuki Yamashita (commander of the Japanese Fourteenth Area Army), and to the east eliminating organized resistance along routes northward into the Cagayan Valley in the northeastern section of Luzon.[2]

Map 8-1

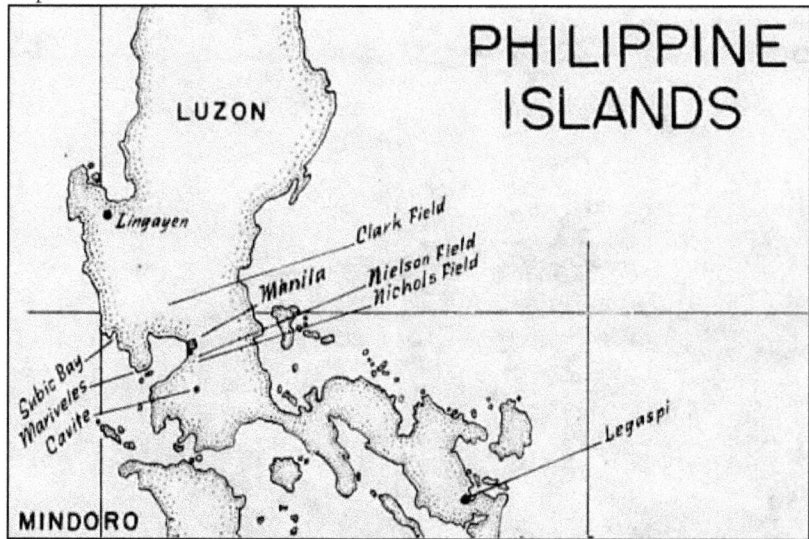

Luzon Island and adjacent areas of the Philippines to the south

In late January, three minor amphibious landings were mounted to provide direct support for the Sixth Army's drive to recapture Manila. General MacArthur wanted to occupy Manila as early as possible in order to free Allied prisoners and internees who were slowly starving to death. These landings were on the west coast of Luzon at:

- San Antonio (Operation MIKE VII) in Zambales Province, located north of Subic Bay, on 29 January
- Grande Island (MIKE VII), located near the mouth of Subic Bay, on 30 January
- Nasugbu Bay (Operation MIKE VI), forty-five miles southwest of Manila, on 31 January[3]

ZAMBALES-SUBIC BAY OPERATION

The mission of this group was to land the assault forces of the XI Corps Headquarters, composed of the 38th Infantry Division and the 34th RCT [Regimental Combat Team] of the 24th Infantry Division together with their supplies and equipment, in the ZAMBALES Area and support the landing by close gunfire and air support, in order to block hostile retirement into BATAAN PENINSULA. An additional mission was to open and occupy SUBIC BAY.

—Commander Task Group 78.3, Report of Amphibious Landings
in Zambales Province, Luzon, P.I., 4 March 1945.

On 29 January 1945, Rear Adm. Arthur Struble's 9th Amphibious Group (Task Group 78.3) landed the U.S. Army's 38th Division and 34th Regimental Combat Team on the west coast of Luzon, in Zambales Province to the north of Subic Bay. The purpose of the MIKE VII amphibious operation was for the 30,000 troops put ashore to take the naval base at Olongapo on Subic Bay, then push forward to the northern shore of Manila Bay.[4]

The seven medium landing ships of LSM Group Nineteen—*LSM-66* (flagship), *63, 64, 67, 68, 268*, and *269*—under the command of Lt. Comdr. William A. Burgett, USN, participated in the operation. They were part of Capt. Erskine A. Seay's (commander, LST Flotilla Fourteen) Task Unit 78.5.4 of forty-five tank landing ships.[5]

The LSMs were combat loaded on 23-24 January in Leyte, with elements of the XI Corps, Eighth Army. Their mission was to take part in the assault landings in Zambales Province, then assist in unloading transports and cargo vessels. In route to the objective, Task Unit 78.5.4 passed through Surigao Strait, south of Bohol and Negros islands, and west of Panay, Mindoro, and Luzon islands.[6]

Arriving off Zambales on 29 January, friendly guerilla officers informed Admiral Struble that no enemy troops were in the area, and that the American flag was flying on Red Beach. After conferring with the commanding general, II Corps, the naval gunfire for the landing was cancelled. During the assault landing, no enemy planes or other forces were sighted, or gunfire of any kind encountered.[7]

The first wave of assault craft landed at 0831 without opposition. The LSMs landing in a later wave between 0850 and 0940, unloaded and retracted in about 20 minutes each. The discharge of wheeled vehicles was slowed because they were unable to negotiate the soft sand of the beach. Each one had to be towed by a tracked vehicle.[8]

The larger, deeper draft LSTs were even more disadvantaged. The beach gradients were such that LSTs had about 50 feet of open water between them and the beach. Accordingly, all vehicles except DUKWs required the assistance of one or two tractors to haul them clear of the beach area to prevent bogging down in the soft sand.[9]

Following the assault landing, the LSMs proceeded to the transports for reloading and thereafter maintained continuous shuttle service from large ships to beach with troops and cargo until 1 February. They collectively made twenty-three trips to the beach carrying about 160 tons of cargo on each trip. At 1515 on 1 February, the LSMs got under way with Task Force 78.3 bound for Subic Bay, Luzon, arriving there and anchoring that evening at about 1830.[10]

LANDING ON GRANDE ISLAND

Photo 8-2

View over lower part of the north side of Grande Island, looking toward the town of Subic Bay, circa early 1900s.
National Archives photograph #USN 903041

At 1000 on 30 January, Rear Adm. Ralph S. Riggs, embarked in the light cruiser *Denver* (CL-58), departed Zambales for Grande Island as Attack Unit commander, together with four APDs (high speed transports) with assigned escorts, supported by a close covering group of the cruiser and two destroyers. The unit landed a reinforced battalion of the 38th Division on Grande Island at 1215. No opposition was encountered, and the transport ships and escorts returned to Zambales.[11]

The mission of the troops was to secure Subic Bay and eventually to reactivate the old American U.S. naval base at Olongapo on its southern shore. This tasking was successfully completed shortly after the landings when troops of the 38th Division walked into town.[12]

Photo 8-3

Aerial photo of the former U.S. Naval station at Olongapo, taken from a USS *Hancock* (CV-19) plane on 15 December 1944.
Naval History and Heritage Command photograph #NH 95603

NASUGBU BAY LANDING

Task Unit 78.2.4 was organized as a part of Task Group 78.2…. The mission of this unit was to transport and land assault troops of the 11th Airborne Division (187th and 188th Regimental Combat Teams) with their supplies and equipment on ships in the Nasugbu Area, Luzon, Philippine Islands at 0815 on 31 January 1945…. The loads carried by LSMs of this unit totaled 30 officers, 356 men, 263 vehicles and 4-3/4 tons of ammunition…. 3 piper cubs [light aircraft well suited for a variety of military uses such as reconnaissance, liaison and ground control] were carried in trucks and are not included in the above total of 263 vehicles. The 263 vehicles are listed as follows: 113 trucks, 43 trailers, 22 howitzers, 8 tractors, 4 ambulances, 3 DUKWs, 1 crane, 1 grader, 1 bulldozer, 45 push-carts, and 22 scooters.

—Comdr. William E. Verge, USN, commander Task Unit 78.2.4, describing the Army troops and vehicles discharged at Nasugbu Bay by the eight LSMs—*LSM-54* (flagship), *41, 52, 53, 65, 169, 218, 203*—under his command.[13]

Photo 8-4

Piper Cub, like those carried aboard LSMs for discharge at Nasugbu Bay, preparing to take off from the flight deck of USS *Ranger* (CV-4), to spot gunfire and carry out reconnaissance near French positions, during Operation TORCH in November 1942. National Archives photograph #80-G-30339

Map 8-2

Manila and surrounding area of southern Luzon Island

Task Group 78.2 under Rear Adm. William M. Fechteler, USN, sortied from Tarragona, Leyte Gulf at 1700 on 27 January, bound for Nasugbu Bay. The passage there was made on schedule and without incident. The approach also proceeded according to plan and at 0619, 31 January, the task group deployed to take assigned positions.[14]

Preliminary bombardment was carried out on schedule, with no return fire. H-Hour was set for 0815, for the landing on a 600-yard stretch of shore about 1,500 yards south of the Wawa River, designated Beach Red. There was a light easterly breeze, calm sea, and no surf. The first assault wave left the line of departure at 0804, and rocket barrage of the beach ended at 0812 as the craft neared the shore. The first wave landed at 0817 with successive waves landing on schedule. No enemy opposition was encountered on the beach, and troops advanced rapidly inland and on both flanks.[15]

LSM LANDINGS

At 0840, Wave 4—consisting of LSMs *54* (flagship), *65*, *52*, and *218*—beached. Five minutes later, the remaining medium landing ships, comprising Wave 5—LSMs *53*, *41*, *169*, and *203*—beached at 0845.[16]

At 0912, the beach was strafed by machine gun fire apparently originating from a godown (warehouse/freight shed) in the village of Wawa. Comdr. William E. Verge, USN, commanding the task unit of LSMs, ordered *LSM-203* to open fire with her 40mm gun.[17]

The ship's commanding officer, Lt. Forrest L. Townsley, USNR, described the ensuing combat action and destruction of the building housing the machine guns:

> The landing at the beach was made with no opposition. After the LSM unit had beached, machine guns started strafing the beach position of this ship and on the left flank nearest the town of Wawa. All strafing came from that direction. Permission was obtained by this ship to open fire on emplacement from which machine gun fire seemed to originate. Fired into barn with 40 mm. The fire ceased and it was supposed that guns were silenced.
>
> Shortly after order to cease firing, machine gun strafing started again. This ship opened fire again and all but blew up the barn. Then an LCI(G) moved in and began shelling the same place with 40mm shells. Later reports from army personnel on advanced patrol in that area revealed that there was a great number of enemy ground forces and machine guns located there. Practically all were killed.

It is believed that this ship was largely responsible for their destruction. Only sporadic machine gun fire resulted after that, these coming from emplacement on the point of Wawa. These were not taken under fire. Mortar fire was encountered while on beach also. Three mortars falling off the port side. Two on the beach and one in the water about 200 yards on the beam. No other enemy action was experienced during the four hours and seventeen minutes on beach.[18]

Unloading of LSMs was slowed owing to beach conditions. Upon grounding the fourth wave had from 3 to 4 feet of water at their ramps. Although the beach fell away rapidly to a depth of about six feet, from there seaward there was little or no gradient. Consequently, the LSMs grounded aft or throughout their length, precluding their bows from reaching shallower water. Adding to difficulties associated with depth of water, soft sand caused vehicles to experience poor traction on the beach, slowing their discharge from ships. However, eventually all cargo was discharged and all LSMs were able to retract.[19]

At 1530, the eight LSMs and other ships—4 APDs, 4 YMSs, 3 SCs, and 36 LCI(L)s—departed for Mindoro. The six LSTs of Task Unit 78.2.5 remained at Nasugbu Bay, awaiting a high tide at about 2400 required in order for them to beach.[20]

ATTACK BY SUICIDE BOATS

Photo 8-5

USS *PC-1129* under way, location and date unknown.
Hyperwar U.S. Navy in WWII

From about 2245 to 0030 that night, the beachhead was attacked by Japanese suicide boats operating from Balayan Bay, located south of Nasugbu. During the attack, the 173-foot sub-chaser, USS *PC-1129* was surrounded and sunk by enemy action of such boats.[21]

Lt. Comdr. Blaney C. Turner, USNR, commanding officer of the larger 306-foot destroyer escort USS *Lough* (DE 586), which sank at least a half dozen of the boats, described the action in a war diary entry:

> Troops of the 11th Airborne Division landed at Nasugbu at 0815 with no serious opposition, supported by fire of this Task Group. This ship established anti-submarine patrol 10,000 yards off Red Beach, between Talin Point and Fortune Island.   At 2300 encountered between twenty (20) and thirty (30) Japanese small boats disposed in a line across our patrol path as an ambush. Took the boats under fire and definitely destroyed six (6). Probably most were destroyed for one half hour later none could be found. A general melee resulted between this ship and the boats. At about 2320 the *PC-1129* about 4,000 yards to the south, was surrounded by the boats and sunk by an explosion at the engine room.
>
> Later, this ship picked up the survivors of *PC-1129*. Expended the following ammunition: nine hundred and fifty-two (952) rounds 40mm service, one thousand, two hundred and twenty-four (1,224) rounds 20mm HEI, six hundred and ten (610) rounds 20mm HET, two hundred and one (201) rounds .45 caliber, seventy-five (75) rounds .30 caliber and two (2) hand grenades. No casualties were suffered to this ship.[22]

Photo 8-6

Destroyer escort USS *Lough* (DE-586) just after launching, at Hingham, Massachusetts, on 22 January 1944.
Naval History and Heritage Command photograph #NH 81349

After *Lough*'s gun crews had reduced the strength of the explosive boat fleet by at least six units, the rest retired.[23]

BATTLE STARS AWARDED LSMs

Manila Bay-Bicol Operations: Zambales-Subic Bay

Ship	Date/Period	Ship	Date/Period
LSM-64	29-31 Jan 45	LSM-68	29-31 Jan 45
LSM-65	31 Jan 45	LSM-268	29-31 Jan 45
LSM-66	29-31 Jan 45	LSM-269	29-31 Jan 45
LSM-67	29-31 Jan 45		

Manila Bay-Bicol Operations: Nasugbu

Ship	Date/Period	Ship	Date/Period
LSM-41	31 Jan 45	LSM-65 (no BS)	31 Jan 45
LSM-52	31 Jan 45	LSM-169	31 Jan 45
LSM-53	31 Jan 45	LSM-203	31 Jan 45
LSM-54	31 Jan 45	LSM-218	31 Jan 45

9

Mariveles – Corregidor

The mission of this Task Group [78.3] was to embark at SUBIC BAY, transport, protect and land the Landing Force, together with its equipment and supplies, at MARIVELES BAY on D-Day [15 February 1945], to make subsequent landing on CORREGIDOR on D plus 1 [16 February], and to support both landings by close gunfire, in order to open the entrance to MANILA BAY.

—Rear Adm. Arthur Struble, USN, commander, Task Group 78.3.[1]

Map 9-1

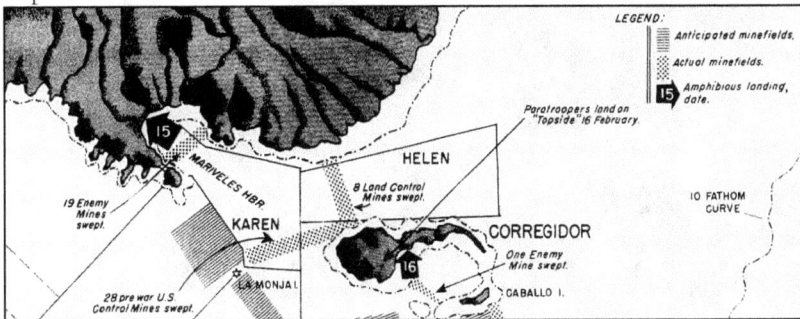

Portion of map showing minesweeping areas associated with U.S. assault landings at Mariveles on the Bataan Peninsula and Corregidor Island (identified by black arrows) on 15 and 16 February, respectively
Commander in Chief, U.S. Pacific Fleet and Pacific Ocean Areas, Operations in Pacific Ocean Areas – February 1945, 27 August 1945

By the middle of February 1945, U.S. troops previously landed at Lingayen; at Nasugbu, just south of the entrance to Manila Bay; and near Olongapo, north of Bataan, were converging on Manila. In order to open that port for the supply of Army forces ashore, and logistic support of future operations, it was necessary to eliminate the threat posed by the Japanese-held fortress of Corregidor blocking the entrance to Manila Bay, and to complete the occupation of adjacent Bataan Peninsula and Cavite shore.[2]

The strength of the Japanese garrison on Corregidor was estimated to be 850 troops (more than 4,000 enemy dead were later counted), while small garrisons were also reported on three other islands at the mouth of Manila Bay: Caballo, Carabao, and El Fraile. These four islands hosted the Japanese-captured U.S. Army military facilities Fort Mills, Fort Hughes, Fort Frank, and Fort Drum, respectively.[3]

At the time, enemy forces on Bataan were estimated at 15,000 troops, with defense preparations believed in progress in and near Mariveles Bay. Air reconnaissance had identified numerous cave and pillbox positions on Corregidor, but large ex-U.S. batteries left when it fell to enemy forces on 2 March 1942 were believed to have been destroyed by later air bombardment. Land mines, and other defenses, were expected on the beaches.[4]

Photo 9-1

Japanese troops celebrate atop a U.S. Army coast defense gun on Corregidor, after the Island's capture on 6 May 1942.
Naval History and Heritage Command photograph #NH 73222

SEA MINE THREAT

Extensive minefields were reported guarding the entrance to Manila Bay, consisting of both pre-war U.S. control (defensive) mines and newer Japanese mines. These fields were expected to pose the major difficulty in opening the bay to shipping, and had to be swept within close range of whatever enemy shore batteries survived the planned pre-assault landing bombardment.[5]

On 14 February, despite Army air cover overhead, enemy shore guns managed to sink the motor minesweeper YMS-48 and damaged the destroyers Fletcher (DD-445) and Hopewell (DD-681). The following day, a naval task group landed Army troops on the peninsula and a short time thereafter resistance ceased on Corregidor and the Bataan Peninsula.[6]

Photo 9-2

Painting by Dwight C. Shepler, 1945, of U.S. Navy minesweepers cleaning a pathway through the mines off Bataan peninsula.
Naval History and Heritage Command photograph #88-199-GK

Photo 9-3

Minesweeper USS *YMS-48* in port on 7 July 1942, location unknown.
Courtesy of Joe Radigan and NavSource

Photo 9-4

Destroyer USS *Hopewell* (DD-681) smoking amidships, just after being hit by four Japanese shore battery rounds while supporting minesweeping operations off Corregidor, Philippines, 14 February 1945.
Naval History and Heritage Command photograph #NH 53565

In early afternoon on 14 February, five YMSs in column order— *YMS-48, 8, 6, 53, 46*—proceeded from Area MABEL (not shown on Map 9-1) northward to Area HELEN, accompanied by the destroyers *Hopewell* and *Fletcher* serving as "shotguns" (providing protection). The YMSs, designated Unit III, were tasked with sweeping the north channel to Manila Bay clear of moored and acoustic mines.[7]

As *YMS-48* led the other sweepers into Area HELEN across its western boundary, enemy guns on Corregidor's north slopes, not yet neutralized by pre-landing bombardment, opened up on her. The first round fell 150 yards short. Of the eight rapid rounds that followed, six were direct hits on the little minesweeper. She was afire after the third one, and dead in the water after the last. *YMS-8* attempted covering fire until forced to withdraw after also being hit. After 1405, when Lt.(jg) Howard A. Kaiser had ordered his crew to abandon, and all able to had done so, two more rounds hit the ship, adding to fires aft.[8]

As the other YMSs quickly cleared the area, *Hopewell* moved in to pick up *YMS-48* survivors. She was hit four times amidships before retiring. A strong tidal current was carrying all survivors toward the enemy, and small arms fire was being directed from the Bataan shore at men in the water. After aircraft laid smoke between the men in the water and Corregidor, *Fletcher* approached to pick up survivors and, while recovering them, took the Japanese batteries under fire.[9]

All hands in the water and afloat in the ship's single undamaged raft were rescued. One officer and two men, reported seriously injured aboard ship, and who had not abandoned, were not recovered. At 1500, *Fletcher* poured 40mm fire into *YMS-48* at the waterline, sinking the small, aflame, unsalvageable 136-foot wooden vessel.[10]

PRE-ASSAULT BOMBARDMENT OPERATIONS

Following minesweeping, fire support ships moving into swept waters took under fire targets in the Mariveles area, and on the islands of Corregidor, Caballo, and El Fraile, while concurrently, heavy bomber strikes were being delivered on Corregidor. Specific targets were hard to distinguish owing to dust and smoke, and because the enemy did not elect to disclose these positions by firing at that time.[11]

Photo 9-5

Light cruiser USS *Phoenix* (CL-46)—flagship of Rear Adm. Russell S. Berkey's Support Group of light cruisers and destroyers—shelling cave gun locations on the north face of Corregidor, 15 February 1945.
Naval History and Heritage Command photograph #NH 122204

The Bataan-Corregidor Attack Group (Task Group 78.3) under the command of Rear Adm. Arthur D. Struble, USN, employed Subic Bay, thirty miles northward of Corregidor, as base of operations for the assembly and embarkation of Army troops, anchorage and replenishment, and temporary repair of naval vessels. The bay had been taken on 30 January 1945.[12]

LSM TRANSPORT UNIT (TASK UNIT 78.3.4)

In early evening on 14 February, Task Unit 78.3.4 got under way from Subic Bay, and joined commander Task Group 78.3 who was aboard the USCGC *Ingram*, and other units of the assault force. Speed of advance was a modest 6 knots.[13]

Photo 9-6

U.S. Coast Guard cutter *Ingram* at U.S. Navy Yard, South Carolina, 11 October 1944.

At 0900 on 15 February, the task group arrived in the transport area off Mariveles Harbor, and assault waves began forming up and proceeding to the line of departure as scheduled. The twenty ships of the LSM Transport Unit under Comdr. Ralph C. Johnson, USN (commander, LSM Squadron Four)—*LSM-18* (flagship), *19, 21, 34, 37, 38, 39, 40, 42, 52, 64, 138, 139, 169, 203, 218, 257, 310, 311, 319*—were scheduled to land on Orange Beach in assigned waves.[14]

At 0953, the Eighth Wave—Lt. Comdr. Everett E. Weire, USN, aboard *LSM-38* (flagship), and the LSMs *37, 39, 169, 203, 311*—departed from the transport area. Arriving at the line of departure at 1031, the wave was halted by the control vessel, the sub-chaser USS *PC-1133*, because of some delay by the Seventh Wave of LCTs (tank landing craft) in retracting. As explained in the next section one of the LSMs of this group was damaged while waiting for orders to proceed.[15]

USS *LSM-169* DAMAGED BY MINE STRIKE

The captain gave the order to abandon ship. This order was passed over all phones. The vessel was afire forward, the mine having ruptured fuel oil tanks and set on fire gasoline from vehicles stowed in the well deck forward of the conn[ing tower]. The ship was listing 10° to port. Life rafts were cast loose and men began jumping overboard. An LCM drew up to the starboard quarter and began taking men aboard the ship. A salvage tug came along the starboard side and poured water from her hoses on the flames. The captain, executive, communications and engineer officers boarded this LCM and were transported to LST 667 together with casualties both Army and Navy. The 5th Officer (Ens. H. H. Foley) and seven men were picked up by LSM 203.

—Acting Commanding Officer, *LSM 169* [*Ens. H. H. Foley*],
Report of Action, 24 February 1945.

While waiting to proceed into the beach, LSM 169 *struck a mine. Flames enveloped the vessel, but the fire was brought under control by the excellent fire fighting service rendered by the [rescue and salvage ship]* GRASP *[ARS-24]. The* LSM 169 *was beached and subsequently towed to SUBIC.*

—Rear Adm. Arthur D. Struble, commander, Task Group 78.3.[16]

Photo 9-7

USS *LSM-169* at Mariveles Bay, 15 February 1945, after striking a mine,
with the rescue and salvage ship USS *Grasp* fighting the fire on board her.
Naval History and Heritage Command photograph #NH-22093

Photo 9-8

Rescue in Manila Bay of a sailor from USS *LSM-169*, after she struck a mine during the landings at Mariveles, 15 February 1945.
National Archives photograph #80-G-273344

The salvage and rescue ship *Grasp*, proceeding into Mariveles Harbor astern of LSMs and LCI(L)s, observed at 1042 an explosion on *LSM-169*, caused by her striking a mine, port side, immediately forward of the bridge. The detonation at about the 15th frame blew up the ship and cargo. Debris was propelled about 200 feet into the air, some fell on the bow of *LSM-39*. (At the time of the explosion, which also set the *LSM-169* aflame, she was about 75 yards off the port bow of *LSM-39*.) Survivors who leapt or were thrown into the water were picked up by LCMs laying to nearby. At 1050, *Grasp* went alongside *LSM-169* to fight fire; five minutes later the infantry landing craft *LCI(L)-688* and *699* also came alongside to assist in this effort.[17]

LSM-169 had loaded at Subic Bay the previous morning, approximately 71 men and four officers of the 24th Cavalry, and their scouting vehicles including 4 armored radio equipped half-track trucks, 5 radio equipped command cars, 2 or 3 jeeps and one 2½ ton truck. These numbers, identified by acting commanding officer Ens. H. H. Foley (5th officer) in a report dated 24 February, were based on the best information available, in the face of the loss of pertinent records.[18]

Casualties reported by Foley in the same report were: 1 dead, 1 missing, and 15 men and 3 officers wounded. Naval crew and embarked Army personnel components comprising this total were not identified.[19]

By 1100 on 15 February, flames topside *LSM-169* which had enveloped the forward part of the ship, were under control but still burning below deck, and ammunition in her magazine was exploding. *Grasp* left the medium landing ship's starboard side at 1110 and made up on her port side, preparatory to towing her onto the beach in order to prevent obstructing the approach of other landing craft. *Grasp*'s firefighting party continued combating fire during towing operations.[20]

BEACHING OF MEDIUM LANDING SHIPS

First reports were that the beach was good but it proved to be very poor and very narrow for LSM's. Most small vehicles had to be towed through the water by large trucks or tractors. U.S.S. LSM 18 experienced no difficulty in retracting.

—Commanding Officer, USS *LSM 18*, Action Report –
Mariveles Operation, 16 February 1945.

LSM-169 was beached by the *Grasp* near Paydaruagan Point. Meanwhile, the remaining five LSMs comprising Wave 8 re-formed and crossed the line of departure at 1100; beached at 1111; and commenced unloading. At completion, each retracted and returned independently to the Transport Area. There were no dry ramps, as LSMs grounded about 30 yards from shore, resulting in an average depth of 1½ to 2½ feet of water at the ramps. Despite this impediment, Wave 8 consumed only about twelve minutes in discharging assault troops and vehicles.[21]

The remaining waves of LSMs landed and discharged at the scheduled intervals except *LSM-218*, which had fouled her port screw with manila line en route to the attack area, and was thus delayed. She beached singly at 1330. There was delay in unloading her, and she retracted two hours later. The five LSTs assigned to Task Group 78.3 were beached singly from 1509 to 1624. Beaching at a standard speed of 9.5 knots, their average distance offshore was 100 feet with 3 feet of water at the bow ramp.[22]

At 1545, Task Unit 78.3.4, less LSMs *169* and *218*, got under way from the Transport Area to return to Subic Bay. The return passage was by route "Shorty," Task Group 78.3 having earlier taken a more circuitous one en route to Mariveles Bay.[23]

SUMMATION

> *Aside from* LSM 169 *striking a probable mine, and some difficulty in beaching due to shallow approaches, the assault presented little difficulty, and troops proceeded to their objectives without opposition. Supporting gunfire against enemy batteries on the north side of CORREGIDOR kept them ineffective.*

—Commander in Chief, U.S. Pacific Fleet and Pacific Ocean Areas – February 1945, Operations in Pacific Ocean Areas – February 1945, 27 August 1945.

Photo 9-9

Entrance to the Mariveles Naval Base, Bataan, photographed after its capture by the Japanese in April 1942.
Naval History and Heritage Command photograph #NH 73549

LSM BATTLE STARS

Manila Bay-Bicol Operations: Mariveles-Corregidor

Ship	Date/Period	Ship	Date/Period
LSM-18	14-28 Feb 45	LSM-64	14-28 Feb 45
LSM-19	14-28 Feb 45	LSM-138	14-28 Feb 45
LSM-21	14-28 Feb 45	LSM-139	14-28 Feb 45
LSM-34	14-28 Feb 45	LSM-169	14-28 Feb 45
LSM-37	14-28 Feb 45	LSM-203 (no BS)	14-28 Feb 45
LSM-38	14-28 Feb 45	LSM-218 (no BS)	14-28 Feb 45
LSM-39	14-28 Feb 45	LSM-257	14-28 Feb 45
LSM-40	14-28 Feb 45	LSM-310	14-28 Feb 45
LSM-42	14-28 Feb 45	LSM-311	14-28 Feb 45
LSM-52	14-28 Feb 45	LSM-319	14-28 Feb 45

1st Filipino Regiment Landed at Catbalogan, Samar

14 February 1945: Commander D. J. WEINTRAUB with Commander LCI Flotilla EIGHT, Commander F. B. C. MARTIN, in LCI 546, surveyed San Juanico Straits for possibilities of sending LSMs to Catbalogan, Samar, Philippine Islands, to load and transport troops to that area.

—Commander LSM Flotilla Two War Diary, February 1945.

1 April 1942:
1st Filipino Battalion activated

July 1942:
Soldiers transferred to the newly constituted 1st Filipino Regiment which replaced the battalion

13 July 1942:
New regiment activated at Salinas, California

10 April 1946:
inactivated at Camp Stoneman, California

Battle honors for New Guinea, Leyte, and the Southern Philippines, and the unit additionally earned the Philippine Presidential Unit Citation

LAGING UNA

Filipino Regiment's Unit Insignia

On the morning of 15 February 1945, Task Unit 76.6.3—LSMs and LCI(L)s under Comdr. Daniel J. Weintraub, USN, (commander LSM Flotilla Two) embarked aboard *LSM-258*—got under way at 0723 from the Red Beach area of Leyte. The ships of the task unit, identified below, were bound first for Tolosa, Leyte, 15 miles south of Tacloban, to load the First Filipino Regiment and their equipment. Upon completion of loading, the unit was to transport these troops northward to Catbalogan, Samar.

- *LSM-258* (flagship), *22, 148, 150, 151, 314, 316, 317*
- LCI(L)s *635, 653, 701, 1003*[1]

Map 10-1

Central Philippine Islands

1ST FILIPINO REGIMENT

When America entered World War II, following the Japanese attack on Pearl Harbor on 7 December 1941, Filipino-Americans wanting to enlist in the U.S. military were unable to do so, because they lacked American citizenship despite their status as American nationals. This policy soon changed when, on 21 December 1941, Congress amended the Selective Service and Training Act to permit enlistment of citizens and "every other male person residing in the United States." Two months later on

19 February 1942, Secretary of War Henry L. Stimson announced the creation of a Filipino battalion to enable Americans of Filipino ancestry as well as resident Filipinos in the United States to serve together in the U.S. Army.[2]

Photo 10-1

Naturalization ceremony for 1,000 soldiers of the 1st Filipino Battalion at U.S. Army Camp Beale, California, on 20 February 1943. In 1948, Camp Beale became Beale Air Force Base.
Camp Roberts Trainer (Vol 2 No 3)- 1st Filipino Infantry p016-17.jpg

On 1 April 1942 the War Department activated the 1st Filipino Battalion, whose existence was short-lived. In July, the unit's soldiers transferred to the 1st Filipino Regiment replacing the battalion, with the new regiment activated on 13 July 1942 at Salinas, California. Red, white, and blue colors on the shield of the regiment's coat of arms represented both the national colors of the Philippines and the United States. The unit motto "LAGING UNA" in Tagalog, a major native language of the Philippines meant "Always First."[3]

Elements of the 1st Filipino Regiment arrived in New Guinea from the United States in April 1944, where they fought until moving to the Philippines in February 1945.[4]

TOLOSA AND MOVEMENT FURTHER NORTHWARD

Returning to the ships dispatched from Leyte, Weintraub's task unit arrived at Tolosa at 0930 on 15 February; whereupon the LSMs and LCI(L)s beached and loading began. Upon completion, the ships anchored off Tolosa for the night.[5]

At 0820 on 16 February, the task unit departed for Catbalogan, Samar, with the ships in a single column with *LSM-258* as the column guide ship. That afternoon upon clearing San Juanico Straits at 1325, the ships formed into two columns with LSMs *258* and *150* as guides.

The task unit arrived at Catbalogan three hours later, and the ships proceeded independently to their assigned beaching stations, and began unloading.[6]

RETURN PASSAGE TO LEYTE
The LSMs and LCI(L)s remained beached at Catbalogan on the 17th. The following morning, 18 February, they retracted, proceeded seaward and formed a double column, bound for San Pedro Bay, Leyte Gulf. Task Unit 76.6.3 anchored off the Red Beach Area that night at 2000.[7]

SERVICE OF THE REGIMENT IN SAMAR AND LEYTE
The troops of 1st Filipino Regiment fought heroically against Japanese troops in Samar, then subsequently were assigned to operations in northern Leyte, where they engaged in heavy combat for nearly two months routing stubborn invaders from their homeland. By August, this was complete in the whole country and with all Japanese eliminated or captured all operations in the Philippines came to an end.[8]

In March 1946, men who chose to remain in the Philippines or were not eligible to return to the U.S. were transferred to the 2nd Filipino Infantry Battalion stationed in Quezon City. This battalion was the former 2nd Filipino Regiment—which had also been formed in the U.S. and sent to the Philippines, but did not see combat there and had been reconstituted. When the 2nd Battalion was disbanded later that month, members were assigned to the Filipino Section of the 86th Infantry Division. Troops of the 1st Regiment returning home were transported aboard the USS *General R. E. Callan* (AP-139), which arrived in San Francisco on 8 April. They were quickly bused to nearby Camp Stoneman in Pittsburgh, California, and discharged.[9]

A few men were present on the morning of 9 April, when the unit flag, hand sewn by the wives of the Filipino officers of the regiment, was folded for the last time. A member of the unit stole into the mailroom where the flag was being stored and took the flag home with him. Thereafter he made it his mission to ensure that it continued to be flown at unit reunions throughout the United States.[10]

11

Assault of Iwo Jima

Photo 11-1

Unloading of general cargo at Iwo Jima on 24 February 1945, by five LSTs and one LSM at Green Beach 1, with Mt. Suribachi in the background. The landing ships are from bottom to center: *LSM-264*, *LST-724*, *LST-760*, *LST-788*, *LST-808* (with an LCT embarked), and *LST-779* (carrying a pontoon causeway).
Naval History and Heritage Command photograph #NH 65314

In late February 1945, as bitter fighting continued between Allied and Japanese forces in the Philippines, further northeast and much nearer the Japanese home islands, an assault of Iwo Jima was carried out. In autumn 1944, the Joint Chiefs of Staff had issued a directive to Gen. Douglas MacArthur and Adm. Chester Nimitz pursuant to planned Allied attacks on Iwo Jima and Okinawa:

> Admiral Nimitz, after providing covering and support forces for the liberation of Luzon, will occupy one or more positions in the Bonins-Volcano Group, target date 20 January 1945, and one or more positions in the Ryukyus, target date 1 March 1945.
>
> General MacArthur will provide support for subsequent occupation of the Ryukyus by Admiral Nimitz's forces.[1]

The strategic concept associated with this directive was to secure island bases for a final assault on the Japanese home islands. Planners considering approaches to Tokyo, recognized that Tokyo, Saipan, and Formosa (today Taiwan) formed an isosceles triangle on a global projection with sides 1,500 miles long. (This shape is not readily apparent when viewing the vertices on a flattened-out map.) B-29s were to begin using the eastern leg (U.S held-Saipan to Tokyo) to bomb the Japanese homeland, but a half-way point was needed. Iwo Jima alone met that requirement (see Map 11-2). Formosa was subsequently rejected as the origin of the western leg, because it was thought to be too difficult to capture, and was replaced with Okinawa, much nearer to Japan's capital city and less strongly defended.[2]

Map 11-1

Portion of Southeast Asia and adjacent Central Pacific; Minamitorishima (also known as Marcus Island) in the upper right of the map, is an isolated Japanese coral atoll in the northwestern Pacific, some 998 nautical miles southeast of Tokyo

Map 11-2

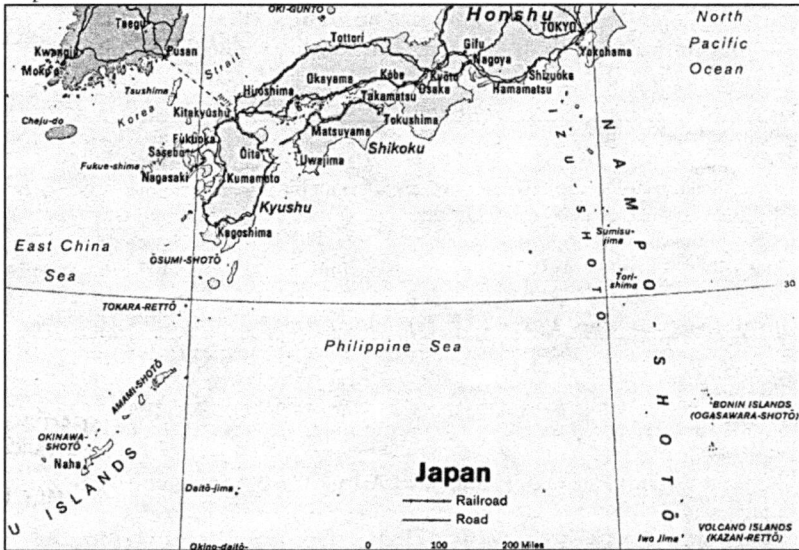

Southern Japanese islands; Tokyo (the capital city on Honshu) is in the upper right of the map; Okinawa (in the Ryukyu Islands), lower left; and Iwo Jima (a part of the Bonin-Volcano Islands Group), lower right

Owing to the unexpectedly prolonged Japanese defense of Leyte and Luzon, the target dates set by the Joint Chiefs of Staff could not be met, which gave the enemy, well aware of its strategic significance, another month to make Iwo Jima almost impregnable.[3]

The assault of Iwo Jima was scheduled before that of Okinawa because it was expected to be easier. Nimitz's Pacific Fleet would have to cover both operations, while MacArthur's Seventh Fleet (previously titled the "Southwest Pacific Force") and associated Amphibious Force was fully engaged in covering and liberating the Southern Philippines.[4]

IWO JIMA TASK ORGANIZATION
Adm. Raymond A. Spruance, USN, (commander Task Force 50, and commander, Fifth Fleet) was in charge of nearly all the naval elements that took part in the assault of Iwo Jima. Subordinate commanders of the main echelons of his command are identified below:

Adm. Raymond A. Spruance, USN
(Commander Task Force 50, and Commander Fifth Fleet)

Special Groups

50.1	Fleet Flagship	Capt. Charles B. McVay III
50.2	Relief Fleet Flagship	Capt. William M. Callaghan
50.5	Search and Reconnaissance Group	Commodore Dixwell Ketcham
50.7	Anti-Submarine Warfare Group	Capt. G. C. Montgomery
50.8	Logistic Support Group	Rear Adm. Donald B. Beary
50.9	Service Squadron 10	Commodore Worrall R. Carter

Joint Expeditionary Force (TF 51): Vice Adm. Richmond K. Turner

52	Amphibious Support Force	Rear Adm. William H. P. Blandy
53	Attack Force	Rear Adm. Harry W. Hill
54	Gunfire and Covering Force	Rear Adm. Bertrum J. Rodgers
56	Expeditionary Troops	Lt. Gen. Holland M. Smith, USMC

Fast Carrier Force (TF 58): Vice Adm. Marc A. Mitscher, USN

Forward Area Central Pacific (TF 94): Vice Adm. John H. Hoover[5]

ATTACK FORCE (TASK FORCE 53)

The mission of Rear Adm. Harry W. Hill's Attack Force was to land assault troops on Iwo Jima on D-Day. His Force included all the transports, cargo vessels, and dock landing ships of two Transport Groups; all the LSTs of the Tractor Flotilla; and all the LSMs of the LSM Flotilla; as well as the Control, Beach Party, and Small Craft Groups; and Pontoon Barge, Causeway, and LCT Group.[6]

**ATTACK FORCE
TASK FORCE 53**

Rear Adm H W Hill

TRANSPORT GROUPS
T.G. 53.1 and 53.2
30 APA,12 AKA,3 LSD,1 LSV

TRACTOR FLOTILLA
T.G. 53.3 - CAPT. BRERETON
3 DD,3 LCI(L),46 LST

LSM FLOTILLA
T.G. 53.4 - COMMANDER CARPENTER
1 LCI(L),30 LSM

CONTROL GROUP
T.G. 53.5 - CAPT. ADELL
1 PCE,6 PC(S),4 PC,8 SC

BEACH PARTY GROUP
T.G. 53.6 - CAPT. ANDERSON

**PONTOON BARGE, CAUSEWAY,
AND LCT GROUP**
T.G. 53.7 - LT. COMDR. RYAN
2 LCI(L),12 LCT

SMALL CRAFT GROUP
T.G. 53.8 - LT. COMDR. NELSON
1 LCI(L),2 LCI(G),2 LST(M)

LSM FLOTILLA (TASK GROUP 53.4)

The LSM Flotilla under Comdr. William H. Carpenter, USN (commander LSM Flotilla 5) consisted of his flagship USS *LCI(L)-628*, and a total of thirty medium landing ships. To make this large number more manageable, the flotilla was divided into subordinate Task Units designated Able and Baker. These were led by Lt. Comdr. T. F. Griswold, USNR, and Lt. Comdr. A. E. Lind, USNR, respectively.

Unit Able (Task Unit 53.4.1): Lt. Comdr. T. F. Griswold, USNR
- *LCI(L)-628* (flotilla flagship)
- LSMs *43, 44, 46, 47, 49, 92, 140, 141, 242, 261, 264* (group flagship), *266* (total 12 LSMs)

Unit Baker (Task Unit 53.4.2): Lt. Comdr. A. E. Lind, USNR
- *LSM-60* (group flagship), *48, 59, 70, 74, 126, 145, 201, 202, 206, 207, 211, 216, 238, 239, 241, 260, 323* (total 18 LSMs)[7]

D-DAY AT IWO JIMA

IWO JIMA was an island of volcanic origin about 4.5 miles long by 2.3 miles wide, shaped roughly like a heart, acorn, or tear-drop, with its larger end to the NE, and its long axis running almost exactly NE and SW. Except for Mount SURIBACHI, an extinct volcano which rose some 560 feet in height at the extreme southwestern tip, the terrain was terraced rather than hilly, but nevertheless sloped upward rather sharply from the beaches, to the long interior plateau where three airfields had been leveled.

—Commander in Chief, U.S. Pacific Fleet and Pacific Ocean Areas,
Operations in Pacific Ocean Areas – February 1945,
27 August 1945.

Iwo Jima was known to have been heavily fortified with coastal defense guns, anti-aircraft artillery, and numerous pill boxes, with the vulnerable beach areas protected by interlocking defense systems, from which mutually supporting fields of fire could be laid down. There were two finished airfields from which both bombers and fighters could operate, and one unfinished field. No naval facilities existed, but the island was garrisoned with an organization of Army and Navy troops estimated to be between 13,000 and 14,000 with about 1,050 civilians.[8]

Map 11-3

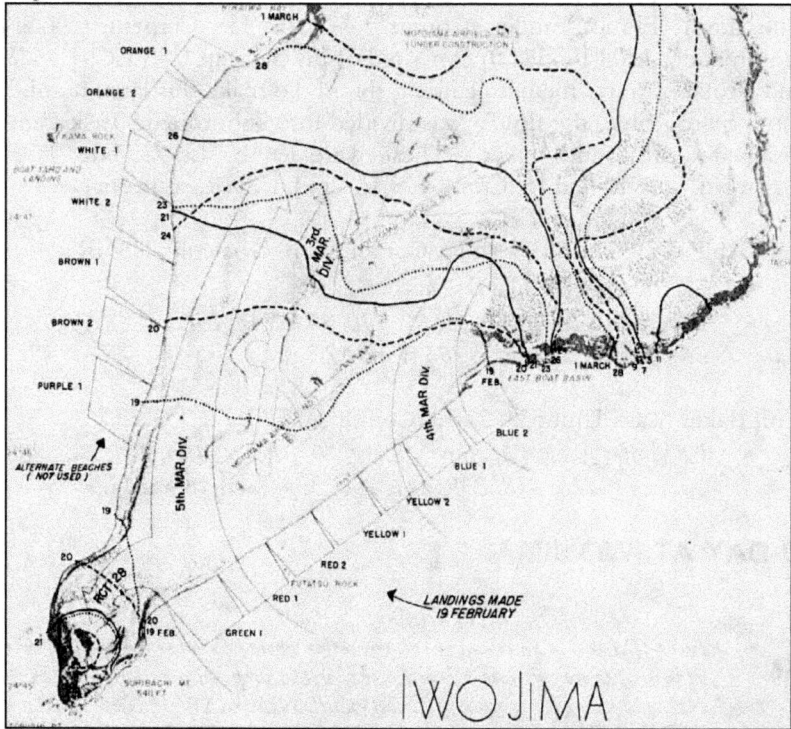

Iwo Jima landing beaches and day-by-day frontline positions through 1 March 1945;
the alternative beaches running roughly north-south at the left of map were not used
Commander in Chief, U.S. Pacific Fleet and Pacific Ocean Areas,
Operations in Pacific Ocean Areas – February 1945, 27 August 1945

The Attack Force, with other units of the Joint Expeditionary Force
(TF 51) not already at the objective, arrived off the southeastern beaches
of Iwo Jima prior to daylight on 19 February, and took station for
debarking the Landing Force. The two Transport Groups hove-to
about 15,000 yards off the southwestern beaches, with Transport Group
53.1, carrying the 5th Marine Division on the left, and Transport Group
53.2, carrying the 4th Marine Division on the right.[9]

The Tractor Flotilla (46 LSTs) proceeded to its designated area
nearer the Line of Departure (LOD). As the Transports lowered their
LCMs and LCVPs and debarked their troops into them, the LSTs and
LSMs launched their LVTs, DUKWs, etc., into the water. The initial
waves formed up at the LOD, which was parallel to and about 4,000
yards off the southeast beaches.[10]

Supported by intense naval gunfire and air bombardment, the first waves made the beach almost exactly at H-Hour (0900), landing over practically the whole width of the southeastern beaches on a front of about 3,000 yards wide. Initially, only a small amount of gunfire was received in the boat lanes during the approach. However, heavy mortar and artillery fire soon developed on the beach and in the boat lanes, with some fire also in the LST areas.[11]

Additionally, adverse beach conditions made landings difficult as detailed in Commander in Chief, U.S. Pacific Fleet and Pacific Ocean Areas' report of Operations in Pacific Ocean Areas – February 1945, dated 27 August 1945:

> With the steep gradient, the surf broke directly on the beach, and it was impossible to keep some of the landing craft from broaching. With each wave, boats would be picked up bodily and thrown broadside onto the beach, where succeeding waves swamped and wrecked them and dug them deeply into the sand, beyond hope of salvage in most cases. Losses had to be accepted until the beachhead was secured, and LSTs, LSMs, and LCTs could be employed. The resultant accumulation of wreckage piled higher and higher, and extended seaward to form underwater obstacles which damaged propellers, and even bilged a few of the landing ships. Several 105mm howitzers loaded in DUKWs were lost en route to the beach due to the rough water.

LSM LANDINGS

At H-Hour plus 30 minutes, six medium landing ships of Unit Baker—LSMs *70, 74, 126, 211, 216,* and *323*—carrying tanks of the 4th Marine Division landed on Blue and Yellow Beaches. The beach areas were then being subjected to heavy enemy mortar and artillery fire, and four ships suffered damage:

- *LSM-323*: minor hit on engine room; one engine knocked out, but subsequently repaired
- *LSM-216*: seven hits on starboard side, wrecking radio room; no damage to machinery
- *LSM-74*: direct hit on engine room, both engines completely disabled; two men killed; sixteen men wounded
- *LSM-211*: five hits below waterline, forward of Frame 17; no casualties to personnel; repair ship personnel subsequently attempted to cement holes below water line in order to make ship seaworthy[12]

During the remainder of the day, few LSMs beached because of continued mortar and artillery fire on the beaches, and because the beach area was littered with wrecked equipment. Commander, Joint Expeditionary Force (Vice Adm. Richmond K. Turner) directed that two LSMs completely unloaded be identified for towing duty south. LSMs *126* and *70* were assigned, and *LSM-126*, after receiving a partial load of cargo from a transport, proceeded with her designated tow.[13]

At sunset on D-Day, the transports and cargo ships retired seaward for the night; the LSMs and other designated vessels remained in the assault area.[14]

D-DAY PLUS 1 (20 FEBRUARY)

During the night, fire support ships kept the island illuminated with star shells and, at daylight on 20 February, heavy fire support ships moved into assigned areas and commenced bombardment of the areas of the island still in enemy hands. The situation on the beaches was slightly improved and LSMs were sent in during the day to unload equipment, returning to assigned transports for additional cargo when empty. In late morning, the weather deteriorated with intermittent showers, and wind increasing slightly. Although beaching conditions remained tenable, weather concerns resulted in cancellation of the movement orders of four LSMs which had been scheduled to depart the area.[15]

LSM-323 reported that her engine had been repaired, and that she was now ready to operate. *LSM-216* was directed to proceed to the amphibious force command ship *Eldorado* (AGC-11) at first light, to receive replacement radios and assistance in installing them. Later that day, as before, designated ships retired at sunset, while LSMs remained in the assault area.[16]

D-DAY PLUS 2 (21 FEBRUARY)

On 21 February, LSMs *323* and *216* received orders to proceed south from Iwo Jima, with LSMs *211* and *74* in tow. The use by repair ship personnel of concrete to patch holes in the *211*'s underwater hull had been unsuccessful, necessitating her being towed stern first. These ships proceeded south, bound for Saipan, before dusk; once again the other LSMs at Iwo Jima remained in the assault area overnight.[17]

D-DAY PLUS 3 (22 FEBRUARY)

Upon return of the transports to the assault area the morning of 22 February, the LSMs continued loading cargo from them and discharging it ashore. Shortly after dusk, Japanese planes were detected and ships in the anchorage were ordered to make smoke. This was the first occasion of enemy aircraft in the area, and there was much indiscriminate firing by ships at them, particularly with 40mm and 20mm AA guns. The planes were at an altitude of a least 5,000 feet, and commander, Joint Expeditionary Force, subsequently directed that no ship covered by smoke should open fire; only those ships which actually had an enemy plane in sight could open fire without permission.[18]

During the raid, *LSM-46*, which was beached at the time, reported having been hit by a bomb. Subsequent information revealed that she was hit by gunfire from high ground at the northern end of the island.[19]

SUBSEQUENT BEACHING OPERATIONS

A Garrison Force has to be kept intact to take over the defense and development of an island after its capture. Hence it is not supposed to take active part in the fighting. It starts landing in successive echelons as fast as the situation ashore permits, however, and takes over varying functions. It therefore comes under the commander of the Landing Force until the capture of the island is completed.

—Commander in Chief, U.S. Pacific Fleet and Pacific Ocean Areas,
Operations in Pacific Ocean Areas – February 1945,
27 August 1945.

As was anticipated, LSM's suffered severe damage while unloading alongside the transports. The weather was not as good as expected, D-Day being the only day of ideal weather. In addition, beaching conditions left much to be desired, and, as the assault phase progressed, more and more ships suffered casualties to screws and other underwater damage from debris in waters immediately off the beach. In addition to weather, resultant surf precluded the use of anything smaller than LCT's [tank landing craft]. Consequently, the latter and the LSM's were responsible for placing practically all assault equipment ashore.

—Commander Task Group 53.4, Action Report,
Attack on Iwo Jima, 19 February 1945.

The unloading of transports at Iwo Jima continued on 23 February and, upon the arrival of Army garrison echelons, LSMs landed equipment carried aboard convoy vessels. *LSM-143* arrived with the Reserve Detachment and was assigned duty with the LSM Flotilla.[20]

BATTLE ASHORE

At great cost, you'd take a hill to find then the same enemy suddenly on your flank or rear. The Japanese were not on Iwo Jima. They were in it! I'd known combat in the Solomons with its sly ambushes and jungle firefights, but Iwo was another kind of war. On Iwo by the 8th day, only two officers of my second battalion (26th Marines, 5th Marine Division) were standing....

—Col. Thomas M. Fields, USMC (Ret.).

Photo 11-2

American flag on Mount Suribachi, Iwo Jima.
Naval History and Heritage Command photograph

To balance the foregoing story of the naval landings a brief description of the exploits of marine divisions that took the island is provided. On 19 February, as naval gunfire pounded the island, more than 450 ships massed off Iwo Jima. Marines of the 4th and 5th Divisions hit the four assault beaches shortly after 0900, initially finding little enemy resistance. Coarse black, volcanic sand hampered their movement as they struggled to move up the beach from the surf zone. As the protective naval gunfire subsided to allow for troop advancement, the

Japanese emerged from fortified underground positions to begin a heavy barrage of fire against the invading force. The 4th Marines continued to push forward against heavy opposition to take the Quarry, a Japanese strong point, while the 5th Marine Division's 28th Marines isolated Mount Suribachi that same day.[21]

The 3rd Marine Division joined the fighting on the fifth day, charged with securing the center sector of the island. The fortified enemy defenses linked miles of interlocking caves, concrete blockhouses and pillboxes, which required frontal assaults to gain nearly every inch of ground. Maj. Gen. Harry Schmidt, commanding the Fifth Amphibious Corps—of which the 3rd, 4th, and 5th Marines were a part—declared Iwo Jima secured on 16 March. Ground fighting, however, continued between then and the official completion of the operation on 26 March 1945.[22]

PERSONAL AND UNIT AWARDS

Comdr. William Hubbard Carpenter, USN, was awarded the Bronze Star Medal (with Combat V) for his actions as commander of the LSM Flotilla at Iwo Jima. The associated medal citation follows:

> For meritorious achievement as Commander of LSM Flotilla Five during the assault and capture of Iwo Jima, Volcano Islands from February 19 to March 3, 1945. Handicapped by heavy seas and high winds which made the handling and beaching of LSMs extremely difficult and caused them considerable damage, Captain (then Commander) Carpenter capably directed his ships in landing troops, supplies and equipment onto beaches under intense enemy fire. By his rapid and efficient evacuation of casualties he contributed materially to the saving of many lives. His aggressive leadership, sound judgment and untiring devotion to duty throughout this period were in keeping with the highest traditions of the United States Naval Service.[23]

LSM BATTLE STARS

Iwo Jima Operation: Assault and Occupation of Iwo Jima

LSM-43	19 Feb-16 Mar 45	LSM-201	19 Feb-16 Mar 45
LSM-44	19 Feb-16 Mar 45	LSM-202	19 Feb-16 Mar 45
LSM-46	19 Feb-16 Mar 45	LSM-206	19 Feb-16 Mar 45
LSM-47	19 Feb-16 Mar 45	LSM-207	19 Feb-16 Mar 45
LSM-48	19 Feb-16 Mar 45	LSM-211	19-21 Feb 45
LSM-49	19 Feb-16 Mar 45	LSM-216	19-21 Feb 45
LSM-59	19 Feb-16 Mar 45	LSM-238	19 Feb-16 Mar 45
LSM-60	19 Feb-16 Mar 45	LSM-239	19 Feb-16 Mar 45
LSM-70	19 Feb 45	LSM-241	19-20 Feb 45
LSM-74	19-21 Feb 45	LSM-242	19 Feb-14 Mar 45
LSM-92	19 Feb-16 Mar 45	LSM-260	19 Feb-16 Mar 45
LSM-126	19 Feb 45	LSM-261	19 Feb-16 Mar 45
LSM-140	19 Feb-16 Mar 45	LSM-264	19 Feb-16 Mar 45
LSM-141	19 Feb-16 Mar 45	LSM-266	19 Feb-16 Mar 45
LSM-143	20 Feb-16 Mar 45	LSM-323	19-21 Feb 45
LSM-145	19 Feb-16 Mar 45		

Commanding Officers

LSM-43 Lt. C. R. Hooff Jr., USNR	LSM-201 Lt. A. J. Buchinsky, USNR
LSM-44 Lt. B. A. Rubin, USNR	LSM-202 Lt. D. Thurlow, USNR
LSM-46 Lt. F. R. Edwards, USNR	LSM-206 Lt. G. C. MacKenzie, USNR
LSM-47 Lt. F. J. Chokel, USNR	LSM-207 Lt. R. Allman, USNR
LSM-48 Lt. M. T. Graugnard, USNR	LSM-211 Lt. H. R. Geyelin, USNR
LSM-49 Lt. R. Greenwood, USN	LSM-216 Lt. C. P. Haber, USNR
LSM-59 Lt. D. C. Hawley, USNR	LSM-238 Lt. D. M. McIntosh, USNR
LSM-60 Lt. W. W. Doar, USNR	LSM-239 Lt. E. W. Jokisch, USNR
LSM-70 Lt. R. C. Whalin, USN	LSM-241 Lt. W. T. Brooks, USNR
LSM-74 Lt. S. M. Prewitt, USNR	LSM-242 Lt. (jg) C. O. Gardner, USNR
LSM-92 Lt. J. Grandin, USNR	LSM-260 Lt. R. J. Grier II, USNR
LSM-126 Lt. G.E. Stricker, USNR	LSM-261 Lt. A. J. Smith Jr., USNR
LSM-140 Lt. R.F. Duff, USNR	LSM-264 Lt. F. M. Parrish, USNR
LSM-141 Lt. E. A. Quinlan, USNR	LSM-266 Lt. W. H. Rutledge, USNR
LSM-143 Lt. R. C. White, USNR	LSM-323 Lt. J. C. Watt, USNR[24]
LSM-145 Lt. R. P. Palmer, USNR	

12

Palawan Island Landings

All beaches used were studded with coral heads. There were many sunken planes in the approaches to the beaches used by LSMs just east of the PUERTO PRINCESA jetty. As a result considerable damage was done to propellers.

—Rear Adm. William M. Fechteler, USN, commander,
Palawan Attack Group (Task Group 78.2).[1]

Photo 12-1

Destroyer USS *Drayton* (DD-366) shelling Palawan Island, 28 February 1945.
National Archives photograph #80-G-305590

As elements of the U.S. Sixth Army under Lt. Gen. Walter Krueger moved into the city of Manila in 1945 to retake it from well dug-in Japanese forces, Gen. Douglas MacArthur issued orders for the start of a series of operations (all code-named VICTOR) to recapture the entire southern Philippine archipelago. These were followed by three operations undertaken near war's end to recapture Borneo (OBOE series), as a first step toward freeing the Netherlands East Indies.[2]

The Victor operations were to be conducted entirely by troops of the U.S. Eighth Army, while Australian forces were to assume responsibility for the seizure of Borneo, Java, and adjacent islands. The numerical code names of these operations did not necessarily coincide with the dates on which they began (D-days).

Operation	Name	D-day	Operation	Name	D-day
Palawan	VIII	28 Feb	SE Negros	VII	26 Apr
Zamboanga	VIV	10 Mar	Mindanao	VV	17 Apr
Panay & W. Negros	VI	18 Mar	Tarakan	OBOE I	1 May
Cebu	VII	26 Mar	Brunei Bay	OBOE VI	10 Jun
Bohol	VII	11 Apr	Balikpapan	OBOE II	1 Jul[3]

The Eighth Army was assigned the task of liberating the Philippine Islands bordering the Sulu Sea-Palawan Island region to the north and west, the Sulu Islands to the south, and Zamboanga Peninsula and Basilan Island to the east. The first of the series of Victor operations on 28 February involved the invasion of Puerto Princesa, Palawan; followed shortly thereafter by the seizure of Zamboanga, Basilan Island, and the Sulu Archipelago. At the time the operations were planned it was determined that possession of these land areas and utilization of captured airfields, would ensure control of two vital sea lanes—the north-south route between the Netherlands East Indies and Japan, and the east-west route from the central and southern Philippines to Singapore. Large-scale operations would then be conducted against the Japanese on Panay and on Negros Occidental, with Cebu, Negros Oriental, and Bohol as the targets to follow.[4]

Map 12-1

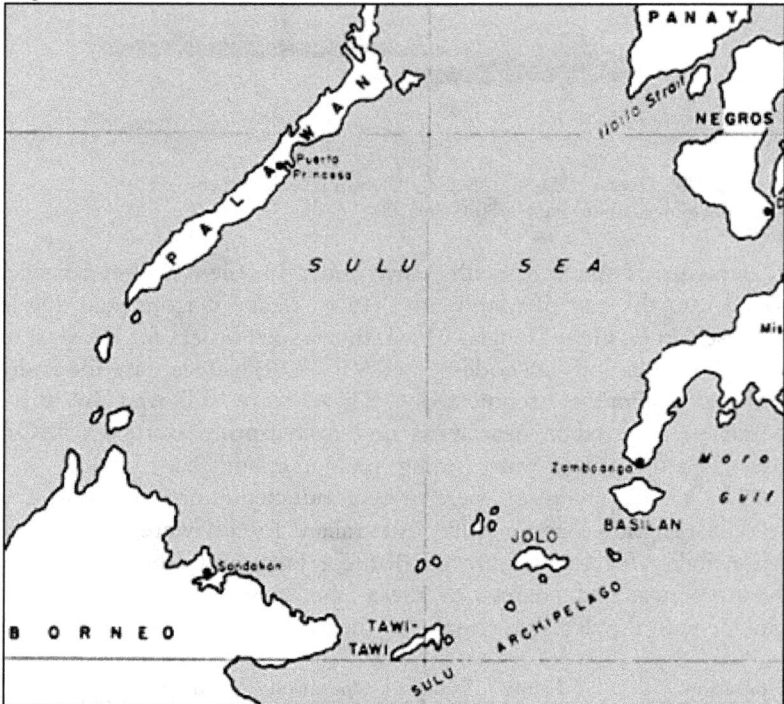

Southern Philippine Islands; Borneo located to the southwest (the third largest island in the World), today consists of three countries: Malaysia, Brunei, and Indonesia

The 41st Infantry Division, under Maj. Gen. Jens A. Doe, was assigned the tasks of liberating Palawan, Zamboanga, and the Sulu Archipelago. Its 186th Infantry Regimental Combat Team was assigned to the Palawan invasion, while the 162nd and 163rd Infantry were scheduled for the Zamboanga and Sulu operations.[5]

PALAWAN ATTACK GROUP (TASK GROUP 78.2)

On the evening of 26 February, Task Group 78.2 sortied from Mindoro and proceeded to the objective area. The passage was made on schedule and devoid of any enemy action.[6]

The collective load carried by the twenty LSMs upon departure from Mindoro, en route to Palawan, was 95 officers, 1,368 men, and 349 vehicles of the 186th Regimental Combat Team, 41st Infantry Division. Comprising the 349 vehicles were 203 trucks, 114 trailers, 7 bulldozers, 6 tractors, 6 graders, 3 cranes, 2 wreckers, 1 track shovel, 1 reefer (refrigerator), 4 DUKWs, and 2 LVTs. Additionally, 19 LCMs (mechanized landing craft) were towed astern of LSMs.[7]

Map 12-2

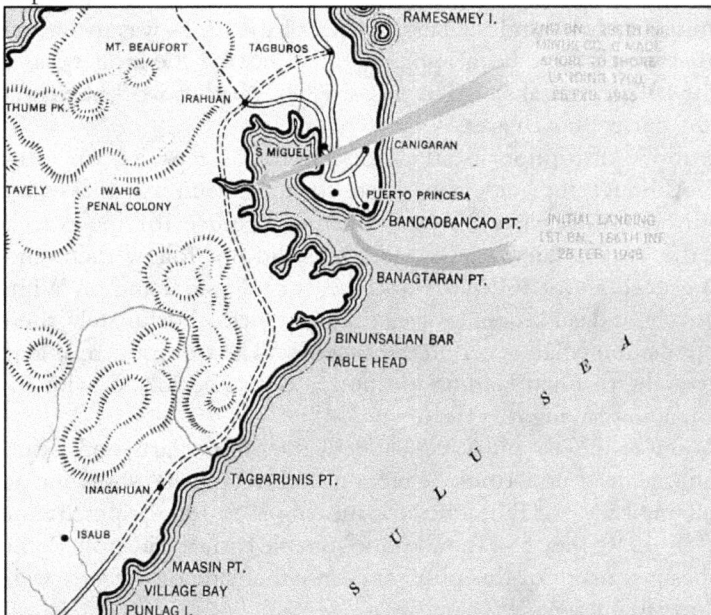

Central east coast of Palawan Island, Philippines; the lower arrow on the map identifies the initial landing on D-Day by the 1st Battalion, 186th Infantry, and the upper arrow, a second landing made by the 2nd Battalion at 1700 that day
William F. McCartney, *The Jungleers: A History of the 41st Infantry Division* (Washington, D.C.: Infantry Journal Press, 1948)

After arriving off the southwest shore of Puerto Princesa early on the morning of the 28th, the task group deployed to carry out the entrance plan. At 0715, pre-landing bombardment began. Even though the landing beaches had already been under air bombardment for forty-eight hours, an additional naval gunfire and rocket barrage was laid down just before H-hour (0845).[8]

At 0820, the assault LSTs began unloading LVTs, allowing the first wave of LVTs to leave the line of departure on time for their respective White Beach 1, White Beach 2, and White Beach 3 landings. Because wave guide boats leading the first wave for White Beach 1 to the immediate vicinity of the correct beach, stopped short of the reef offshore, the troop wave commander turned the wave sharply to the left, and landed about 250 yards west of the designated beach. The three remaining LVT waves for that beach followed the first wave.[9]

The fifth (LCVPs from APDs) and subsequent waves for White Beach 1 did not follow the deviation and were able to land on the correct beach area. It was vital to have the troops of the 5th and 6th waves land there, and not follow the LVT waves to the adjacent westward area, to get them ashore ahead of artillery landing in waves of LCMs. The terrain immediately behind the landing area of the LVTs was mangrove swamp that would have been impassible for moving the artillery, as it was by the LVTs (amtraks). As it was, the latter had to work their way back to the correct beach area.[10]

The above disruption in attack direction was repeated on other beaches. Although the guide sub-chaser for the assault waves assigned to land on White Beaches 2 and 3 steered a course for the correct beaches, the wave guide LCVPs and LVTs did not follow them and, instead, beached about 300 yards to the east of White 2 and on White 3, respectively, and subsequent waves followed them. Fortunately, there was no opposition whatsoever on the beaches. The troops were able to assemble at the planned landing location and pushed inland, with the errors of landing having no effect.[11]

As soon as the assault waves landed, the Shore Party and Beach Party commanders undertook a reconnaissance of the shoreline to locate suitable LSM/LST beaches for moving in more equipment and supplies. By 1030, they had found none suitable east of Tidepole Point; the beaches just north of this point and on either side of the jetty were the only possibilities.[12]

At that time, commander, Task Group 78.2 directed commander, Task Unit 78.2.4 (Comdr. William E. Verge, USN) to beach in *LSM-54* at White Beach 3 to determine the feasibility of unloading LSMs at that point. Verge, commanding the LSM Unit of twenty medium landing ships—*LSM-54* (flagship), *41, 50, 53, 63, 65, 66, 67, 127, 128, 129, 131, 133, 168, 219, 224, 225, 237, 268, 269*—assessed the beach, when *LSM-54* beached at that location at high tide, as fair.[13]

Subsequently, the Beachmaster requested that *LSM-54* retract and beach to the right of the pier at Puerto Princesa town, which transpired. This beach was found to be strewn with wreckage of sunken planes and boats; nevertheless, LSMs landed at both beaches and unloaded their equipment. Verge noted under Special Comments in his action report:

> The beaches were all hard coral with many coral heads and beaching was extremely difficult. The beaches most free of coral contained the sunken wreckage of many Japanese planes. Nearly all the LSMs involved had one or both propellers damaged in beaching.[14]

RETURN TO MINDORO

At 1900 on 28 February, the first echelon returning to Mindoro departed; it included all LSMs unloaded at that time, less two retained for consolidation operations. By 0730 the following morning, 1 March, all remaining LSMs had unloaded except two, which were completing. Two of six LSTs had unloaded and were anchored ready for return, one was beached and unloading, three had retracted and were unloading remaining cargo bulk offshore and lightering to shore. That evening, the second returning echelon of ships sailed for Mindoro. It included 5 of 6 LSTs (the remaining one was unloaded, but unable to retract), and 9 LSMs (seven under tow). Two other LSMs requiring tow were held awaiting towing ships.[15]

The following morning, 2 March, *LST-912*, which had been stuck on the beach, was able to retract at 0130. That evening, a third returning echelon departed at 1850; it included 2 LSMs (towed by LSTs) and all unloaded LSTs. (Other LSTs, in addition to the original six, had arrived on 1 March as part of a reinforcement echelon.)[16]

VICTOR III OPERATION A GREAT SUCCESS

The Palawan landings and their strategic significance were summarized in General Headquarters, Southwest Pacific Area Communique No. 1060, of 2 March 1945:

> We have landed on Palawan and seized control of this fifth largest and most westerly island of the Philippine Archipelago. Engrossed in operations elsewhere the enemy again failed to diagnose our plans and properly prepare his defense. Elements of the 41st Division of the Eighth Army, coordinated with naval and air support, landed near Puerto Princesa, the capital and major city of the island, and

pushed swiftly inland to seize the town and two nearby airfields. The enemy fled to the hills and our losses were very light. The air bases of Palawan command the western end of the southern water passage through the Philippines by way of the Sulu Sea and interdict the north and south channel of the South China Sea, the enemy's main water transportation line to Indo China, Thailand, Malaya, Singapore, Burma, and the East Indies. It places us within 500 miles of the enemy bases of Brunei Bay and Tarakan in North Borneo. It will therefore not only help to ensure the safe passage of our own sea transport but render hazardous that of the enemy. The progressive securing of the Philippines as a base thus tends to cut the enemy in two and condemn all his conquests to the south to recapture.

LSM BATTLE STARS

Consolidation of Southern Philippines: Palawan Islands Landings

Ship	Date/Period	Ship	Date/Period
LSM-41	28 Feb-1 Mar 45	LSM-129	28 Feb-1 Mar 45
LSM-50 (no BS)	28 Feb 45	LSM-131	28 Feb 45
LSM-53	28 Feb-1 Mar 45	LSM-133	28 Feb 45
LSM-54 (no BS)	28 Feb 45	LSM-168 (no BS)	
LSM-63 (no BS)	28 Feb 45	LSM-219	28 Feb-2 Mar 45
LSM-65 (no BS)	28 Feb-1 Mar 45	LSM-224	28 Feb-1 Mar 45
LSM-66	28 Feb-1 Mar 45	LSM-225	28 Feb
LSM-67 (no BS)	1-2 Mar 45	LSM-237	28 Feb-1 Mar 45
LSM-127	28 Feb-1 Mar 45	LSM-268	28 Feb-1 Mar 45
LSM-128	28 Feb-1 Mar 45	LSM-269	28 Feb-1 Mar 45

Note: Apparently there is a mistake in *Navy and Marine Corps Awards Manual Department of the Navy NAVPERS 15,790 (Rev. 1953)* regarding *LSM-168*. She participated in the Palawan operation as a group flagship, but is not listed for that operation, which should be the case, even if she did not earn a battle star.

13

Mindanao Island Landings

Embark at Mindoro, troops, equipment and supplies of the 41st Infantry Division, transport them to the objective [Zamboanga, Mindanao]...and, commencing at H-Hour [0915] on J-Day [10 March 1945], land troops, equipment and supplies on Yellow and Red Beaches.

—Commander Task Unit 78.1.12, Action Report – Victor-Four Operation, 16 March 1945, describing the mission of twenty--one LSMs under Comdr. Daniel J. Weintraub, a part of Rear Adm. Forrest B. Royal's Zamboanga Attack Group (Task Group 78.1).

Task Unit 78.1.12

LSM	LINE OF DEPARTURE	BEACHED	RETRACTED
18(GF)	1114	1124	1209
19	1022	1048	1132
21	1018	1040	1116
22	1021	1040	1112
* 34	1135	1146	1233
* 37	1210	1228	1335
* 38	1020	1040	1155
* 39	1015	1041	1110
* 40	1015	1042	1121
* 42(GF)	1015	1040	1107
* 130	1125	1147	1210
138	1114	1127	1219
139	1114	1127	1250
* 205	1210	1223	1250
* 218	1051	1106	1150
257	1021	1040	1126
258(FF)	1022	1040	1111
310	1119	1136	1157
311	1122	1142	1223
* 314	1205	1215	1245
* 319	1015	1027	1152

* Red Beach Unit

Assault landings by LSMs at Zamboanga, Mindanao beaches on 10 March 1945. Commander Task Unit 78.1.12, Action Report – Victor-Four Operation, 16 March 1945

Photo 13-1

Lt. Gen. Robert L. Eichelberger, commanding General 8th Army, is welcomed aboard the amphibious force command ship USS *Rocky Mount* by Rear Adm. Forrest B. Royal, commander Amphibious Group Six, 7 March 1945.
Commander Task Group 78.1, Amphibious Attack on Zamboanga, Mindanao – Report of, 26 March 1945

The assault echelons of Rear Adm. Forrest B. Royal's Zamboanga Attack Group (TG 78.1) departed Leyte and Mindoro on 8 March 1945, rendezvoused in the late afternoon the following day, and then proceeded in company to the objective. The sea was rough during the passage, causing considerable seasickness to both Army and Navy personnel. As she arrived off Zamboanga at 0636 on 10 March, Royal's amphibious force command ship *Rocky Mount* (AGC-3) executed the signals, "Commence the approach"; "All Task Unit Commanders take charge of their units"; and "Disregard the movements of the *ROCKY MOUNT*."[1]

Following intensive air bombardment, naval bombardment by the Cruiser Covering Group began at 0645. Forty minutes later, when the assault LSTs, APDs (high speed transports), and dock landing ship *Rushmore* (LSD-14) were in proper position behind the Line of Departure (LOD), the launching of embarked assault craft began and continued as follows:

- 0729: APDs launched LCVPs (Higgins boats)
- 0732: LSTs *630* and *753* began launching assault LVT waves
- 0734: *Rushmore* launched LVTs[2]

Photo 13-2

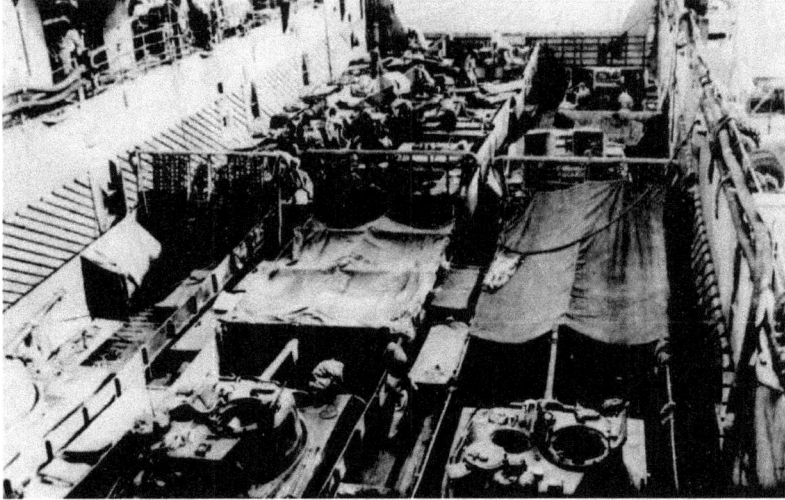

Heavily loaded LCMs in welldeck of USS *Rushmore* (LSD-14), 10 March 1945.
Commander Task Group 78.1, Amphibious Attack on Zamboanga,
Mindanao – Report of, 26 March 1945

Photo 13-3

Heavy deck load of DUKWs and "J" boats on board *Rushmore*, 10 March 1945.
Commander Task Group 78.1, Amphibious Attack on Zamboanga,
Mindanao – Report of, 26 March 1945

Map 13-1

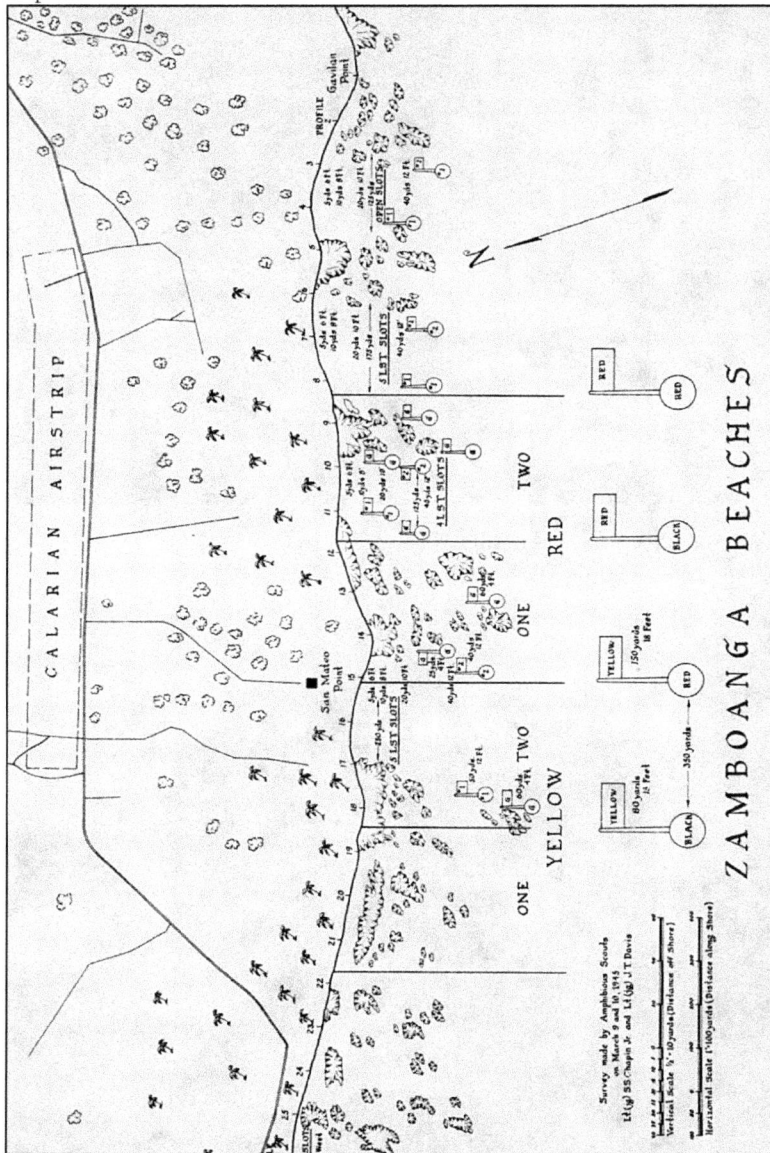

Adjacent Zamboanga Yellow 1, Yellow 2, Red 1, and Red 2 assault beaches
Commander Task Group 78.1, Amphibious Attack on Zamboanga,
Mindanao – Report of, 26 March 1945

As shown on the preceding map, all landings were made on Red and Yellow Beaches. On invasion day, preparatory to the landings, the eleven YMSs of Task Unit 78.1.5 carried out a final sweep of waters close to the beach. One moored mine was cut free from its tether and upon surfacing, destroyed by YMS gunfire. It was similar to a USN Mk. 6 type, having 4 to 5 horns visible.[3]

Lt. Ernest Saltmarsh's minesweepers had begun operations in the approaches and off the beaches two days earlier on 8 March. At 0824 the preceding morning, after receiving enemy fire from Red Beach 2, they had returned it with their 40mm anti-aircraft guns. A few minutes later, all the YMSs engaged in the clearance were firing all along their tracks, both 40mm, and 3-inch rounds from their deck guns, against enemy fire on the beach. There were no personnel casualties, and the only damage to ships was superficial damage to the bow of *YMS-50*, caused by small bits of shrapnel.[4]

Photo 13-4

Yard minesweeper USS *YMS-71*, location unknown, circa 1942.
National Archives photograph 80-G-49330

At 0750, the order was given to "Land the Landing Force." The first assault wave was dispatched from the Line of Departure at 0847, with the second wave following at 0850, and the third at 0853. At 0900, Naval Amphibious Scouts reported to the Landing Craft Control and Beach Master Unit, favorable hydrographic conditions on Yellow and Red Beaches, and this information was relayed to LCI(L) waves, LSMs and LSTs before they commenced their run-ins.[5]

The fourth and fifth waves left the Line of Departure at 0910 and 0912. A little later, the first LCI(L)s (Sixth Wave) landed on Red 2 and Yellow 2 Beaches at 0933.[6]

Photo 13-5

LCI(L)s with troops approaching the beach at Zamboanga, 10 March 1945. Commander Task Group 78.1, Amphibious Attack on Zamboanga, Mindanao – Report of, 26 March 1945

Photo 13-6

Painting by Carlos Lopez, 1943, of Navy commandos who carried out reconnaissance, scout or demolition missions, normally conducted at night, against enemy-held shores. Naval History and Heritage photograph #88-159-HD

The seventh wave, LCI(L)s, landed on Red 2 and Yellow 2 Beaches at 0955, followed by the eighth wave, LCMs, on those same beaches at 1010. At 1012, enemy mortar or artillery batteries took LCI(L)s *1025*, *1071*, and *1075* under fire. LCI(L)s *710* and *779* later reported being taken under fire also and hit, resulting in a few personnel casualties, but no damage to the large infantry landing craft themselves.[7]

Photo 13-7

Soldiers from *LCI(L)-771* have to wade ashore at Red Beach.
Commander Task Group 78.1, Amphibious Attack on Zamboanga,
Mindanao – Report of, 26 March 1945

LSM LANDING OPERATIONS

Most of the LSMs landed finally with a dry or nearly dry ramp. However, the beach immediately off the ramp consisted of loose cobblestones and a rather steep gradient just ahead of the ramp. The vehicles had a difficult time clearing the LSMs. As was known for this operation, the condition mentioned above, it is imperative that steps be taken to organize and plan for equipment to keep the vehicles moving once they leave the LSM's ramp. The LSMs were thereby subjected to the hazards of fire encountered for two to three times the normal length of time.

—Comdr. Daniel J. Weintraub, commander, Task Unit 78.1.12.[8]

The first LSMs to land comprised Wave 9, which were split into two groups—at 1022: LSMs *42*, *38*, *39*, *40*, and *319* headed into Red Beach 2—and two minutes later at 1024: LSMs *258*, *21*, *22*, *19*, and *27* going into Yellow Beach 2. The table at chapter's head provides the times individual LSMs arrived at the Line of Departure (but not when they left it); when they beached; and when they retracted.[9]

Comdr. Daniel J. Weintraub, the LSM Unit commander, explained the reason for split waves:

Originally the 22 LSMs were to be sent in waves of 11 each on Yellow TWO and Red TWO. From the timely information given by the Beach Parties it was recognized by the Flotilla Commander and Commander LSM Group Six [Weintraub], in charge of Yellow TWO and Red TWO LSMs respectively, that no more than 5 or 6 LSMs [could] be sent in to each Beach as a wave. This turned out to be correct. Had 11 LSMs been sent in on Yellow TWO, and due to lack of space for proper beaching been forced to lie off they would have come into the mortar and artillery fire falling just astern of the beached LSMs.[10]

Photo 13-8

USS *LSM-138* and *LSM-18* unloading over the beach at Zamboanga, Mindanao, 1 April 1945.
National Archives photograph #80-G-359833

A house on the beach between Yellow 2 and Red 1 beaches provided an excellent navigational aid for the approach of landing craft. Plans called for the non-destruction of this house, and the cooperation of forces involved in maintaining this landmark aided markedly in the beachings.[11]

Photo 13-9

View of house that marked the boundary between Yellow 2 and Red 1 beaches, San Mateo Point, Zamboanga, looking seaward, 10 March 1945.
Commander Task Group 78.1, Amphibious Attack on Zamboanga, Mindanao – Report of, 26 March 1945

The LSM Unit suffered only one personnel casualty during landings on 10 March, and there was no damage to ships. A mortar round landed in the water near *LSM-19* during her approach to the beach, and crewman Signalman Third John Raymond Murray suffered a wound to his left leg caused by a piece of shrapnel.[12]

RETURN OF LSM UNIT TO MINDORO

At 1830 that evening, in the first returning echelon, the twenty-one ships of the Task Unit 78.1.12 (LSM Unit) departed Zamboanga, Mindanao, for Mangarin Bay, Mindoro. Sailing in company as screening ships were the high-speed transports *Lloyd* (APD-63), *Newman* (APD-59), *Cofer* (APD-62), and *Kephart* (APD-61), and destroyer *Sigourney* (DD-643).[13]

The task unit arrived Mindoro at 1400 on 12 March, and anchored in assigned berths in preparation to load and return as J+7 Echelon to Zamboanga on 17 March.[14]

41ST INFANTRY DIVISION PROGRESS ASHORE

Photo 13-10

Top: Front of concrete pillbox near beach 1,200 yards east of Baliwasan River, and bottom, the rear of the same pillbox. Commander Task Group 78.1, Amphibious Attack on Zamboanga, Mindanao – Report of, 26 March 1945

Reinforced units of the 41st Division, less the 186th Regimental Combat Team which was still "mopping up" on Palawan, poured ashore at San Mateo Point (site of the landing beaches), just west of Zamboanga City, against light opposition. Consolidation of the beachhead following the landing proceeded rapidly against sporadic enemy resistance, because many strong defensive positions had been abandoned by the Japanese who had become jittery and thoroughly demoralized by the heavy air and naval bombardment.[15]

The Japanese troops withdrew to the heights north of the city and their only defense of the landing area came from sporadic mortar and artillery fire directed from well-constructed gun emplacements in the hills outside Zamboanga. The assault forces secured Wolfe Airstrip, an initial objective, before noon on 10 March, and took San Roque Airfield and Zamboanga City the following day even though the roads to and within the city were heavily mined, planted with booby traps and flanked by concrete pillboxes protected by wire entanglements.[16]

Grim and stubborn Japanese resistance slowed the advance of the 41st Division into the mountains. However, with the arrival of the 186th Regimental Combat Team in late March, the drive gained fresh vigor. By early April organized resistance had ceased. Scattered elements were later sealed off and decimated either by killing or capture by a series of American landings along the western coast of the peninsula.[17]

LSM BATTLE STARS

Consolidation of Southern Philippines: Mindanao Islands Landings

Ship	Date/Period	Ship	Date/Period
LSM-18	10 Mar-16 May 45	LSM-138	10 Mar-23 Apr 45
LSM-19	10 Mar-16 May 45	LSM-139	10 Mar-23 Apr 45
LSM-21	10 Mar-3 May 45	LSM-205	10 Mar-3 May 45
LSM-22	10 Mar 45	LSM-218	10-31 Mar 45
LSM-34	10 Mar-16 May 45	LSM-257	10 Mar-23 Apr 45
LSM-37	10 Mar-3 May 45	LSM-258	10 Mar-3 May 45
LSM-38	10 Mar-16 May 45	LSM-310	10 Mar-3 May 45
LSM-39 (no BS)	10 Mar-16 May 45	LSM-311	10 Mar-3 May 45
LSM-40	10 Mar-16 May 45	LSM-314	10 Mar-16 May 45
LSM-42	10 Mar-16 May 45	LSM-319	10 Mar-16 May 45
LSM-130	10 Mar-5 May 45		

Operation VICTOR I
Amphibious Landings

Photo 14-1

USS *PT-490* with General Douglas MacArthur aboard, carrying him
and his staff from Negros Island to Iloilo, Panay, in 1945.
National Archives photograph #SC 262349

Following the 10 March 1945 amphibious landing at Zamboanga on
Mindanao Island, came landings that month on the islands of Panay,
Negros, and Cebu, as well as on the minor islands of:

- Basilan (south of Zamboanga)
- Romblon and Simara (north of Mindoro)
- Inampulagan and Guimaras (southeast of Iloilo)
- Mactan and Cauit (east of Cebu)
- Caballo (near Corregidor)[1]

BASILAN ISLAND LANDING

At 0830 on 16 March, an Attack Unit (TU 78.1.2)—organized at
Zamboanga by commander, Task Group 78.1 for the purpose of
carrying out an assault on nearby Basilan Island (see Map 14-1)—
departed Zamboanga. Movement to the objective was without incident,
and the landing at Lamitan by Company F., 162th Infantry in three LCM
waves, was made without enemy opposition.[2]

Map 14-1

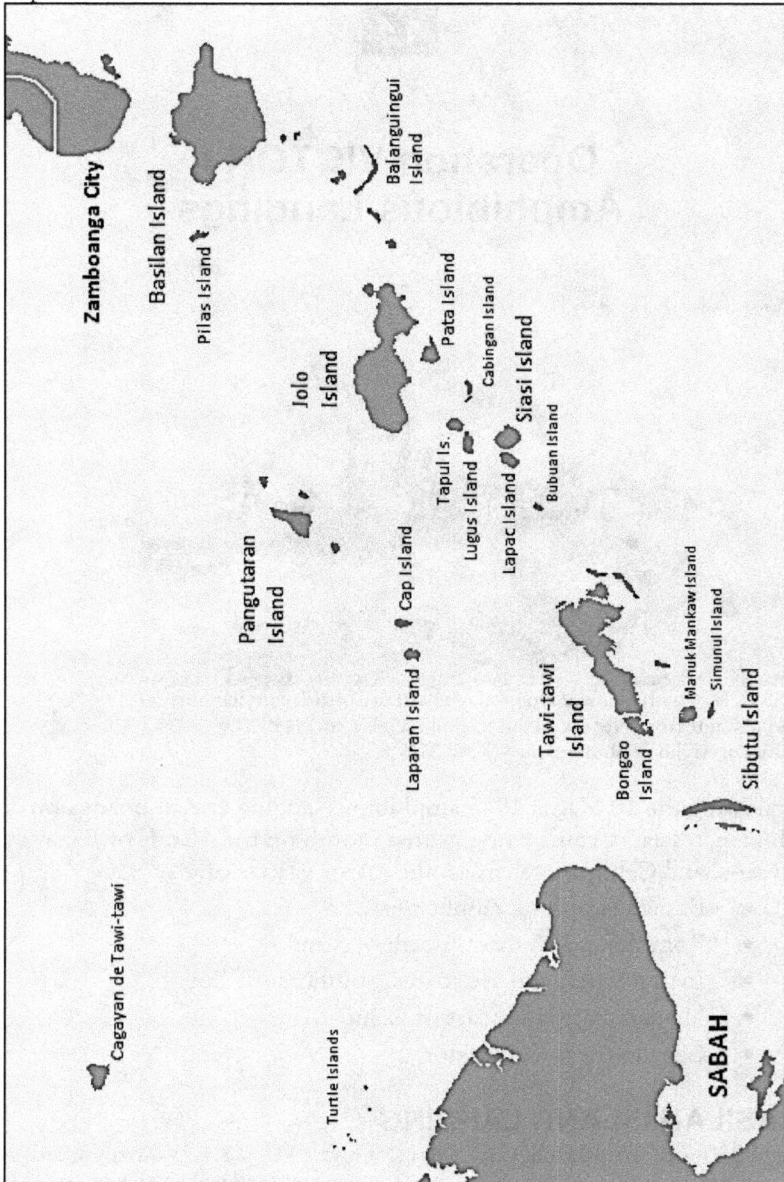

Sulu Archipelago, Philippines

PANAY (VICTOR I) OPERATION

By this point in the March assaults, guerrilla forces on Panay in the Central Philippines had practically cleared the island of Japanese, except for a concentration of troops near the city of Iloilo. In order to eliminate remaining enemy forces, and to establish radar and air navigation and transportation facilities, and minor naval facilities (particularly for PT boats), an amphibious assault was staged from Lingayen Gulf. D-Day was 18 March for landing the 40th Infantry Division (reinforced), less one Regimental Combat Team.[3]

Map 14-2

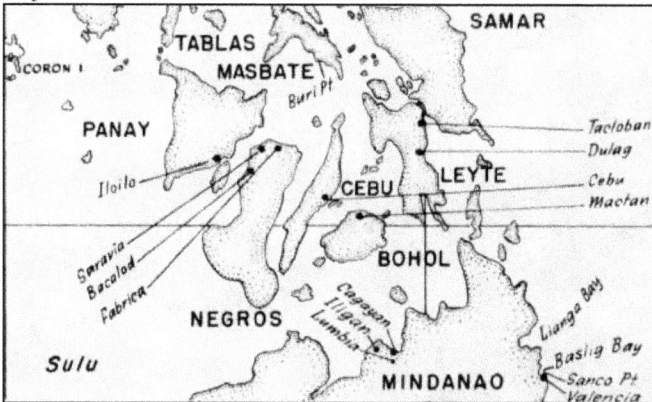

Central Philippine Islands
Commander in Chief, U.S. Pacific Fleet and Pacific Ocean Areas,
Operations in the Pacific Ocean Areas - September 1944, 7 March 1945

The mission of the Victor One Attack Group (TG 78.3) under Rear Admiral Struble was to embark and land the 40th Division, together with its equipment and supplies in the Iloilo area of southern Panay; with subsequent landings at Guimaras Island, Negros Occidental (western side of Negros Island), and adjacent small islands. The Panay and other landings comprising the VICTOR I Operation were undertaken to assist in the reoccupation of the Visayas—islands primarily surrounding the Visayan Sea with some in the northeast extremity of the Sulu Sea. The major islands of the Visayas are Panay, Negros, Cebu, Bohol, Leyte and Samar.[4]

At 0700 on 15 March, the bulk of Task Group 78.3 left Lingayen for Panay. The remaining ships of the task group joined at 2150 the following evening off Mangarin Bay, Mindoro. At 0755 on 18 March, the Attack Group arrived off Iloilo. Landing ships and craft were ordered to cast off LCM tows, and the attack group ordered to deploy.

Scheduled pre-landing gunfire was cancelled after groups of natives, waving white flags, were sighted collecting on Red Beach.[5]

Photo 14-2

Painting by James Turnbull, 1945, of a Filipino guerrilla waving an American flag while standing in the surf preceding amphibious assault landings for a different operation. This man was spotted by an observation plane waving a flag during a concentrated pre-invasion bombardment a few minutes before H-Hour. He was attempting to signal American forces that the Japanese had retreated and that troops offshore would be able to land without bombardment.
Naval History and Heritage Command photograph #88-159-LD

At 0850, the designated LSTs began discharging LVTs into the boat lane. The first wave landed unopposed at 0906, followed closely by the second and third waves of LVTs, and the fourth wave of LCMs. The LCI(L)s, comprising the eighth wave, were unable to land closer than 75 yards from shore when beaching.[6]

LSM UNIT (TASK UNIT 78.3.3)

At 0935, *LSM-267*, a member of the LSM Unit under Comdr. William E. Verge, USN, was directed to Red Beach to test beaching conditions which proved to be deficient. It had been believed that landing beaches "Red" and "Blue" which both afforded proximity to the objective, had acceptable landing conditions. The Army preferred Red Beach to the east of the Skbalom River at Tigbauan, because it would avoid a troop crossing of the river. As such, it was selected for the assault landing. However, the suitability of Red Beach for unloading LSMs and LSTs proved untenable because of the gradient, and operations were shifted to Blue Beach (to the west of the river).[7]

The Beachmaster began calling LSMs into Blue Beach at 1113. Carried aboard the ten LSMs of Task Unit 78.3.3—*LSM-54* (flagship), *53, 63, 65, 66* (group flagship) *128, 131, 224, 267, 269*—were a total of 23 officers, 416 men, and 137 vehicles—40 trucks, 39 tanks, 33 trailers, 13 bulldozers, 11 halftracks, and 1 carryall. In addition, each of the LSMs had towed an LCM astern while in transit to the objective.[8]

By mid-afternoon, all the LSMs had unloaded and retracted from Blue Beach, and were anchored off Red Beach. That evening, they moved seaward for "night retirement" to minimize the possibility of enemy attack; before returning to anchorage off Red Beach at 0900 the following morning. That evening, the LSM Task Unit was dissolved, and individual ships carried out their new orders.[9]

ACTIVITIES OF MOTOR TORPEDO (PT) BOATS

Photo 14-3

Motor torpedo boat tender USS *Portunus* (AGP-4) with PT boats alongside.
U.S. Navy photo from the collections of the U.S. Navy Memorial

Earlier, at noon on assault day, 18 March, the motor torpedo boat tender *Portunus*, with ten PT boats and two motor gunboats (PGMs) arrived off Blue Beach. That afternoon, pairs of PTs, working with aircraft, searched the coastline of Panay from the landing beach south and west, and the coastline of southern Guimaras Island and Negros from Hinigaran, south. Commencing that night, PTs carried out regular night patrols in north Guimaras Strait, in south Iloilo Strait, and off the coast of southwestern Panay as far as San Jose.[10]

PROGRESS ASHORE

Iloilo was secured on 20 March by the troops ashore. The Japanese garrison had hastily withdrawn the previous night after razing approximately seventy percent of the city. Fortunately, the docks were undamaged and the harbor area was clear. By 22 March, organized enemy resistance had ceased, leaving only isolated enemy pockets to be dealt with by guerrillas and Army patrols.[11]

ASSOCIATED OPERATIONS

On 21 March, patrols landed on Guimaras Island, located across Iloilo Strait, and found it clear of the enemy. The following day, another patrol landed on Inampulugan Island in Guimaras Strait, and destroyed an enemy mine control station while eliminating the small garrison.[12]

On 29 March, the 185th Regimental Combat Team of the 40th Division proceeded, by shore-to-shore movements (referred to by the Army as "leap frogging"), from Iloilo to Pulupandan Point on northern Negros Oriental. As no opposition was encountered coming ashore, initial progress inland was rapid. Bacolod town and airstrip were captured on the 30th. The Japanese fought tenaciously at Talisay, but the town and airfield fell to American troops on 2 April.[13]

BATTLE STARS

Consolidation of Southern Philippines: Visayan Island Landings

Ship	Date/Period	Ship	Date/Period
LSM-35	2 Apr 45	LSM-150	2 Apr 45
LSM-50	26 Mar-2 Apr 45	LSM-151	28 Mar 45
LSM-53 (no BS)	18-31 Mar 45	LSM-168	2 Apr 45
LSM-54	18-26 Mar 45	LSM-224 (no BS)	18 Mar 45
LSM-63	18-29 Mar 45	LSM-265	28 Mar 45
LSM-65	18 Mar-1 Apr 45	LSM-267	18 Mar-1 Apr 45
LSM-66 (no BS)	18 Mar-1 Apr 45	LSM-269 (no BS)	18-19 Mar 45
LSM-128 (no BS)	18 Mar-1 Apr 45	LSM-316	29 Mar-2 Apr 45
LSM-131 (no BS)	18 Mar-1 Apr 45	LSM-317	28 Mar-2 Apr 45

Assault Landing on Cebu's Central Eastern Coast

Establish naval facilities and initiate MTB [motor torpedo boat] operations in the CEBU City area, establish facilities for air operations, and destroy enemy forces in the vicinity.

—Purpose of an amphibious assault landing on 28 March 1945, near Cebu City, on the island of Cebu, Philippines.[1]

CEBU City was occupied on the day after the landing, and the docks were found essentially undamaged. Progress from the beaches to CEBU City, and thence inland, was impeded by extensive land mines, booby traps, and demolitions fired by electric contact. LAHUG airstrip was secured on 28 March, but a strong enemy position nearby continued to dominate the field.

—Commander in Chief, U.S. Pacific Fleet and Pacific Ocean Areas, Operations in Pacific Ocean Areas – March 1945, 31 August 1945.

Map 15-1

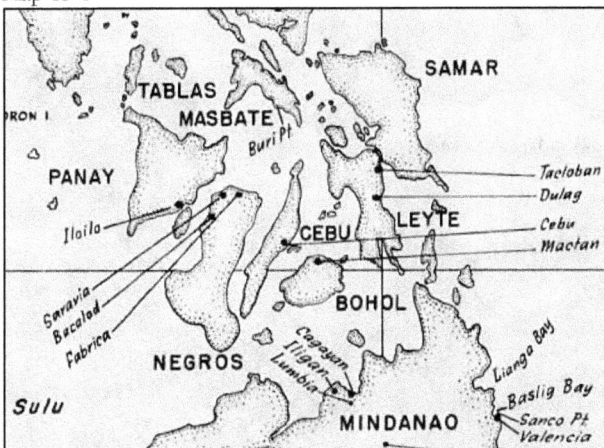

Cebu City, the capital of Cebu Island (located in the center of the Map), is identified by a black dot with a line to "Cebu" annotation

Following the earlier Zamboanga and Iloilo amphibious assaults in March 1945, came one at Cebu City, involving almost the same number of troops as those landings; approximately 14,000 combat and service troops of the Americal Division (reinforced), less one Regimental Combat Team. These troops were staged from Leyte, and landed at Talisay Beach, 4½ miles southwest of Cebu City on 26 March.[1]

AMERICAL INFANTRY DIVISION

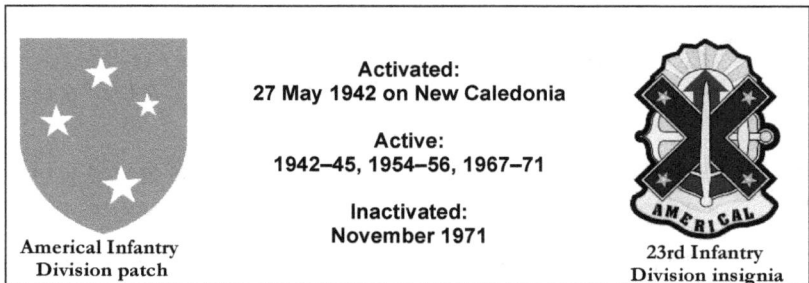

Americal Infantry Division patch	**Activated:** 27 May 1942 on New Caledonia **Active:** 1942–45, 1954–56, 1967–71 **Inactivated:** November 1971	23rd Infantry Division insignia

Photo 15-1

American Division troops on board the tank landing ship USS *LST-1035* eating, while enroute to the Cebu landing, on 25 March 1945.
National Archives photograph #80-G-259229

The Americal Division of the United States Army was activated 27 May 1942 on the island of New Caledonia, the only division formed outside of United States territory during World War II (a distinction it would repeat when reformed during the Vietnam War), and the only one with a name and not a number. In the immediate emergency following Pearl Harbor, the United States had hurriedly sent three orphaned infantry regiments split from National Guard divisions to defend New Caledonia against a feared Japanese attack. These were the 132nd Infantry Regiment from the 33rd Infantry Division of Illinois; the 164th Infantry Regiment from the 34th Infantry Division of North Dakota; and the 182nd Infantry Regiment from the 26th "Yankee" Infantry Division of Massachusetts.[2]

At the suggestion of a subordinate, the division's first commander, Maj. Gen. Alexander Patch, requested that the new unit be known as the Americal Division—the name a contraction of "American, New Caledonian Division." After World War II the Americal Division was officially re-designated as the 23rd Infantry Division.[3]

CEBU ATTACK GROUP (TASK GROUP 78.2)

The Attack Group assembled for the landing at Cebu was commanded by Capt. Albert T. Sprague, USN. Typically, "flag officers" headed these types of operations, not captains, and in fact, Rear Admiral Fechteler was originally named the task commander, but had been unexpectedly detached for duty as Assistant Chief of Naval Personnel in Washington, D.C. Sprague was chosen to lead in his place.[4]

Task Group 78.2, and the Cruiser Covering Group (Task Group 74.3) commanded by Rear Admiral Berkey, consisted of the following numbers and types of ships:

- TG 78.2: 1 AGC, 4 APD, 15 LCI(L), 11 LSM, 17 LST, 5 LCI(R), 4 LCS(L), 2 PC, 8 YMS, 1 LCI(D), and 1 ATA; screened by 5 DD
- TG 74.3: 3 CL and 6 DD[5]

AGC: amphibious force command ship	LCI(R): rocket infantry landing craft
APD: high-speed transport	LCS(L): large support landing craft
ATA: auxiliary fleet tug	LSM: medium landing ship
DD: destroyer	LST: tank landing ship
CL: light cruiser	PC: sub-chaser
LCI(D): demolition infantry landing craft	YMS: yard minesweeper
LCI(L): large infantry landing craft	

LSM UNIT (TASK UNIT 78.2.4)

The LSM component of the Assault Group (Task Unit 78.2.4 under Lt. Comdr. George F. Baker) consisted of LSMs *35*, *50*, *150*, *151*, *168*, *219*, *225*, *237*, *268*, *316*, and *317*. On the evening of 21 March, these ships collectively embarked at Leyte, specialist portions of the Eighth Army's Americal Division scheduled to participate in the invasion of Cebu:

- Company B, 716 Tank Battalion
- Personnel of the 247th Field Artillery Battalion[6]

On the evening of 24 March, the assault group departed Leyte Gulf for Cebu. Three of the eleven LSMs sailing in company had an LCM landing craft in tow astern, in addition to their embarked troops. The passage was without incident, and the group arrived at the objective area at daylight on 26 March. Upon the order "Deploy," Task Unit 78.2.4 proceeded to the transport area off Talisay Beach.[7]

Following pre-landing bombardment by cruisers and destroyers, and minesweeping of nearshore waters with negative results, the LSTs began launching LVTs (amtraks) and LCVPs (Higgins boats). Because LVTs were "amphibious tractors" (although normally called amtraks or alligators), operation orders often titled groups of LSTs carrying them to the objective as "tractor groups."[8]

H-Hour was 0830. The first wave (LVTs) landed at 0828, followed by the second wave (LVTs) at 0831, and third wave (LCVPs) at 0835.[9]

Photo 15-2

Amphibious tractors (LVTs) approaching the beach under the cover of naval bombardment.
National Archives photograph #80-G-259254

Photo 15-3

Landing craft (LCVPs) approach the Cebu invasion beach, 26 March 1945.
National Archives photograph #80-G-259247

At 0837, the commander of the close support unit reported enemy mortar fire on the left flank of the beach. Of equal or greater concern was the discovery by the landing force of the presence of large quantities of land mines on the beach, from the high-water mark to the edge of the coconut grove back of the beach.[10]

Photo 15-4

Scene on the Cebu invasion beach, three hours after the landing, 26 March 1945.
National Archives photograph #80-G-259243

The fourth and fifth waves (LCVPs) landed on schedule, followed by the sixth and seventh waves (LCMs) carrying artillery, which was unloaded without difficulty.[11]

In the absence of enemy troop opposition on the beach, land mine clearance efforts began, and troops worked their way inland. At 0900, the eighth wave (DUKWs) landed on time, as a continuous series of explosions in Cebu City made it apparent that Japanese forces were destroying the city. Sporadic mortar fire landed on the beach, but only in a small section, which was kept clear, and no damage resulted.[12]

At 0917, the air observer reported two enemy planes taking off from Lahug Airstrip. The Combat Air Patrol could not find them; they were not picked up on radar, nor seen again; and it was believed that they flew across the island at low altitude escaping.[13]

LANDING OF LSMs DELAYED

Wave nine, LCI(L)s, was delayed because they could not beach, owing to a submerged log boom obstacle that had not hampered earlier craft with shallower drafts. The large infantry landing craft were unloaded just off the beach into LCVPs, LCMs, and LCTs which carried their troops into the beaches.[14]

LSMs were held up from beaching until UDT (Underwater Demolition Team) personnel could clear the obstacle. Pontoon sections (five 2x18 sections) were launched from LSTs, and towed to a position just off the beach. High priority LSTs were brought in, and ramp-to-ramp unloading into LCTs commenced.[15]

At 1045, the Beachmaster called in the first medium landing ship; *LSM-168* reported unloading without difficulty.[16]

Photo 15-5

A Sherman tank wades ashore from *LSM-168* on 26 March 1945 during the invasion of Cebu Island.
National Archives photograph #80-G-259238

However, conditions were not ideal as commander, Task Force 78.2 detailed in describing the challenges which LSMs/LSTs faced in discharging their embarked personnel, equipment, and supplies:

> It was apparent that the beach gradient would in general prevent the satisfactory beaching of LSMs and LSTs for unloading. Not only was the gradient too low, but a small sand bar off the beach caused both types to ground aft with ramps in varying depths from 5 to 7 feet of water. For a limited width, LSMs could beach fairly well. They beached three at a time and unloaded throughout the day but slowly and with the assistance of bulldozers to haul out drowned vehicles.[17]

SIGHTING OF ENEMY MIDGET SUBMARINE

> *Ten of the new Type C boats were sent to the Philippines on D-type destroyer transports in 1944. Based in the southern Visayas at Davao, Cebu, and Zamboanga, the midgets were commanded by Captain Kaku Harada, one-time skipper of [the light aircraft carrier] Chiyoda and the "father" of the program. Hammered by American attacks, the bases were abandoned in favor of Cebu, where Harada was located at the end of the war at the 33rd Naval Special Base. There the last of the midgets fought to the close of the Philippine campaign from an advance base at Dumaguete at the southern side of Negros Island, where they sortied to ambush US forces coming through Surigao Strait into the Mindanao Sea.*

—Article "Japanese Midget Submarine Operations 1942-45 II."[18]

Photo 15-6

Japanese midget submarine beached in the southwest Pacific.
Naval History and Heritage Command photograph #NH 74772

At 1535, the destroyer *Conyngham* (DD-371) reported sighting a possible periscope in the channel from Cebu Harbor, and the sub-chaser *PC-1133* was dispatched to investigate. The subchaser may, or may not have reported positive results. In any case, a short time later, *Conyngham* and *Flusser* (DD-368) opened fire on an object in the channel, reported to be the conning tower of a small submarine that had broached, apparently from grounding on a sand bar while submerged. Inexplicably, the midget, though straddled with naval gunfire, escaped, evidently having received only slight or no damage.[19]

Hours later at 0035 on 27 March, the high-speed transport *Newman* (APD-59) spotted a midget on the surface some 7 miles south of the previous day's encounter. Approaching the sub, *Newman*'s crew opened fire with automatic weapons at 100 yards, scoring many hits, then she attempted to ram, but the submarine submerged. Two patterns of depth charges were dropped, one with explosives set for shallow detonation, and a second pattern with deep settings destroying the midget submarine.[20]

Then unknown, by February 1945 the midgets at Cebu were the last Japanese submarine forces left in the Philippines. Following the loss on 27 March of the midget fired on and depth charged by the *Newman*, the remaining three subs were scuttled, and supporting base personnel and submarine crews joined land forces defending Cebu.[21]

DEPARTURE OF LSMs
At 1850 on 26 March, the first echelon departing for Leyte, sailed from Cebu. It consisted of the destroyer *Abbot* (DD-629); high-speed transport *Kephart* (APD-61); LSMs *150*, *168*, *219*, *225*, and *316*; and LCI(L)s *965*, *984*, and *980*. *LCI(L)-965* was in tow astern of *LSM-316*.[22]

The following evening, 1900 on 27 March, the remaining medium landing ships—LSMs *35*, *50*, *151*, *237*, *268*, and *317*—left Cebu. They were part of the second echelon returning to Leyte, which also included the high-speed transports *Newman* (APD-59) and *Cofer* (APD-62); subchasers *PC-1133* and *1134*; and three LSTs.[23]

Assault and Occupation of Okinawa

Enemy forces encountered were limited to shore batteries, submarines, planes, baka bombs, mines and suicide boats, rafts and swimmers. Other than the above, the minesweepers had few worries, except for reefs, shortage of fresh water and a deplorable and serious shortage of diesel spares, which was more often than not a lack rather than a shortage.

—Rear Adm. Alexander Sharp Jr., commander, Minecraft, U.S. Pacific Fleet and commander, Mine Flotilla, remarking on the duties of his forces and conditions experienced during the capture of Okinawa. These same threats and challenges were posed to other ships.[1]

Map 16-1

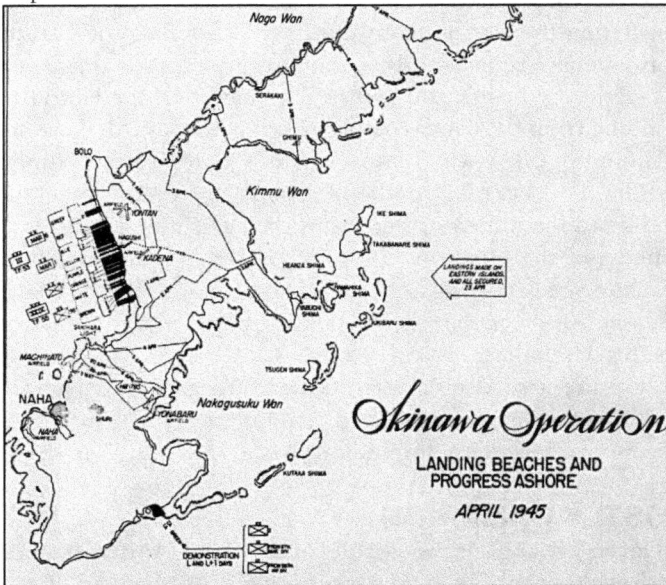

Southern area of Okinawa Island, including the landing beaches on the southwest side Commander in Chief, U.S. Pacific Fleet and Pacific Ocean Areas, Operations in Pacific Ocean Areas – April 1945, 16 October 1945

On the morning of 1 April 1945 (L-Day), U.S. Army and Marine Corps troops landed over the Hagushi beaches on Okinawa in two corps abreast: the XXIV Army Corps on the southern flank, and the III Amphibious (Marine) Corps on the northern one. The Northern Attack Force (TF 53) with the 1st and 6th Marine Divisions and the Southern Attack Force (TF 55) with the US Army 7th and 96th Infantry Divisions, landed the assault waves simultaneously, on schedule.

Northern Attack Force (Task Force 53):
Rear Adm. Lawrence F. Reifsnider, USN
III Amphibious Corps (Reinforced): Maj. Gen. Roy S. Geiger, USMC
1st Marine Division, 6th Marine Division (III Amphibious Corps)

Southern Attack Force (Task Force 55):
Rear Adm. John L. Hall Jr., USN
XXIV Army Corps: Maj. Gen. John R. Hodge, USA
7th Infantry Division, 96th Infantry Division (XXIV Army Corps)[2]

Okinawa is the largest island of the Okinawa Gunto ("Gunto" means islands), which is part of the Ryukyu Islands. The Ryukyus are a component of the even larger, arc-shaped Nansei Shoto island group which stretches 790 miles between Kyushu, Japan, and Formosa (today Taiwan). Separating the Pacific from the East China Sea, the Nansei Shoto comprises eight large islands, about twenty smaller ones, and numerous islets, exposed reefs, and rocks. The chain is divided into five groups. Beginning from the south and progressing northward, these are the Sakishima Gunto, Okinawa Gunto, Amami Gunto, Takara Gunto, and Osumu Gunto. The two southern groups are collectively, the Ryukyu Islands, and the three northern ones the Sakishima Islands.[2]

The members of the Okinawa Gunto incorporate Okinawa Shima (island) and many smaller islands, including the Kerama Retto (island group). The assault and occupation of Okinawa began in this cluster of small islands fifteen miles west of Okinawa. There, a preliminary operation to capture a roadstead was necessary to gain an advanced naval base for refueling, repairs, and ammunition replenishment necessary to support the largest amphibious force of World War II.

LONG, COSTLY CAMPAIGN
On 21 June, eleven weeks after the assault landings on 1 April, when the Tenth Army drove through the southernmost point of Okinawa, it was announced that organized resistance had ceased. Gen. Mitsuru Ushijima, commanding the 32nd Army, which fought in the Battle of

Okinawa, committed suicide the following day. An overall account of the grim details leading to this end is beyond the scope of this book.[3]

However, the capture of Okinawa, which helped to bring the war to a close, cost the U.S. Navy 34 naval vessels and craft sunk, 368 damaged, and 4,900 sailors killed or missing in action, and over 4,800 wounded. Most of these losses resulted from Kamikaze plane attacks. Tenth Army casualties were 4,412 soldiers killed in action and 17,689 wounded; the Marines suffered 2,779 killed and 13,609 wounded.[4]

This chapter is devoted primarily to the losses of six U.S. Navy LSMs/LSM(R)s at Okinawa. As recounted in Chapter 1, USS *LSM(R)-193* emerged unscathed from waves of Kamikaze attacks, a uniquely rare occurrence, considering her heroic actions that earned her a Presidential Unit Citation. However as shown in the following table, several LSMs/LSM(R)s were lost, suffered damage and/or personnel casualties at Okinawa; those highlighted by shading in the table were lost. *LSM-12* foundered after being damaged by a Japanese suicide boat off Okinawa and was determined to be a total loss. The other five ships were sunk by suicide aircraft attacks.

U.S. Navy LSMs/LSM(R)s Lost in World War II

Date	Ship	Cause of Loss
5 Dec 44	USS *LSM-20*	Kamikaze attack off Ormoc, Leyte
7 Dec 44	USS *LSM-318*	Kamikaze attack off Ormoc, Leyte
4 Apr 45	USS *LSM-12*	Operational - broached at Okinawa
3 May 45	USS *LSM(R)-195*	Kamikaze attack off Okinawa
4 May 45	USS *LSM(R)-190*	Kamikaze attack off Okinawa
4 May 45	USS *LSM(R)-194*	Kamikaze attack off Okinawa
25 May 45	USS *LSM-135*	Kamikaze attack off Okinawa
21 Jun 45	USS *LSM-59*	Kamikaze attack off Okinawa[5]

ROCKET SHIPS LSM(R)s AT OKINAWA

LSM(R)s of the Command have been assigned to act as radar picket fire support ships… It is believed that these ships are not particularly suited for this duty. Since their primary function is to deliver rockets during invasion operations, it seems feasible that subjecting them to continual enemy air attack will allow a secondary duty to seriously affect their ability to perform their primary function due to mechanical damage. They have no great value in combating enemy aircraft due to the absence of air search radar, adequate director control for the 5"/38 main battery, and director control for the 40 MM single guns. The fact that they carry a considerable quantity of high explosive rockets in their magazines presents another hazard. In general, it is believed that assigning them to this duty should be avoided since it means risking the operation of a limited number of specialized ships for duty which could be performed by any number of other landing craft whose primary function is more closely coincident with screening operations.

—Comdr. Dennis L. Francis, USN, commander, LSM Flotilla Nine.[6]

LSM(R) GROUP 27 OF LSM FLOTILLA NINE

Present at Okinawa were twelve LSM(R)s—consecutively numbered from *188* to *199*—comprising a new class of rocket ships. The former LSMs had been converted for their new role by covering the well deck, sealing the bow doors, increasing the number of guns and adding rocket launchers. With their greatly increased weaponry came a new mission, providing supporting fire to amphibious landing operations, superseding the role of landing troops, equipment, and supplies ashore.[7]

At noon on 19 March 1945, the LSM(R) Unit—twelve ships of LSM(R) Group Twenty-Seven of LSM Flotilla Nine, designated Task Group 52.21)—left Leyte as part of a convoy termed the Western Islands Tractor Flotilla. The mission of the LSM(R)s was to carry out rocket firing assignments in the Kerama Retto (island group) west of Okinawa, and then at Okinawa on Assault Day. They were to fire rockets on Aka Shima and Zamami Shima on 26 March; Aware Town on Tokashiki Shimaon on 27 March; then on 1 April, hit Guzukuma and Takushippo on Okinawa. In addition, the ships were to carry out patrols and special assignments.[8]

On 25 March, the convoy arrived in the Kerama Retto Area. For the forthcoming operations, the LSM(R)s were organized into two units, under the overall command of Comdr. Dennis L. Francis, USN, commander, LSM Flotilla Nine:

Unit One: Lt. Comdr. John H. Fulweiller, USNR
LSM(R)s *188, 189, 190, 191, 192, 193*

Unit Two: Comdr. Dennis L. Francis, USN
LSM(R)s *194, 195, 196, 197, 198, 199*[9]

LSM(R)-194 RESCUES DESTROYER CREWMEN

On the morning of 26 March, following a rocket firing mission against Zamami Shima, LSM(R)s *193, 194,* and *195* were assigned to patrol off the east and west coasts of the southern half of Tokashiki Shima. LSM(R)s *188, 189,* and *192* patrolled the east and west coasts of the northern half of the same island. That evening, *LSM(R)-194* went to the aid of the destroyer *Halligan* (DD-584) which, while supporting minesweeping operations, struck a mine. The detonation exploded the forward magazines and blew off a forward part of the ship including the bridge, back to the forward stack. The sub-chaser *PC-1128* and *LSM(R)-194* arrived soon after the explosion to aid survivors.[10]

By rapid actions, *LSM(R)-194* rescued 72 crewmembers before the destroyer sank. Commander Francis described the incident in a report, and recommended that her crew receive special recognition:

> The Commanding Officer and entire ship's company of the U.S.S. *LSM(R) 194* are deserving of Unit Citation for their joint act of heroism in connection with rescue work on the U.S.S. *HALLIGAN* (DD 584) on 26 March 1945. Noting the latter to be in distress with flames covering her deck, the *LSM(R) 194* despite the fact that her rocket racks were loaded, proceeded alongside the *HALLIGAN*. Turning her hoses on the flames she extinguished them and at the same time took aboard 72 survivors, caring for some until they were delivered aboard the [amphibious force flagship] U.S.S. *BISCAYNE* [AGC-18] some hours later. For this action which was over and above the call of duty, this command feels the ship's company of the *LSM(R) 194* to be worthy of special commendation.[11]

Commander Francis' recommendation was successful; USS *LSM(R)-194* was awarded the Navy Unit Commendation.

LSM(R)-189 ATTACKED BY SMALL BOATS AND SUICIDE AIRCRAFT

> *The boats attacking us were contacted by radar at 1200 to 1500 yards and sighted at 500 to 600 yards. They did not appear to be suicide boats as they returned to attack their objective. The boats were relatively high-powered for they made over 15 knots and appeared to be twenty-five to thirty-five feet long, looking much like our Higgins Boats in type. The personnel manning them seemed to vary. One boat reported by our look-outs had a crew of four, and as the others, no estimate can be made. It was very dark and there were so many explosions, covering this ship with water, that it was difficult to get a detailed description.*

> *There is a possibility of another boat being destroyed accordingly to our gunnery officer's report, however, this reporting officer did not see it, nor did the quartermaster and we can only definitely report three (3) boats destroyed.*

—Lt. James M. Stewart, USNR, commanding officer, USS *LSM(R)-189*.[12]

In early morning on 29 March, *LSM(R)-189*, under the command of Lt. James M. Stewart, was attacked by Japanese small boats which she destroyed. She was sharing a patrol with *LSM(R)-188*, which had the northern half of their sector, and like her sister ship was charged with aggressive harassment (taking under fire targets of opportunity ashore) in addition to her defensive mission.[13]

Details of the action follow: At 0300 that morning, Stewart called his crew to General Quarters, after receiving a report of a small boat dropping depth charges near the gunboat *LCI(G)-589*. While proceeding to the gunboat's assistance, *LSM(R)-189* picked up on radar a contact believed to be the boat in question. At 0308, she opened fire on a small boat dead ahead with her 40mm guns. The boat, apparently unhit and undeterred, turned and sped directly toward the rocket ship, dropped a depth charge in front of her bow, which exploded, and then passed down her starboard side. At 0316, *LSM(R)-189*'s guns opened on a boat sighted astern (presumably the same one), and blew it up with a direct hit from a 5-inch round.[14]

Between 0318 and 0440, *LSM(R)-189* sank at least two more enemy boats, and also took under fire and scored hits on an attacking aircraft:

0318: [Detected] Second target by radar

0319: Circling area containing target

0320: Sighted boat and opened fire

0325: [Detected] Third target by radar

0330: Sighted boat off port quarter – opened fire with guns #22 and 41

0331: Boat exploded depth charges and began speeding toward beach

0335: Have boat trapped – guns opened fire

0348: Guns #22 and 24 scored hits when a shot from gun #41 demolished it

0400: Target by radar – anti-aircraft fire dead ahead

0401: Opened fire on enemy plane – plane downed by fire from ships ahead – we did get hits from 20MM guns – plane identified as RUFE [Nakajima A6M2-N Navy Type 2 interceptor/fighter-bomber]

0428: Target [detected] off starboard quarter by radar

0432: Boat sighted – opened fire

0438: Boat coming up fast on our stern ready to let go depth charge under our stern

0440: 5" gun made direct hit on craft astern, 75 feet away, demolishing it completely[15]

At 0500, Lieutenant Stewart gave the order for his crew to "stand easy" (meaning relax, but don't go anywhere) at their General Quarters stations. After nearly an hour of respite, there came at 0555, the sound of anti-aircraft fire ahead, followed by the sighting of an enemy plane. A crossfire of AA fire from *LSM(R)-188* and other ships in the area sent it (lead aircraft of two or three other places of the same attack group) down in flames.[16]

At 0600, a burning plane crash dived into *LSM(R)-188*, tearing off her 5-inch gun director and causing other damage unidentifiable from *LSM(R)-189*'s bridge, which started fires on her decks. *LSM(R)-189* immediately altered course and at full speed went to *LSM(R)-188*'s assistance. Arriving on scene only minutes later at 0607, she found that the *188*'s crew had put out the fire, and the ship was proceeding at full speed, bound for the Kerama Retto anchorage.[17]

LSM(R)-188 SUFFERS DAMAGE AND CASUALTIES

Steaming at patrol speed (one-third on one engine) on an easterly course. Enemy aircraft were sighted to starboard and the AA battery opened fire with the ships in company. Speed increased to flank. Target possibly hit. A second plane sighted and taken under fire and probably hit. This plane circled ahead from starboard to port and was again taken under fire on our port beam. All guns were hitting and he was badly afire at one hundred fifty (150) to two hundred (200) yards. As he passed our director, part of his plane was knocked off which caused an explosion on deck. The plane crashed about seventy-five (75) yards to starboard and burned a few minutes before sinking.

—Lt. Horace A. Bowman, commanding officer, USS *LSM(R)-188*.[18]

Throughout the night of 28-29 March, *LSM(R)-188* carried out an "aggressive harassment patrol" going to General Quarters as necessary to fire on one target or another, then shifting back to a lower state of readiness to allow crewmembers not on watch some rest. (Rocket ships on night patrol were using only one-third speed and a single engine, 350 turns. Moving slowly, they did not give much of a silhouette, and it was hard for the enemy to spot them when there was no screw wash to create a ship's wake.) Her crew, as a matter of routine, was alerted prior to sunrise on the 29th, because enemy aircraft attacks were common at this time as morning twilight revealed to attacking pilots, ships on the horizon, while aircraft higher in the sky were still shielded to defending gunners by rapidly disappearing darkness.[19]

Dawn on this morning brought an attack by three and possibly four planes as observed by Lt.(jg) W. H. Turner, USNR, the executive officer, at his watch station, battery officer for the 5"/38 gun mount. The first plane was fired on by other ships operating in the vicinity. The second plane attacked *LSM(R)-188* from her starboard side. The ship's two 40mm guns took the aircraft under fire, scored hits, and it turned away burning. It was then lost from sight until seen dead ahead, and both 40mm guns and the port 20mm gun opened fire. The plane was hit and burning, but continued straight toward the ship, and struck the director tub holding the director for the 5-inch gun.[20]

The rocket ship suffered extensive topside damage, including a hole, approximately 14 feet by 9 feet, blasted in the main deck over the after magazine, apparently caused by the explosion of an aircraft bomb somewhere above the deck. Resultant fires were extinguished by magazine sprinklers, and the use of fire hoses in other areas above and below deck. Despite burns on both hands and face, Gunner's Mate Second Class Walter R. Venters had the presence of mind to turn on the sprinkler system in the Rocket Assembly Room. This act on his own initiative was instrumental in controlling the spread of fire.[21]

Personnel casualties were high because some 5-inch rocket bodies exploded, covering topside areas with high velocity metal shards. Of the ship's complement of six officers and seventy-seven enlisted men, 57 percent were casualties as follows:

- Killed in Action – 8
- Missing in Action – 6
- Died of Wounds received in action – 1
- Wounded in Action – 32[22]

The identities of these individuals may be found in Appendix A.

Photo 16-1

USS *LSM(R)-188* alongside the landing craft repair ship USS *Egeria* (ARL-8) on 29 March 1945, after being damaged during a Japanese aircraft attack. National Archives photograph #80-G-342587

BOATS AND CAVES HOUSING THEM DESTROYED

At 1730 on 31 March, LSM(R)s *189*, *190*, *191*, *192*, and *193* were dispatched to the eastern coast of Mae Shima. Their mission was to destroy suicide boats suspected to be hidden in caves, and to neutralize these caves for future use. Three suicide boats were destroyed and numerous caves offering potential cover closed by "cave ins" caused by weapons fire.[23]

ASSAULT DAY AT OKINAWA

At 0806 on 1 April, the landing craft flotilla flagship *LC(FF)-535* led LSM(R)s *194*, *195*, *196*, *197*, *198*, and *199* in a rocket attack on the town of Takushippo. Their mission was to disrupt nearby transportation facilities. The expenditure of approximately 900 fin-stabilized rockets and 2,100 spin-stabilized rockets resulted in the destruction of the town as well as neutralization of local defenses and transportation facilities. There was also collateral damage to the town of Hanza caused by rockets landing south and southeast of the target area.[24]

Minutes later at 0820, *LSM(R)-193* in company with LSM(R)s *189*, *190*, *191*, and *192* carried out a rocket attack on the town of Guzukumu. Their mission was to destroy railroad and highway infrastructure to disrupt troop movements. The result was the destruction of about 200 yards of railroad and primary highway, and almost complete obliteration of the town proper. There was also some possible destruction of local defenses and troop concentrations by rockets landing outside the target area on either side of the town.[25]

REORGANIZATON OF LSM(R)s

On 2 April as ordered, LSM(R) Group Twenty-Seven under Comdr. Dennis L. Francis, USN, less *LSM(R)-188*, reported to commander Task Group 51.5 (Transport Group) for duty. Its ships received orders to patrol stations in the inner screen around the transport area, or to serve as close support ships to destroyers on radar picket stations. As before, the rocket ships were split into two task units under the overall command of Francis.

Task Unit 52.21.1: Lt. Comdr. John H. Fulweiler, USNR
LSM(R)s *188, 189, 190, 191, 192, 193* (flagship)

Task Unit 52.21.2: Comdr. Dennis L. Francis, USN
LSM(R)s *194, 195, 196, 197, 198, 199*[26]

THREE LSM(R)s SUNK IN TWO DAYS

As the eighty-two-day-long Battle of Okinawa continued to be fought ashore, at sea, and in the skies overhead, rocket ships were assigned to picket stations off the island. Some Japanese accounts of the battle refer to it as *tetsu no ame* or *kou no kaze*, "iron rain" or "steel rain," respectively, owing to the intensity of Kamikaze attacks.

In an effort to achieve early detection and engagement of inbound waves of suicide aircraft from outside the area, a ring of radar picket stations was established around Okinawa to cover all possible approaches to the island. Initially a typical picket station had one or two destroyer types supported by two or more landing ships or landing craft—large support landing craft LCS(L) or rocket ships LSM(R)—for additional AA firepower.

USS *LSM(R)-195*

On 3 May, *LSM(R)-195* was patrolling on Radar Picket Station 10, seventy-three miles west of Okinawa. The destroyer minelayer *Aaron Ward* (DM-34) working with the high-speed transport *Little* (APD-4) were the principal ships of the station. For support in company with *LSM(R)-195* were the LCS(L)s *14, 25*, and *83*. At about 1815, the rocket ship received a "Flash Red Control Green, enemy planes approaching from the West" warning from *Arron Ward* over the Fleet Common radio circuit. The term "Control Green" denoted that a friendly plane was also in the area.[27]

Aboard *LSM(R)-195*, General Quarters was sounded and battle stations manned. *Aaron Ward* and *Little*, about 7 to 9 miles away, then opened fire. Shortly after, as was seen from the rocket ship, the *Aaron*

Ward was crashed by a plane and the *Little* was hit by a plane or bomb. As *LSM(R)-195* and the three LCS(L)s proceeded toward them at flank speed to render aid, the starboard engine of the rocket ship broke down and had to be secured, causing her to fall behind the LCS(L)s by 500 to 1,000 yards.[28]

Two planes approached *LSM(R)-195* from astern and off her port quarter. One was a "Nick" (Kawasaki Ki-45 Toryu Army type 2 fighter), and the other a probable Nick or "Dinah" (Mitsubishi Ki-46-III-Kai Army type 100 air defense fighter). As the planes closed in, the aircraft separated in preparation for carrying out a coordinated attack; one circled off the rocket ship's starboard beam at 500 feet elevation, the other came in very low, from abaft her port beam, using fast, evasive tactics. *LSM(R)-195* opened fire on the plane to starboard with 5"/38 and 40mm guns, as it appeared to be closer.[29]

Simultaneously, the plane on the port side began to close, and was taken under fire by the two shorter range 20mm guns. It dove into the port side of *LSM(R)-195* at Frame 17. The impact ripped rocket launchers from the deck, while plane wreckage landed in the midship and forward rocket magazines and forward crew's quarters. Lt.(jg) William E. Woodson USNR, the ship's commanding officer, described in his action report, the resultant ignition of numerous rockets causing associated damage, and the inability to combat fires because fire main water was unavailable:

> An unusual amount of shrapnel resulted from burning rockets which were loaded topside. These burning rockets were propelled only short distances from the ship with numerous hits about the deck lighting small fires and causing the additional amount of shrapnel. Order was given to fight the fire and turn on sprinkler system and it was discovered that both the fire main and auxiliary pumps were broken and inoperative. When it seemed that nothing could be done with the fire and loaded and ready service rockets were hitting all parts of the ship, the order was given (at approx. 1920) to abandon ship. Ten to 15 minutes later, the ship after numerous explosions went down bow first.[30]

After two life rafts had been put over the side with almost 20 men in each and the commanding officer was in the water, tremendous explosions from the 5-inch gun powder magazine blasted underwater. At about 2145, a ship was sighted and the survivors' quartermaster signaled for help by use of a flashlight. The ship was the destroyer *Bache* (DD-470) which directed its whaleboat to the lifeboats.[31]

A list of *LSM(R)-195* crewmembers killed or wounded, and other survivors may be found in Appendix B.

The following day brought the losses of LSM(R)s *190* and *194*.

USS *LSM(R)-190*

On 4 May, *LSM(R)-190*, under the command of Lt. Richard H. Saunders, USNR, was patrolling on Radar Picket Station 12, at which the destroyer *Luce* (DD-522) was in charge. Other ships in company on the station were the LCS(L)s *81*, *84*, and *118*. The patrol disposition was a box formation with the destroyer in the center, and the other four ships positioned around her.[32]

At 0800, the *Luce* detected and reported enemy planes approaching from the north, distance twenty miles. Ens. Lyle S. Tennis, USNR, communications officer in the Conn, reported the finding to the commanding officer. The next report from the *Luce* indicated that the planes were fifteen miles away and closing. With the commanding officer and gunnery officer in the Conn, General Quarters was ordered. Shortly afterwards, two Kamikaze planes attacked the *Luce*; the first coming from high out of the clouds, the other flying low over the water. The latter crashed the destroyer amidships leaving her severely damaged in a sinking condition.[33]

Meanwhile, a Dinah flew in over the stern of *LSM(R)-190* and dropped a bomb, which missed. Hit by gunfire, the plane initially turned away, but then returned and dove into the 5"/38 mount, setting it on fire. Shrapnel from the plane crash severely injured the commanding officer, leaving him in a prone position, and also killed the gunnery officer. Ship control was assumed by Radioman Third Class William J. Nuber (the telephone talker on watch) for the next four or five minutes until Ensign Tennis was able to take over the Conn. (Having "the conn" is the status of being in control of a ship's movements while at sea. It is also a verb describing the act of controlling a ship. For LSMs/LSM(R)s, this term was also used as a general reference to the bridge or pilot house.)[34]

LSM(R)-190's Executive Officer, Lt.(jg) George T. Harmon, USNR, described in an Action Report initial damage suffered by the rocket ship and ensuing injury from additional aircraft attacks, which collectively resulted in her loss.

> The sprinkler system to the 5/38 magazines and the after rocket assembly room were ordered turned on and fire hoses broken out from amidships and played [water sprayed] on the 5/38 mount. However, as fire mains [piping] had been ruptured pressure was

negligible, and the Damage Control Parties commenced breaking out lines from the auxiliary fire pump. The fire meanwhile spread to the powder and handling rooms.

A second plane (VAL) [Aichi D3A Navy type 99 carrier bomber] came in on the port beam very low and crashed into the upper level of the engine room. Wreckage of this plane remained stuck in the side of the ship. Fires immediately broke out in the engine room and shortly smoke was so thick that it was impossible to see the controls. This second attack disabled the auxiliary fire pump.

The ship continued at flank speed, zigzagging, while a third plane (DINAH), crossing from port to starboard at masthead height, dropped a bomb which missed by 700 yards. By this time all guns except the starboard 20mm were inoperative as a result of material and personnel casualties.

A fourth plane attacked in "sneak" fashion releasing a bomb which hit in the area of the Mk. 51 Director tub.

A fifth plane, a VAL, dove from considerable height pursued by [U.S. Navy F4U] CORSAIRS of the CAP [Combat Air Patrol] which had arrived on the scene at 0815. This plane crossed from port aft of the Starboard 20mm causing no damage.[35]

The destroyer *Luce* sank at this time. On board *LSM(R)-190*, fire was spreading through the entire engine room, and it had to be vacated. Because fires were now beyond control and the *190* had a decided port list, it was decided to abandon ship.[36]

Ensigns G. E. Etter and J. R. Benner directed a working party dropping cargo nets over the side. The body of Ens. S. C. Bjorklund and the wounded commanding officer were brought down from the Conn by Ensigns Tennis and Etter. The executive officer, Lt.(jg) Harmon, reported to the captain that fire had spread throughout the 5-inch gun magazine, aft stowage space, and the engine room; that all power was off; and the auxiliary fire pump inoperative, and advised that the order be given to abandon ship. The captain although seriously wounded gave the order, which was carried out at about 0830.[37]

All hands abandoned ship except Ensign Tennis and two crewmen, both of whom were wounded. They remained behind to cut free the last life raft before going over the side. Once launched, two life rafts were lashed together and the commanding officer and other wounded were put aboard them. At approximately 0850, the rocket ship sank;

forty minutes later the *LCS(L)-84* started to pick up survivors who were subsequently transferred to the rescue escort patrol craft *PCE(R)-852*.[38]

A list of *LSM(R)-190* KIA, WIA and other survivors may be found in Appendix C.

PERSONAL AND UNIT AWARDS FOR VALOR

Navy Cross Medal	Navy Unit Commendation
Ensign Lyle S. Tennis, United States Naval Reserve, for extraordinary heroism and distinguished service in the line of his profession while serving as Communications Officer on board the USS *LSM(R)-190*	USS *LSM(R)-188* USS *LSM(R)-189* USS *LSM(R)-190* USS *LSM(R)-194*

Ens. Lyle S. Tennis, USNR, was awarded the Navy Cross, which is second only to the Congressional Medal of Honor in precedence among American military decorations, for his actions aboard USS *LSM(R)-190*, His medal citation follows:

> The President of the United States of America takes pleasure in presenting the Navy Cross to Ensign Lyle S. Tennis, United States Naval Reserve, for extraordinary heroism and distinguished service in the line of his profession while serving as Communications Officer on board the U.S.S. *LSM(R)-190*, a close-in fire support ship, in action against the enemy on 4 May 1945, off Okinawa in the Ryukyu Islands. After three enemy suicide planes crashed into the ship, wounding the Commanding Officer, he, although suffering from shrapnel wounds himself, assumed direction of the ship and calmly and efficiently maneuvered the ship and directed the firing of the anti-aircraft batteries. When it became necessary to abandon ship, he aided in evacuating his wounded Commanding Officer and was the last to leave the sinking vessel. By his outstanding initiative and inspiring leadership, he contributed materially to minimizing the number of casualties. His conduct throughout was in keeping with the highest traditions of the United States Naval Service.

USS *LSM(R)-190* was awarded the Navy Unit Commendation (NUC) and, although she sadly lay on the seafloor off Okinawa, her port and starboard side ribbons boards unadorned by the NUC, her crew were able to proudly sport their ribbons on uniform blouses.

Five LSM(R) rocket ships earned unit commendations in World War II. These were USS *LSM(R)-193*, highlighted in Chapter 1 for her receipt of the highest award, the Presidential Unit Citation (PUC), and four LSM(R) recipients of the Navy Unit Commendations. All of these awards were earned at Okinawa during the Allied costly, ultimately victorious, assault and occupation of that island.

World War II LSM(R) PUC and NUC Recipients

Ship	Award	Date/Period
USS *LSM(R)-193*	PUC	11 May 1945
USS *LSM(R)-188*	NUC	29 March 1945
USS *LSM(R)-189*	NUC	29 March - 12 April 1945
USS *LSM(R)-190* (sunk 4 May 1945)	NUC	7 April - 1 May 1945
USS *LSM(R)-194* (sunk 4 May 1945)	NUC	26 March - 4 May 1945[39]

The preceding pages cover the heroic actions of LSM(R)s *188, 189, 190,* and *194* that singularly warranted or contributed to their eventual receipt of Navy Unit Commendations. Sadly, additional material is devoted to *LSM(R)-194* because, she like *LSM(R)-190*, was sunk on 4 May 1945 by suicide aircraft. After the next section describing her loss, there follows accounts of the losses of the medium landing ships *LSM-135* and *LSM-59*, also sunk at Okinawa by Kamikaze aircraft attacks.

USS *LSM(R)-194*

USS LSM(R) 194 *was patrolling on radar picket station 1…in company were the USS* MORRISON *(DD 560), the USS* INGRAHAM *(DD 694), and the LCS 21, 31 & 23. The* MORRISON *was acting OTC [Officer in Tactical Command] for the entire company and the LCS 31 was OTC for the small craft. The ships were maneuvering in accordance with flaghoist received from DD 560. The four gunboats were in column formation with a destroyer on each beam of the formation.*

—Commanding Officer, USS *LSM(R) 194*, Action Report –
Battle of Okinawa – 4 May 1945, 6 May 1945.

On the morning of 4 May 1945, *LSM(R) 194*, along with two destroyers and three large support landing craft LCS(L)s were on Radar Picket Station 1. At 0758, General Quarters was ordered on board the rocket ship after "Flash Red Control Green, enemy planes approaching from the north" was reported by the OTC, commanding officer of the destroyer *Morrison*. At that time, there were twelve Combat Air Patrol aircraft above, and OTC called commander, Task Force 51 requesting additional planes. Subsequently, twenty-four more arrived.[40]

At 0814, the destroyers were hit by suicide planes, with the *Morrison* taking three planes. She immediately listed, was abandoned, and sank at 0837. At Okinawa, given the opportunity as might be expected, the pilots of suicide aircraft chose "high value" units to crash. On picket stations, these were the radar-equipped destroyers able to detect and report to the task force, the approach of waves of enemy aircraft. Their next priority, given the choice to attack other type ships on station were the 203-foot LSM(R)s bristling with high-explosive rockets, whose detonation would likely hasten their demise. The smaller, less valuable LCS(L)s were the least valuable targets for Kamikaze planes.[41]

A Tony (Kawasaki Ki-61 Hien Army type 3 fighter) crossed over *LCS(L)-21* and came in on the starboard beam of *LSM(R)-194*. The ship's 40mm and 5"/38 guns opened fire—with the latter gun "checking fire" to avoid hitting the LCS(L). (Check Fire means to stop firing, but continue tracking targets, and be ready to recommence firing.) As the plane came closer, *LSM(R)-194*'s 20mm and .50-caliber machine guns also opened fire, and scored hits. The aircraft, carrying a bomb, swerved, then crash dived into the rocket ship at frame 27 inflicting mortal damage to the ship. Relatively little time passed between the plane strike at 0838, and when *LSM(R)-194* sank as a result of initial damage, and that suffered from fires and explosion of the boiler. The ship's commanding officer, Lt. Allan M. Hirshberg, USNR, described this in his Action Report:

> Fires were started in aft steering and engine room. The boiler blew up. The handling room was in flames. Fire and flushing system was ruptured. Sprinkler systems all turned on but it is questionable that much water was forthcoming. The after damage control party [personnel] were all badly burned and Commanding Officer called forward damage control to proceed aft and take over. The ship immediately started to settle by the stern with a list to starboard. Before the hose could be rigged to pump out, the ship had settled too far to save, with water washing up on main deck aft. The order was given to abandon ship for all hands except 40 mm gun crews. Then ordered 40 mm gun crews to abandon ship, following which the commanding officer abandoned ship.[42]

LSM(R)-194 sank stern first and, about five minutes after she went down, a terrific under water explosion occurred. Three life rafts had been launched, the others being unavailable because of damage and fire in the after portion of the ship. At 0935, *LCS(L)-21* recovered the commanding officer and forty-eight crewmembers; the remaining crew were picked up by *LCS(L)-23*.[43]

The names of *LSM(R)-194* KIA, WIA and other survivors, and three LSM(R) Group 27 Staff members aboard WIA, may be found in Appendix D.

LOSS OF *LSM-135* AT IE SHIMA

At 0835 on 25 May, General Quarters was sounded [in the Ie Shima anchorage area]. One suicide plane dived on a Dutch merchantman, KODA ENTEN, and missed. Shortly afterwards, a suicide plane hit [the minesweeper] AM 305 (SPECTACLE) while she was patrolling an inshore screening position off MOTOBU Peninsula. The LSM 135 was dispatched to her assistance. About 15 minutes after arriving at the AM 305, the LSM 135 was hit by a third suicide plane. The ship burst into flame, was beached, abandoned, and eventually declared a total loss. By this time (0930) five ships were in the area of the AM 305 and a fourth plane dived, leveled out, strafed the ships, and then continued at maximum speed out of the area. The Captain and eleven men on the LSM 135 were either killed or missing in action. In addition, fifteen men from the AM 305 who had been rescued from the water were also killed or missing in action.

—Commander LSM Flotilla Eight, Action Report, Ryukus,
24 March – 1 June 1945, 3 June 1945.

On the morning of 25 May, USS *LSM-135* was laying alongside the Dutch merchant vessel *Koda Enten* off Ie Shima, a tiny island west of Okinawa. The medium landing ship was there doing lighterage work under LSM Flotilla Eight (Task Unit 31.1.14).[44]

The weather was misty with low hanging clouds, visibility about three miles, when without warning a Kamikaze dove from the overcast, apparently aiming for the cargo ship. The pilot missed crashing into the ship directly, but shot across her deck, narrowly missed the LSM and crashed 30 feet off her beam and exploded. Fortunately, the two ships were unharmed, and there were no personnel casualties.[45]

LSM-135 then got under way to allow both ships a clear field of fire against further attack. The medium landing ship had six 20mm anti-aircraft guns, but neither 40mm nor .50-caliber machine guns. At this time, a suicide plane crashed the minesweeper USS *Spectacle* (AM-305) about three miles distant from the LSM. *LSM-135* was ordered to proceed to her assistance. Approaching the "sweeper," it was seen that *Spectacle* was burning, and there were many men in the water.[46]

Photo 16-2

Painting by Richard DeRosset of USS *YMS-311* shooting down four attacking Japanese Navy bombers on 6 April 1945 while engaged in minesweeping off Okinawa.

The commanding officer of *LSM-135*, Lt. Harry L. Derby Jr., USNR, ordered the vessel's ramp lowered, and crewmen began retrieving survivors from the water. As some were hurt, Boatswain's Mate First Class Robert J. Lee, USNR, Coxswain Ralph W. Lawhead, USNR, and Storekeeper First Class S. J. Gorchov, USNR, swam out and assisted them on board. Two seriously injured men were placed on stretchers in the tank deck awaiting medical care. The other 12 to 15 survivors went below to the forward crew's compartment under the tank deck. There, crewmen gave them coffee and wrapped them in blankets.[47]

This operation complete, *LSM-135* got under way to search for other survivors in the water. Unfortunately, after an order was passed to raise the ramp, it jammed. Attempting to free it, the engineering officer, Lt.(jg) B. N. Jenkins Jr., USNR, went below to the control room forward—an action which he credited for saving his life. He had scarcely reached the control room when a suicide plane struck topside.[48]

Its left wing crashed into the conn—the tower-like structure on the starboard side from which the ship was controlled—and the aircraft plunged into the tank deck forward. The impact propelled the engine and bomb through the deck into the living compartment where Lee, Lawhead and the survivors had taken refuge, and exploded. The conning tower, deluged with burning gasoline, flared up like a giant torch.[49]

Jenkins was hurled against the control room bulkhead by the bomb explosion. Dazed and choking in the then smoke-filled compartment, he found the passage normally used for egress blocked with debris.

However, he was able to squeeze his way through and make his way aft through connecting compartments, then went topside where he found an unabated raging inferno:

> When I reached deck amidships, I found the entire forward half of the ship in flames. The conning tower was a furnace. There was no water pressure because of broken fire mains. Extinguishers were played on the flames but had no appreciable effect. Driven by the heat, the surviving men had already begun to abandon ship, dropping overboard far aft to escape the oil burning on the water up forward.[50]

The crews of the after 20mm guns remained at their stations and, although *LSM-135* was sinking, drove off a second Japanese plane which swept in low over the ship. Only two wounded survivors from the minesweeper had miraculously escaped further injury in the bomb explosion and fire. They were gently lowered over the side into a raft and taken to a rescue ship on scene by *LSM-135* survivors.[51]

With the ship down by the bow, and with a heavy list to starboard, and the gun crews off the ship, Jenkins quickly made his way through all accessible compartments searching for survivors. Finding none, he went over the side, the last of ship's company to leave *LSM-135*.[52]

When the order was given to abandon ship, all wounded personnel had been placed in the water wearing life jackets and the men in the water got them to life rafts. Two officers and thirty-seven men were picked up by the destroyer escort *William C. Cole* (DE-641), two officers and nine men by the fleet tug *Tekesta* (ATF-93), and one enlisted man by the mortar infantry landing craft *LCI(M)-353*. The abandoned and adrift *LSM-135* grounded on a reef in the southeast corner of Ie Shima. It was judged to be a total loss, with only very minor salvage to be carried out by commander, LSM Flotilla Eight, to recover usable items.[53]

The commanding officer and ten men of *LSM-135* were killed or missing, and two officers and eight men were wounded. An undetermined number of the crew of the minesweeper, which had just been rescued from the sea, were lost with the LSM. Information about the officers and men of the medium landing ship killed in action or missing in action may be found in Appendix E.[54]

LOSS OF *LSM-59*

The evening of 21 June 1945, *LSM-59* stood out of Kerama Retto Harbor in company with the fleet tug *Lipan* (ATF-85) which was towing the high-speed transport *Barry* (APD-29). Severely damaged by

Kamikaze attack on 25 May northwest of Okinawa, *Barry* had been taken to Kerama Retto, stripped, decommissioned and struck from the Naval Register. She was being towed out to sea for use as a Kamikaze decoy. Conditions were ideal: weather clear, visibility excellent, and the sea calm.[55]

At 1841, as *LSM-59* was preparing to go alongside the *Barry* to pass a signal blinker tube to her, she was hit on the starboard side by a suicide plane that had approached undetected low over the water. The ship was at Condition III with three-section watches, and the commanding officer, Lt. D. C. Hawley, USNR, was at the conn. There were several friendly planes in the area, and lookouts on watch had not reported the enemy one, nor had it been engaged by the Combat Air Patrol.[56]

Within a minute of the *LSM-59* hit, a second suicide plane crashed the *Barry*. This plane was clearly seen by the medium landing ship, and was believed to be a Judy (Yokosuka D4Y Suisei Navy carrier dive bomber). It approached low over the water at a high rate of speed.[57]

The plane that hit *LSM-59* plunged through her tank deck down into the engine room and tore a large hole in the bottom of the ship. All electrical power and both main engines were knocked out, and the stern, engulfed in flame and smoke, began to settle immediately. Five 15-lb CO_2 fire extinguishers and the ship's two hoses for the 50-lb hose reel CO_2 system were brought into play within two minutes. The fire was put out at 1845.[58]

However, the ship was sinking rapidly with damage too great to attempt any damage control operations. The commanding officer gave the order to launch life rafts, then to abandon ship. Life Rafts 1 and 3 on the starboard side, and 2 and 4 on the port side were cut loose and put over the side and boarded by the crew. At 1846, the stern disappeared and the bow rose to a vertical position. At 1854, the bow slipped beneath the water.[59]

The destroyer escort *Swearer* (DE-186) and the minesweeper *Steady* (AM-118), patrolling nearby, came quickly to the rescue of survivors. Within 45 minutes from when *LSM-59* was abandoned, the majority of ship's company and embarked personnel were aboard these ships. All personnel were picked up except for crewmember Electrician's Mate Third Class C. W. Frey, USNR, and Aviation Structural Mechanic Third Class C. H. Fazer, USNR, from TDD Unit #41. Eight men received burns or wounds, and were treated on board the amphibious attack transport *Gosper* (APA-170).[60]

Assault on Japanese-held Fort Drum

Embark at beach, Subic Bay, Army Engineer demolition platoon, proceed to Corregidor; embark Infantry Assault Detachment, proceed to FORT DRUM (EL FRAILE), go alongside starboard side to disembark Army personnel and equipment, wait for the placing of demolitions, re-embark all Army personnel. Lay off until explosion occurred, thus destroying Japanese forces in interior of FORT; making the entrance of Manila Bay secure from observation and possible communications to Japan, giving information on our shipping going in and out of Manila Bay.

—Mission of USS *LSM-51* which, on 13 April 1945 in conjunction with USS *LCI(L)-547*, was to support an assault by U.S. Army combat infantry personnel on American-built, heavily-fortified Fort Drum, captured by the Japanese earlier in the war.[1]

Photo 17-1

Fort Drum in 1983, with the battleship USS *New Jersey* (BB-62) in the background. U.S. Navy photograph DN-SN-83-09891 (PH2 Paul Soutar)

On the afternoon of 10 April 1945, Lt. James Potts Jr., USN, the commanding officer of USS *LSM-51*, landed her at 1609 on Rifle Range Beach at Subic Bay. Minutes later, a platoon of demolition men from Company B, 113th Engineer Combat Battalion came aboard with the necessary equipment to install a wooden-hinged ramp (brow) on the starboard side of the conning station (atop the tower). Following completion of this work the following evening, the ramp was tested to ensure that it would operate properly. *LSM-51* then retracted and proceeded to anchorage with the Army Combat Engineers on board.[2]

On the morning of 12 April, after Comdr. Samuel H. Pattie, USN, boarded *LSM-51* at 0827, she immediately got under way for Corregidor. Pattie was in charge of the Fort Drum Attack Unit (Task Unit 78.9.16), which included in addition to *LSM-51*, the large infantry landing craft *LCI(L)-547* assigned as an as-needed rescue unit, two PT boats (MTBs) in support, and two mechanized landing craft (LCMs) to work directly with/assist the medium landing ship.[3]

TASK ORGANIZATION
EL FRAILE ("FORT DRUM") OPERATION
13 APRIL 1945

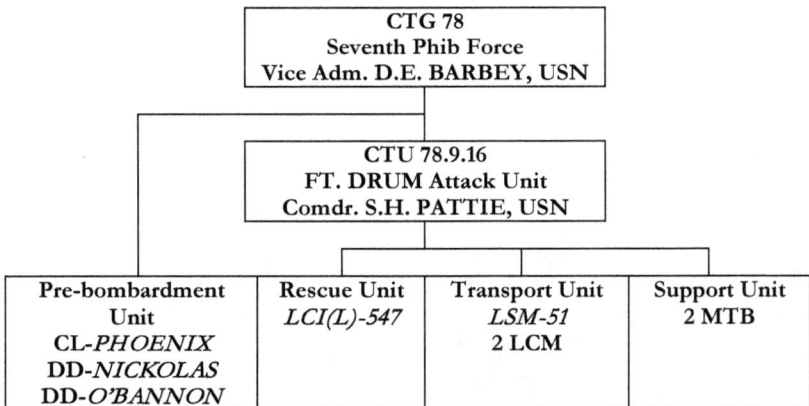

CTG 78
Seventh Phib Force
Vice Adm. D.E. BARBEY, USN

CTU 78.9.16
FT. DRUM Attack Unit
Comdr. S.H. PATTIE, USN

Pre-bombardment Unit	Rescue Unit	Transport Unit	Support Unit
CL-*PHOENIX*	*LCI(L)-547*	*LSM-51*	2 MTB
DD-*NICKOLAS*		2 LCM	
DD-*O'BANNON*			

Seventh Amphibious Force History Task Organization Sheet 36

At 1600, after *LSM-51* moored starboard side to the dock at Corregidor, an Army Infantry Combat Detachment came aboard for rehearsal of the assault on Fort Drum. This involved the reinforced platoon of riflemen from Company F, 151st Infantry, practicing manning their stations, and rapidly disembarking the ship as they would have to onto Fort Drum. At 1630, the detachment left *LSM-51* for the night.[4]

The following morning, 13 April, the Infantry Combat Detachment came aboard at 0815 bringing with them all required equipment. *LSM-51* got under way at 0825; and after setting General Quarters at 0859, started her approach to Fort Drum at 0932. She went alongside the U.S. Army's unsinkable "concrete battleship" at 0935. Currently occupied by Japanese forces, it had been constructed in the early 1900s on the entirety of the islet El Fraile, located at the entrance to Manila Bay. An islet is a small island of less than one acre in area.[5]

PRECEDING NAVAL BOMBARDMENT

A small group of Japanese, well protected inside of Fort Drum, have withstood continuous bombings and have fired small arms at craft which pass, killed and wounded PT-Boat personnel who attempted to land, and probably reported ship movements in the harbor entrance. Our mission is to fire on the southern 6" casemate of the fort in an attempt to open it and fire the magazines. If penetration is obtained, we shall repeat the performance on the northern 6" casemate.

—USS *Phoenix* War Diary, April 1945.

There were no defensive actions by Japanese defenders against *LSM-51* as she approached, then came alongside Fort Drum, because its once-impressive gun batteries had been knocked out of action by air and naval bombardment. The most recent attack on the fort had been carried out by the light cruiser *Phoenix* (CL-46), accompanied by the destroyers *Nicholas* (DD-449) and *O'Bannon* (DD-450), two days earlier.[6]

In early afternoon on 11 April, upon reaching a firing position off El Fraile at 1342, *Phoenix* launched observation and spotting planes and sounded General Quarters (GQ). She commenced bombardment of Fort Drum at 1404, and ceased fire at 1520, having expended 177 rounds of 6"/47 caliber ammunition. Her gunfire penetrated the casemate (fortified gun emplacement), and some rounds were heard exploding inside the fort, but it was evident that she had not fired the magazine. At 1529, she secured from GQ and left the area accompanied by the two destroyers.[7]

PRECEDING TRANSFORMATION OF THE SMALL ISLAND INTO AN ARMY "CONCRETE BATTLESHIP"

On the evening of 30 April 1898 during the Spanish-American War, as Commodore George Dewey attempted to lead the U.S. Navy Asiatic

Squadron into Manila Bay, Spanish guns on El Fraile Islet fired upon the three-masted cutter USS *McCulloch*. She returned fire, and her illumination of the area with a flare also enabled the protected cruisers USS *Boston* and USS *Raleigh*, and gunboat USS *Concord*, to fire back at the islet. Despite the islet's guns, the American ships were able to pass into the bay through the south entrance off Luzon.[8]

The following day, 1 May, Dewey's squadron destroyed the Spanish Pacific Fleet in the Battle of Manila Bay. The United States went on to win the war, which ended Spanish colonial rule in the Americas and resulted in U.S. acquisition of territories in Latin America and the western Pacific, including the Philippines.[9]

Photo 17-2

El Fraile Islet, circa 1909, before removal of much of its upslope area to allow transformation into a concrete sea fort.
U.S. Army photograph

When the United States annexed the Philippines in 1898, defense of the archipelago became its responsibility. In order to protect Manila Bay, the U.S. fortified four islands at its mouth—Corregidor, Caballo, Carabao and El Fraile—which became the sites of Fort Mills, Fort Hughes, Fort Frank, and Fort Drum, respectively.[10]

As part of this strengthening, the War Department decided to level El Fraile and have the U.S. Army Corps of Engineers build a 20-foot-thick steel-reinforced concrete deck atop it, armed with large guns mounted in twin armored turrets. Secondary armament was provided by two pairs of 6-inch guns mounted in armored casemates on either side of the main structure.[11]

The American Board of Fortifications also planned for El Fraile to be developed into a mine control and casemate station as part of the Harbor Defenses of Manila and Subic Bays. The defensive chain that was devised included the four forts in Manila Bay, and Fort Wint on Grande Island in Subic Bay.[12]

This work, begun in April 1909, produced a 40-foot-high structure with reinforced concrete exterior walls (between approximately 25 feet and 36 feet thick) that followed the natural shoreline of the rocky islet, and were topped by a deck 20 feet thick. The deck housed casemated 6-inch guns and a 60-foot-tall fire control cage mast. Additionally, Fort Drum boasted four 14-inch guns, mounted in pairs in armored turrets.[13]

Diagram 17-1

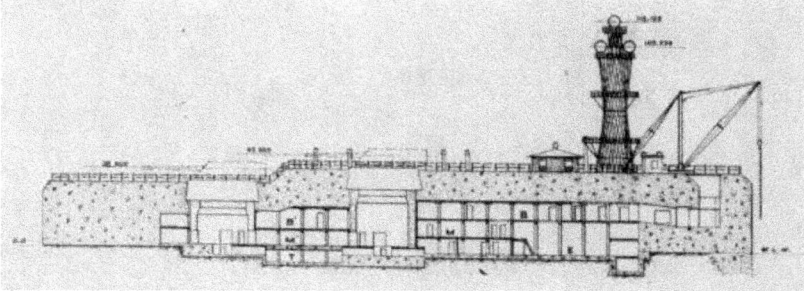

Drawing of longitudinal section of Fort Drum, Manila Bay, updated 1 January 1920. U.S. Army Corps of Engineers

Photo 17-3

14-inch turret for Fort Drum (El Fraile Islet, Philippines) undergoing tests at the Sandy Hook Proving Ground. The turret has two M1909 14-inch guns, developed solely for Fort Drum.
National Parks Service photograph

The Army Corps of Engineers had not purposefully designed the resultant 350 feet long by 144 feet wide fort, to resemble a warship. However, the citadel—with "bow" pointed westward, "stern" eastward, "port side" southward, and "starboard" side northward—did so, and it was thus dubbed "the concrete battleship."[14]

ASSAULT BY U.S. ARMY COMBAT ENGINEERS AND INFANTRY PERSONNEL ON FORT DRUM

At 0935, 13 April 1945 alongside FORT DRUM, *Army personnel went aboard. No difficulty was encountered in staying alongside due to having three (3) LCVP's, manned by the Army, pushing us against the side of the* FORT *and our having put over two (2) lines, one (1) forward and (1) one aft, hooking the lines in place on the* FORT *with grapnels. These lines did not last long due to the chafing on the concrete sides and surging of the ship.*

—Commanding Officer USS *LSM 51*, Action Report – Submission of – Fort Drum (El Fraile) Operation, 14 April 1945.

Friday, 13 April 1945 was the day of the assault on Fort Drum. Aboard *LSM-51* the engineers were ready with 600 pounds of explosives brought aboard earlier that morning, and the infantrymen equipped with rifles and bandoliers of ammunition. At 0935, as *LSM-51* inched up to Fort Drum, starboard side to, three LCVPs came along her port side bow first, and pushed her against the fort. Her crew were at their battle stations, and soldiers topside with their weapons at the ready.[15]

U.S. Army
113th Engineer Battalion
patch

U.S. Army
151st Infantry Regiment
patch

Crewmembers let down the ramp by means of a block and tackle, and two sailors (Milton C. Browne and William B. McGuffle) leapt onto the fort from the ramp, and fastened lines to available projections. Immediately after them the infantry riflemen scurried along the ramp, followed by the engineers. At this point, no Japanese resistance was encountered or signs of surrender evident.[16]

An LCM, aboard which was a large tank filled with a diesel oil/gasoline mixture, was then brought in astern of *LSM-51*. A messenger line attached to a hose on the landing craft was thrown up to Army engineers on the medium landing ship, then passed to other engineers on the fort, who pulled up the hose.[17]

As riflemen covered every opening from which the Japanese inside the fort could direct small arms fire, the engineers planted explosives and the LCM pumped its diesel oil/gasoline mixture (3,000 gallons in all) into vents and other opening on the otherwise, impregnable "concrete battleship."[18]

Photo 17-4

American soldiers embarked aboard USS *LSM-51* quickly run down a wooden ramp affixed to the ship's conning station, onto the deck of Japanese-occupied Fort Drum. U.S. Army photograph

Photo 17-5

Different view of soldiers gaining access to Fort Drum from *LSM-51*. Her superstructure being offset to starboard made this type of ship ideal for the operation, there being only a very short span to the fort.
U.S. Army photograph

At 1000, all Army personnel returned aboard *LSM-51*. The fuses had been lit, but were then extinguished because of a break in the hose by which the mixture of gasoline and diesel was being pumped into the fort through a vent. At 1003, Army personnel again boarded the fort, repaired the break in the hose, shifted the nozzle to another vent, relite the fuses, then returned to the ship at 1017.[19]

A short time earlier, *LSM-51* had begun to receive sniper fire from the fort through a six-inch gun port which the *Phoenix* had previously shelled and knocked in. At 1019, Seaman 1st Class Steve Bukovics, the gunner on the ship's No. 4 gun was wounded in the neck. *LSM-51* left Fort Drum's side at 1021, accompanied by the other vessels, and lay to nearby awaiting results. There was an initial explosion from Fort Drum at 1046, followed four minutes later by a series of major explosions. (It was later learned that all defenders inside the fort were killed by the explosions or resultant fires.) At 1104, *PT-376* came alongside the medium landing ship, and Bukovics was put aboard her for further transfer to the amphibious force command ship *Blue Ridge* (AGC-2).[20]

Less than an hour later, *LSM-51* moored starboard side to the Corregidor dock and discharged Army personnel and equipment. She then got under way for Subic Bay in company with *LCI(L)-547*, the designated rescue vessel which had stayed within a thousand yards of the medium landing ship throughout the entire operation.[21]

Both of these ships were awarded a battle star for the assault on Fort Drum.

Manila Bay-Bicol Operations: El Fraile (Fort Drum), Manila Bay

Ship	Date	Ship	Date
LSM-51	13 Apr 45	*LCI(L)-547*	13 Apr 45

Invasions of Sadau and Tarakan Islands, Borneo

The Sadau Attack Unit, Task Unit 78.1.16, of which this ship was a part, transported, protected and established units of the 26th Australian Brigade Group on Sadau Island, Dutch Borneo, on 30 April 1945. On the same day units of the Royal Australian Engineers were disembarked and supported by the Sadau Attack Unit while demolition teams cleared paths on the beaches off Lingkas Town, Tarakan Island. On 1 May 1945 PHILIP joined Task Group 74.3, the fire support group, in support of the major landings on Tarakan Island by the 26th Australian Infantry Brigade, Reinforced.

—Commanding Officer USS *Philip* (DD-498), describing his ship's role in a preliminary amphibious landing made on 30 April 1945 against no opposition on Sadau Island (in the channel west of Tarakan) for the purpose of siting shore-based artillery to cover the main landings the following day on Tarakan Island.[1]

Photo 18-1

Lt. Frederick William McKittrick, watched by men of the 2/4 Commando Squadron, hoists an Australian flag at Sadau Island, off Borneo, 30 April 1945. Australian War Memorial photograph 090925

Map 18-1

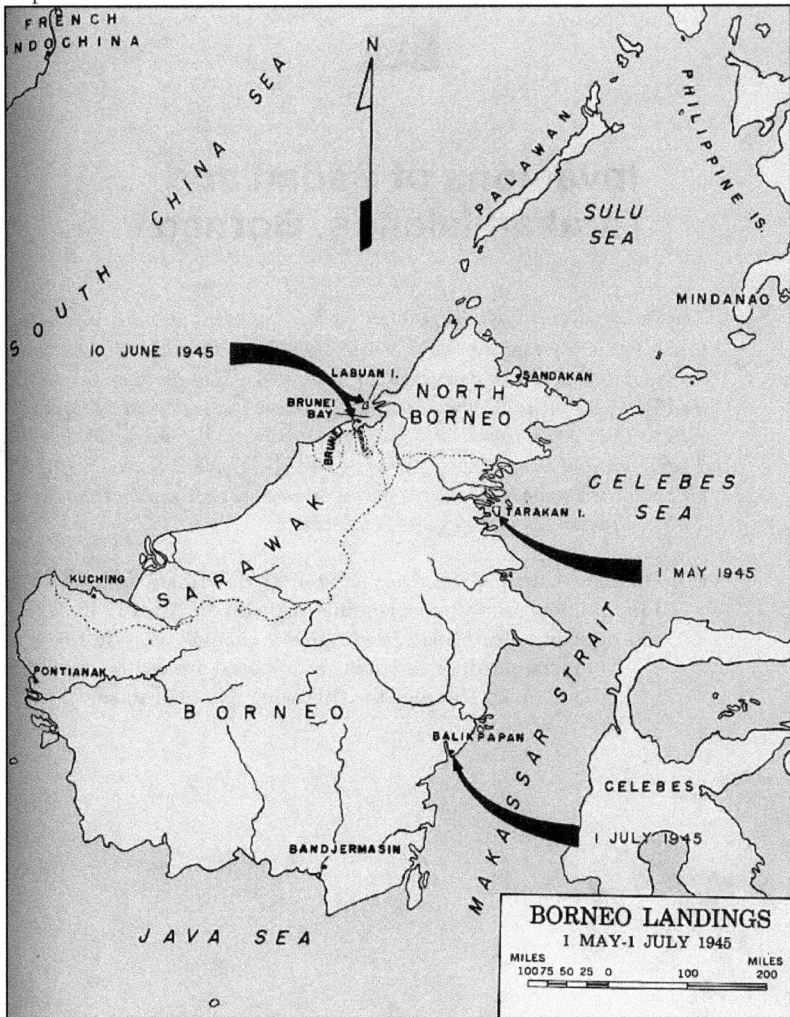

Movement of Australian assault forces en route to landings at Tarakan Island,
at Labuan Island in Brunei Bay, and at Balikpapan during the 1945 Borneo Campaign.
https://www.navy.gov.au/history/feature-histories/borneo-1945-amphibious-
success-story

With the recapture of the Philippines well advanced, Allied operations
against Borneo began with an amphibious landing at Sadau Island on 30
April 1945. This action, carried out to land supporting artillery ashore,
was a precursor to the main landing at Lingkas Town on Tarakan Island,
located a little to the east in the channel, the following day.

The objectives of the Allied Borneo Campaign of 1945 (1 May-15 August) were to deny Japan the continued fruits of its conquests in the Netherlands East Indies, and use of the approaches to those areas. To achieve these aims, an Australian-led force was to capture Tarakan Island to provide an airfield for support of an assault on Balikpapan, and for recapture of seized Brunei Bay for use as an advanced fleet base that could protect resources in the area. The final objective and phase of these assaults was to occupy Balikpapan for its naval air and logistic facilities as well as its petroleum installations.[2]

SADAU ATTACK UNIT

The Sadau Attack Unit (Task Unit 78.1.16) under Capt. Charles W. Gray, USN, consisted of the following seven ships and craft:

- Destroyer USS *Philip* (DD-498) – flagship
- Tank landing ship USS *LST-667*
- Medium landing ship USS *LSM-151*
- Large infantry landing craft USS *LCI(L)-712*
- Large support landing craft USS *LCS(L)-50*
- Tank landing craft USS *LCT-1331*
- Sub-chaser USS *PC-1120*[3]

The following brief account of the unopposed landing at Sadau Island focuses on the role of *LSM-151*. Days earlier on 22 April, she had loaded at Morotai Island, Netherlands East Indies (today Indonesia), five officers and 61 enlisted personnel of the 158th Australian Field Battery; their 25-pounders (artillery pieces); four 40mm anti-aircraft guns; and 22 tons of ammunition and provisions. Other ships of the Attack Unit transported assault troops and a demolition squad assigned to clear landing spots on the beaches at Tarakan Island. The job of this squad was to demolish beach obstacles such as steel stakes and pilings driven into the shallow waters in front of the proposed landing beaches. The mission of the field battery was to provide protection for the demolition squad, and cover the assault landings the following day on Tarakan Island.[4]

Following a rehearsal operation at Morotai, the Attack Unit departed the island in mid-afternoon on 26 April. The small group of ships arrived off Tarakan Island at 0400 on 30 April, and proceeded through the channel across Tarakan Bay to a point off Sadau Island. At 0617, Captain Gray shifted his pennant from flagship destroyer *Philip* to

PC-1120 preparatory to the assault on Sadau Island. *Philip* began firing at predesignated targets on the island at 0712, and ceased firing at 0731.[5]

At 0745, the first wave landed. Less than an hour later, *LSM-151* beached at 0840 and began discharging her carried personnel and cargo.[6]

Photo 18-2

Troops of 2/4 Commando Squadron going ashore from the landing craft USS *LCI(L)-712* on Sadau Island, Borneo, 30 April 1945. The landing was unopposed and there were no Japanese found on the island.
Australian War Memorial photograph 090861

Photo 18-3

At left: USS *LSM-151*, carrying 25-pounders and 57 Battery, 2/7 Field Regiment, Royal Australian Engineers, personnel beaching at Sadau Island on 30 April 1945; and at right: Men of 57 Battery unloading supplies.
Australian War Memorial photographs 090864 and 090928

After unloading, *LSM-151* retracted from the beach and proceeded to a point 3,500 yards off Tarakan Island, anchoring while *Philip* shelled the beach near her position off that island. The destroyer had earlier (after pre-landing bombardment of Sadau Island) taken station off Tarakan at 0928, preparatory to support of demolition personnel—which included a plane laying smoke to shield them from view of Japanese forces ashore.[7]

Photo 18-4

Plane laying smoke to cover breaching by Royal Australian Engineers of obstacles off the Tarakan Island landing beaches, 30 April 1945. Commander Task Group 78.1, Action Report, CTG 78.1 (ComPhibGruSix) – Tarakan, Borneo, Operation (1-3 May 1945), 5 May 1945.

Photo 18-5

Engineers attach demolition charges to beach obstacles. Commander Task Group 78.1, Action Report, CTG 78.1 (ComPhibGruSix) – Tarakan, Borneo, Operation (1-3 May 1945), 5 May 1945.

At 1713 on 30 April, the Sadau Attack Unit (Task Unit 78.1.16), its mission completed, got under way in formation and proceeded out of the harbor. Early the following morning, its ships met up with the main body of Task Group 78.1 (Tarakan Attack Group)—which had left Morotai a day after them on 27 April—and transited back to Tarakan Island as part of this Attack Group.[8]

TARAKAN ATTACK GROUP

As previously mentioned, the Allied amphibious landings at Tarakan on 1 May were undertaken for the acquisition of its rich petroleum fields (thereby denying them to the enemy) and the establishment of an airfield for support of an assault on Balikpapan. Rear Adm. Forrest B. Royal, USN, embarked in the amphibious force command ship *Rocky Mount*, commanded the Tarakan Attack Group (Task Group 78.1); Rear Adm. Russell S. Berkey, USN, commander, Cruiser Covering Group (Task Group 74.3), was second in command.[9]

Photo 18-6

Rear Adm. Russell S. Berkey, USN, speaking to another ship via Megaphone (or loud hailer) from the bridge of his flagship, USS *Phoenix* (CL-46), during the pre-landing bombardment of Corregidor, 15 February 1945.
National Archives photograph #80-G-273279

The seaward approaches to the roughly pear-shaped island of about 15½ miles long by 11 miles wide were extremely treacherous, with extensive banks of sand and mud extending outward for several miles. The two main channels were heavily mined, making clearance operations dangerous. Lt. Comdr. James R. Keefer's Minesweeping Unit (78.1.5) consisted of the high-speed transport *Cofer* (APD-62) carrying four LCVPs equipped as shallow-water sweepers, and eleven 136-feet, wooden-hulled YMS minesweepers. Over a five-day period, one of the YMSs was sunk, two were extensively damaged, and two suffered minor damage as a result of mine explosions and enemy shore battery fire while sweeping.

YMS Casualties at Tarakan Island

Date	Ship	Cause
28 Apr 45	YMS-329	Extensive damage from exploded magnetic mine
30 Apr 45	YMS-51	Minor damage from exploded Mk 26.1 mine
30 Apr 45	YMS-363	Minor damage from exploded enemy contact mine
2 May 45	YMS-481	Sunk by enemy shore battery fire
2 May 45	YMS-334	Extensive damage from five or six 75mm enemy shells
2 May 45	YMS-364	Minor damage from 75mm enemy shell[10]

In addition to mines, enemy coast defense and anti-aircraft guns, with the usual defense positions, were in place. Presenting another challenge was an effective anti-tank barrier above the beaches—constructed of oil pipeline and scrap metal covered with earth—which had to be breeched to create openings upslope from the landing beaches.[11]

ASSAULT DAY (1 MAY 1945)

Photo 18-7

Pre-landing naval bombardment on assault day, 1 May 1945, hits fuel storage and ammunition dump (on right).
Commander Task Group 78.1, Action Report, CTG 78.1 (ComPhibGruSix) – Tarakan, Borneo, Operation (1-3 May 1945), 5 May 1945.

Photo 18-8

LSTs beached in gaps blown in obstacles by demolition personnel, commence unloading operations on 1 May 1945, as the tide rapidly recedes. A Japanese-constructed anti-tank ditch in foreground slowed operations.
Commander Task Group 78.1, Action Report, CTG 78.1 (ComPhibGruSix) – Tarakan, Borneo, Operation (1-3 May 1945), 5 May 1945

On 1 May, the initial assault landings at Tarakan commenced on schedule at 0815 (H-Hour). Succeeding waves landed on time, in spite of heavy currents encountered off the beaches, and put ashore elements of the famed 9th Australian Division ("The Rats of Tobruk"). No enemy opposition was encountered until about two hours later when ineffective mortar and artillery fire developed.[12]

Included among the ships assigned to the supporting Transport and Landing Craft Unit were 21 LSTs and 4 LSMs. Pontoon causeways were carried by 7 of the LSTs for use over the shallow, muddy beaches. The 328-foot tank landing ships of the LST Unit, and smaller, 203-foot medium landing ships of the LSM Unit are identified in the table.[13]

```
78.1.1  Transport and Landing Craft Unit - Captain SINCLAIR

   78.1.12  LST Unit - Captain SINCLAIR
            (LSTFlot 7 (modified) - Captain SINCLAIR)

            LST 466 (FF), 67, 171, 467, 562, 584 (GF),    21 LST
            585, 590, 613, 626, 637, 667, 697, 711,
            742, 743, 924, 993, 1025, 1027, 1035.

            (LSTs 584, 585, 590, 711, 743, 993, 1027
            carry pontoon causeways)
            (LST 67 is logistic LST)

   78.1.14  LSM Unit - Lt. Comdr. BURGETT
            (LSM Group 19 (less 8 LSMs) - Lt. Comdr. BURGETT

            LSM 269 (GF), 224, 267, 151                    4 LSM
```

Light, folding assault boats were towed in by each LCVP ("Higgins boat") and used to get troops ashore by paddling after the LCVPs had grounded as the water was too deep because of the beach topography for the troops to wade ashore. After bulldozers opened exits through the tank barrier, Marston matting and iron plates had to be used to make the roads passable.[14]

Photo 18-9

Folding assault boats being mass produced in a South Australian factory, circa 1941.
Australian War Memorial photograph 010794

Photo 18-10

Men of the 11th Field Company, Royal Australian Engineers, carrying a MK1 Folding Assault boat, circa 1940-1942.
Australian War Memorial photograph P01105.021

LSTs IMPORTANT, LSMs LITTLE UTILIZED

> *Unloading was extremely slow due to beach and shore conditions. The LSMs were given last priority of unloading which permitted them only a minimum of usefulness and did not use to best advantage the ability of these craft to assist in unloading larger craft.... There were no casualties to personnel. The performance of duty by all hands was very good.*

—Lt. Comdr. William A. Burgett, commander, Task Unit 78.1.14.[15]

At 0450 on 1 May, the LSM Unit entered the channel with the Assault Force and, arriving off the Tarakan beaches, anchored at 0600 in LST Area Two. At 1005, *LSM-151* was directed to load cargo from the Royal Australia Navy infantry landing ship HMAS *Manoora.* That evening, the LSM Unit shifted to an anchorage closer to the beaches, with *LSM-151* joining sister ships at 1900 upon completion of loading from *Manoora.*[16]

The LSM Unit remained anchored off Lingkas Beach, Tarakan, until 6 May, when LSMs *267* and *269* landed the first assault cargo. On the 7th, LSMs *224* and *151* beached; as did the *267* and *269* later that day after mooring alongside the infantry landing ships HMAS *Manoora* and HMAS *Westralia* to load cargo.[17]

LSMs *269* and *224* completed unloading, retracted, and went to anchorage on 7 May, and LSMs *257* and *151* the following day. In late afternoon on 9 May, the LSM Unit got under way for Morotai as part of Task Unit 78.1.97.[18]

Photo 18-11

HMAS *Westralia* at Sydney Harbour, 1944.
Australian War Memorial photograph 107129

COMBAT ASHORE

Despite difficult coastal approaches, extensive minefields and strongly fortified defenses, the amphibious assault of Tarakan on 1 May 1945, was accomplished with marked success. A heavy concentration of naval and air bombardment prior to the landing, as well as naval gunfire support to ground forces once ashore neutralized most of the Japanese resistance. Hard fighting by 9th Australian Division troops secured the area. Capture of Tarakan with its airfields ensured that fighter aircraft coverage extended past Balikpapan, which would prevent Japanese shipping from entering the area. For the first time, all land and sea areas within MacArthur's Southwest Pacific command came under Allied air superiority.[19]

LSM BATTLE STARS

Borneo Operation: Tarakan Island Operation			
LSM-151	27 Apr-5 May 45	LSM-267	27 Apr-5 May 45
LSM-224	27 Apr-5 May 45	LSM-269	27 Apr-5 May 45

19

Invasion of Brunei Bay, Borneo

Photo 19-1

General view of the Brunei Bay area, British North Borneo, in 1945.
Australian War Memorial photograph 045064

The campaign against Borneo by Australian troops—begun on 30 April at Sadau Island in support of the main landings the following day, 1 May, at Tarakan Island—continued on 10 June with landings at Brunei Bay on the northwest coast of Borneo. The Brunei Bay area boasted extensive oil and rubber resources, where the Japanese had developed a protected anchorage over an area of approximately 16 by 14 miles, as a forward naval base. The seaward side of the bay is protected by Labuan and associated islands. Entry to it is gained by two main channels; one south of Labuan Island, and the other east of it. At the time of attack, there were a number of piers, mostly with a modest depth of water alongside, at several small harbors around the bay.[1]

In addition to naval facilities, there were three airfields in the vicinity; two of them on Labuan Island, and one about three miles from the town of Brunei, but possible air opposition was considered to be negligible. The number of enemy troops in the immediate area were estimated at only 2,000 to 2,500; and it was believed there were possibly a few coast defense and AA guns, pill-boxes, and entrenchments. The greatest danger to landing forces were extensive enemy and Allied minefields known to exist, which would require protracted sweeping.[2]

As U.S. Navy minesweepers worked their way down through Tarakan, Brunei, and Balikpapan, they faced both Japanese moored mines and large numbers of U.S. Navy magnetic influence mines. The former were intended by the Japanese to help protect approaches, bays, and harbors from attack by sea. The latter had been dropped by Army Air Force B-24s and far-ranging Australian PBY Catalinas as part of an Allied offensive mining campaign against both the Japanese home islands and other enemy occupied/controlled areas.[3]

During pre-landing sweeping, USS *Salute* (AM-294) struck a mine and sank with the loss of 9 crewmen killed or missing, and 37 wounded. This was the only ship loss/personnel casualties suffered by the minesweepers, although they were fired on by shore batteries in the Mini-Lutong area on 13 June.[4]

BRUNEI ATTACK GROUP (TG 78.1)

Transport, protect, land, firmly establish on shore the 9th Australian Division in the BRUNEI BAY area and support it in subsequent operations in order to secure BRUNEI BAY for use as an advanced fleet base and to protect resources in the area.

—Mission of the Brunei Attack Group.[5]

The Brunei Attack Group under Rear Adm. Forrest B. Royal, USN, numbered 87 ships. Among this Task Group as part of the subordinate Transport and Landing Craft Unit, were all three RAN infantry landing ships—HMAS *Manoora*, HMAS *Westralia*, and HMAS *Kanimbla*—and U.S. Navy LSTs (34 total) and LSMs (20 total). The RAN ships were commanded by Captain Cousin, RAN, and other ships were under USN command.[6]

Infantry, Tank, and Medium Landing Ships

```
78.1.1  Transport and Landing Craft Unit, Captain HUDSON
78.1.11 Transport Unit, Captain COUSIN
        MANOORA (F), WESTRALIA, KANIMBLA                    3 LSI
```

```
78.1.12 LST Unit, Captain HUDSON

        LST Flotilla 24, Captain HUDSON

        LST 640 (FF), 560, 591, 595, 619 (H), 638,      13 LST
            696, 806, 912 (H), 936, 937, 941, 942

        LST Flotilla 15, Captain MANEES

        LST 574 (FF), 573, 709, 751, 922, 626,           8 LST
            1025 (H), 1027

        From LST Flotilla 22

        LST 584, 585, 590, 637, 1035                      5 LST

        LST Flotilla 8, Captain WATTS

        LST 614 (FF), 562, 742, 667 (H), 697, 613 (H),    8 LST
            743, 993
78.1.14 LSM Unit, Commander VERGE

        LSM Flotilla 7, Commander VERGE
        LSM 54 (FF), 50, 51, 52, 53, 63, 64, 65, 67,     20 LSM
            68, 128, 133, 138, 139, 168,(GF), 203,
            219, 225, 237, 269.
```

On Assault Day, 10 June, the Attack Group sailed into Brunei Bay before dawn under the protecting guns of the Fire Support Group. The main body of the assault force was to land on Brown Beach at Victoria Town on Labuan Island, while smaller forces landed at Muara Island and Brunei Bluff on White and Green Beaches, respectively. The beaches in Brunei were wide and sandy, much better suited to amphibious landings than those at Tarakan had been.[7]

Photo 19-2

On Assault Day, 10 June 1945, the 6-inch guns of the light cruiser Royal Australian Navy cruiser HMAS *Hobart* lay down a barrage on Japanese positions in the hills behind the Brunei beachhead. Australian War Memorial photograph 110232

At 0915, the first waves in LCVPs and LVTs landed simultaneously, on schedule, at Brown, Green, and White Beaches. These landings, as far as eighteen miles apart, were carried out rapidly and with precision. The beaches were quickly secured by troops making the shore, with all assault waves landed by 1003, with remaining waves on call.[8]

Photo 19-3

Troops of 2/17 Infantry Battalion running from beached LCVPs through the surf onto Green Beach, as part of the second assault wave on 10 June 1945. Australian War Memorial photograph 110230

LSM ACTIVITIES

The LSMs began unloading at Brown Beach before noon on Assault Day, and the LSTs at mid-afternoon. Prior to arrival of the Attack Group at Brunei Bay, the twenty ships of the LSM Unit had been split among the four assault units:

- Brown Beach: LSMs *50, 51, 52, 53, 63, 64, 65, 128*
- Green Beach: *LSM-237*
- White Beach: LSMs *67, 68, 138, 168, 203, 219, 225*
- Reserve Unit: LSMs *54, 133, 139, 269*[9]

Embarked aboard the twenty LSMs in support of the assault landings by the 9th Australian Division were a total of 58 officers, 914 men, and 565 vehicles. The numbers of personnel and quantities of vehicles carried aboard each ship, and types of vehicles comprising their totals, are identified in the following table.[10]

9th Australian Division Personnel / Vehicles Embarked Aboard LSMs

Ship	Officers	Men	Vehicles
LSM 50	1	49	32
51	1	49	41
52	2	52	21
53	2	50	36
54	5	46	22
63	1	51	35
64	3	51	32
65	2	50	24
67	4	48	28
68	1	21	11
128	2	44	15
133	3	49	25
138	5	47	39
139	6	49	15
168	4	45	27
203	3	43	35
219	2	48	31
225	5	46	54
237	1	28	7
269	5	48	35
TOTALS:	58	914	565

VEHICLES BY TYPE

176	Jeeps
165	Trailers
58	Trucks
47	Dozers
22	Tanks
26	25 pounder guns
12	40mm guns
2	2 pounder guns
3	Auto Patrols
2	Cranes
1	Prime Mover
1	Wrecker
36	Sleds
12	Hand Carts

TOTAL   565

Photo 19-4

USS *LSM-203* and *LSM-68* unloading on White Beach, 10 June 1945.
Commander Task Group 78.1, Action Report, CTG 78.1 (ComPhibGrpSIX) – Brunei
Bay, Borneo, Operation (10-17 June 1945), 19 June 1945.

LSM beaching/unloading operations were unopposed, and there were no combat-related material or personnel casualities. After initially beaching and discharging their preloaded cargo, LSMs, as directed, took cargo from other ships and lightered it ashore.

Lt. S. B. Whitehead, USNR, commanding officer of USS *LSM-64*, summarized in his action report, the activities of his ship as one of the eight LSMs assigned to the Brown Beach Assault Unit.

10 June 1945

0426: Deployed from TU 78.1.14 and joined Brown Assault Unit TU 78.1.16.

0644: Anchored by the stern anchor in 3 fathoms of water at Brunei Bay, British North Borneo in LST Area Five.

0651: A lone plane, resembling a 'Judy' flew across the fleet at about 2000 feet on a course, roughly, 000° True and dropped one bomb doing no damage. Several ships fired at the plane but he was soon out of range and was apparently not hit. Enemy fire was observed from wrecked tanker off Victoria Town as first wave went into Brown Beach.

1121: We beached on Brown Beach II, Labuan Island.

1146: We retracted to make new approach as water was too deep in front of ramp to discharge cargo. Our starboard screw was damaged on a sunken log at this time.

1154: We rebeached.

1227: We retracted, having discharged cargo, and proceeded to HMAS *MANOORA*...

11 June 1945

0017: Cast off from HMAS *MANOORA*...

0654: We were on our way to Brown Beach...

0821: Beached in Slot 1 Brown Beach One on orders from Beach Master.

1020: Ship's crew commenced unloading cargo through deep water... No trucks or troop labor was available, cargo consisted of about 250 tons of rations, ammunition, oil piping, valves and assorted machinery.

1400: Beach Master sent one duck [DUKW] to assist in unloading.

1930: Unloading was completed.

12 June 1945

0928: Retracted from beach and proceeded to anchor at 1104 in Berth T 99...

1606: Underway in company with echelon 0-6-K as ordered by CTG 78.1 to Morotai Island, N.E.I.[11]

COMBAT ASHORE

Australian 9th Infantry troops landed on Labuan Island found Victoria Town abandoned and almost completed destroyed. Infantry personnel and tanks moved inland from Brown Beach against little opposition. By 1129, the 24th Brigade was within sight of the Labuan Airfield. From this point on, enemy opposition increased.[12]

Following the landing at White Beach on Muara Island, the island was completely reconnoitered without finding any enemy. By nightfall, the Australians on Green Beach (Brunei Bluff) had captured Brooketon and advanced 3,000 yards toward Brunei Town.[13]

Photo 19-5

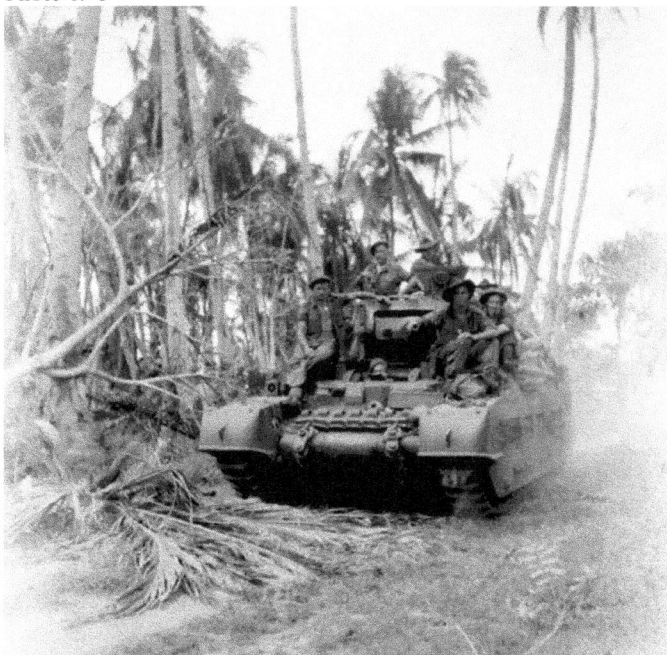

2/17 Infantry Battalion members riding on a Matilda tank, 10 June 1945.
Australian War Memorial photograph 110230

At 1724 on Assault Day, troops were landed on Hamilton Peninsula, Labuan Island, and at 1830, Maj. Gen. George F. Wootten assumed command of the 9th Australian Division ashore. In support of the fighting ashore, USAAF B-24 and RAAF Beaufighters continued to bomb and strafe designated areas. The town and airfield of Labuan were captured on the first day but strong Japanese resistance on the island continued until 21 June.[14]

Photo 19-6

The Sultan of Brunei and his wife, accompanied by Wing Commander K. E. H. Kay, RAF, British Borneo Civil Affairs Unit, walking up from the wharf on 17 June 1945, on their arrival back in the area from the village of Tentayer where they took sanctuary during Allied bombing of Brunei.
Australian War Memorial photograph 109545

LSM BATTLE STARS

Borneo Operation: Brunei Bay Operation

Ship	Period	Ship	Period
LSM-50	10-14 Jun 45	LSM-128	10-14 Jun 45
LSM-51	10-14 Jun 45	LSM-133	10-14 Jun 45
LSM-52	10-14 Jun 45	LSM-138	10-14 Jun 45
LSM-53	10-14 Jun 45	LSM-139	10-14 Jun 45
LSM-54	10-14 Jun 45	LSM-168	10-14 Jun 45
LSM-63	10-14 Jun 45	LSM-203	10-14 Jun 45
LSM-64	10-14 Jun 45	LSM-219	10-14 Jun 45
LSM-65	10-14 Jun 45	LSM-225	10-14 Jun 45
LSM-67	10-14 Jun 45	LSM-237	10-14 Jun 45
LSM-68	10-14 Jun 45	LSM-269 (no BS)	10-14 Jun 45

Invasion of Balikpapan, Borneo

1. *The landing problem for the BALIKPAPAN Operation was a very difficult one due to several unusual features of the site selected for the landing beaches.*

    (a) Shallow water extended out a great distance from shore which made it necessary to locate the Transport Area 14000 yards from the landing beaches.

    (b) Extensive Allied and Enemy minefields were present between the Transport Areas and landing beaches.

2. *To overcome the above difficulties an approach lane was designed to permit the landing craft to traverse the least dangerous and most completely swept part of the minefields. This required two turns in the approach channel. To simplify the boat coxswain's problem the approach lane was buoyed by the [net laying ship] USS MANGO (AN-24) prior to F Day [Assault Day].*

        —Commander Task Group 78.2, Action Report – Balikpapan-Manggar-Borneo June 15-July 6, 1945, 14 August 1945.

Photo 20-1

Large infantry landing craft discharging troops over Green Beach.
Commander Task Group 78.2, Action Report – Balikpapan-Manggar
-Borneo June 15-July 6, 1945, 14 August 1945

On 1 July 1945, assault troops of the 7th Australian Division landed unopposed at Balikpapan, in the final major amphibious operation of the Borneo Campaign. The Australians had departed Morotai on the afternoon of 26 June, aboard ships of the Balikpapan Attack Group (Task Group 78.2)—composed of 121 ships in total—and proceeded to the objective without encountering any enemy resistance. A group of twenty additional ships from Tawi-Tawi Island in the Philippines, joined on 29 June, and proceeded in company.[1]

Rear Adm. Albert G. Noble, USN, commanding the Attack Group, had originally thought it questionable whether the landings could be carried out on time, owing to difficulties in pre-assault minesweeping then in progress at the objective. However, because of subsequent progress made in minesweeping, underwater demolition and reconnaissance, and the cumulative effectiveness of bombardment and air strikes against enemy defensives, he had decided on 28 June to land on the scheduled date.[2]

HEROIC MINESWEEPER AND UDT 11 PERSONNEL

Neither the scope, nor space remaining in this book allow details about the significant efforts/contributions of the Minesweeping Unit and Underwater Demolition Teams 11 and 18. However, it's important to highlight that the below identified U.S. Navy minesweepers were awarded the Presidential Unit Citation, for heroic actions at Balikpapan.

President Unit Citation (Balikpapan, Borneo, 15 June-1 July 1945)		
USS *Scout* (AM-296)	USS *YMS-49*	USS *YMS-335*
USS *Scuffle* (AM-298)	USS *YMS-50*	USS *YMS-336*
USS *Sentry* (AM-299)	USS *YMS-52*	USS *YMS-339*
USS *YMS-9*	USS *YMS-53*	USS *YMS-364*
USS *YMS-10*	USS *YMS-95*	USS *YMS-365*
USS *YMS-39*	USS *YMS-196*	USS *YMS-366*
USS *YMS-46*	USS *YMS-314*	USS *YMS-368*
USS *YMS-47*	USS *YMS-315*	USS *YMS-392*

During the Borneo Campaign (Tarakan, Brunei, and Balikpapan) the U.S. Pacific Mine Force lost *Salute* (AM-294), *YMS-39, 50, 84, 365,* and *481*, and suffered damage to twelve others—*YMS-10, 47, 49, 51, 314, 329, 334, 335, 339, 363, 364,* and *368*.[3]

Underwater Demolition Team 11 earned Presidential Unit Citations for its swimmers' actions in both the Brunei Bay landings (8-10 June 1945) and the Balikpapan operation (26 June-4 July 1945).

In support of the landing at Balikpapan, Task Unit 78.2.11—UDT 11, embarked aboard the fast transport USS *Kline*, and UDT 18 aboard

USS *Schmidt*—arrived in the Balikpapan area on 24 June, and quickly got to work. Lt. L. A. States, USNR (commanding officer of Underwater Demolition Team 11, and commander, Task Unit 78.2.11) summarized the unit's prelanding activities in his Action Report:

> During the morning of 25 June the unit carried out a daylight swimming reconnaissance of Red BAKER and Yellow BAKER Beaches at MANGGAR KETJIL and Green BAKER Beach at MANGGAR. On the following morning the Task Unit returned to these beaches in a demolition operation clearing an 800 yard gap through the enemy obstacles on Red and Yellow BAKER and an equivalent gap on Green BAKER. On 27 June the Task Unit carried out a daylight swimming reconnaissance on the preferred beaches, Red, Yellow and Green, at KLANDASAN, S.E. BORNEO. On 28 June a 1600 yard gap was cleared on the preferred beaches. There was no activity on 29 June. On 30 June UDT 11 returned to the preferred beaches and completed the task assigned this unit...by clearing a gap of 400 yards additional to the 1600 yards cleared on 28 June. On 1 July, Fox Day (Assault Date), selected personnel of this unit acting as wave guides led the first assault wave from their line of departure to the cleared gaps in the beach defenses.[4]

RAN AND USN LANDING SHIPS

The three Australian landing ships *Manoora*, *Westralia*, and *Kanibla* were attached to the Balikpapan Attack Group as part of Capt. Allan P. Cousin's, RANR, Transport Unit (78.2.2) which also included the attack cargo ship USS *Titania* and the dock landing ship USS *Carter Hall*.[5]

78.2.2 Transport Unit - Captain Cousin, RANR(S)

MANOORA(F), WESTRALIA, KANIBLA	3 LSI
TITANIA (AKA 13)	1 AKA
CARTER HALL (LSD 3)	1 LSD

Capt. Daniel J. Weintraub, USN, embarked in the landing craft flotilla flagship USS *LCFF-789*, commanded the twenty-two LSMs comprising Task Unit 78.2.4 (LSM Unit). These ships, identified in the following table, were split into three subordinate groups.[6]

78.2.4 <u>LSM Unit</u> (LSM Flot 2, mod)(22 LSM) - Captain Weintraub

LCFF 789	1 LCFF
<u>LSM Group 4</u> - Lt. Comdr. Johnson LSM 18(GF), 19, 21, 257, 258, 22, 310, 311	8 LSM
<u>LSM Group 5</u> - Lt. Comdr. Smith LSM 36(GF), 37, 130, 148, 150, 151, 205	7 LSM
<u>LSM Group 6</u> (Mod) - Lt. Comdr. Weire LSM 38, 39, 40, 42(GF), 267, 223, 224	7 LSM

The LST Unit under Capt. Francis J. Mee, USN, consisted of thirty-five LSTs of which nineteen participated in Assault Day. Their story follows.[7]

78.2.5 <u>LST Unit</u> (35 LST) - Captain Mee

<u>LST Flot 22</u> - Captain Mee LST 632(FF), 639(P), 714(P), 721(P), 935(P), 938(P),	6 LST
<u>LST Flot 7</u> (15 LST) - Captain Sinclair	
<u>LST Group 19</u> - Commander Van Zandt LST 181(P), 245, 470, 471(P), 474(GF), 466(FF)	6 LST
<u>LST Group 20</u> - Commander Baker LST 452(GF), 454(P), 456(PB), 457(P), 462	5 LST
From <u>LST Group 21</u> LST 66, 168, 206	3 LST
From <u>LST Flot 8 (11 LST)</u>	
<u>LST Group 23</u> - Commander Linthicum LST 395(PB), 397(S)(P), 911, 1016, 1017, 1018(GF)(S)(PB)	6 LST
From <u>LST Groups 22 and 24</u> LST 666(S)(P), 673(PB), 694(PB), 740, 910	5 LST
From <u>LST Flot 15</u> LST 703(P), 753(P), 777(S)(P), 579	4 LST

(P) - Pontoon
(PB) - Pontoon Barges
(S) - Surgical

ASSAULT DAY

At 0554 on 1 July off Balikpapan, Rear Adm. Albert G. Noble, USN (Commander Task Force 78.2) executed the order "DEPLOY," at which time the nineteen LSTs stopped in order for them to cast off the LCTs, one apiece, they had in tow. All tows were cast off by 0616, and nine LSTs assiged to Area Baker proceeded there; the remaining LSTs made their way to Area Able.[8]

Immediately upon anchoring in Area B, LSTs *397*, *632*, and *639* launched wave guide boats, and disembarked wave guide officers for the first waves of 37 LVTs. LSTs *452*, *454*, *694*, and *777* provided wave guide officers and boats for the second wave of 54 LVTs. At 0807 the first and second waves departed Area Baker for the line of departure.[9]

LST-457 subsequently furnished wave guide boats and officers for the 16th wave of 16 LVTs. At 0950, LSTs were directed to launch pontoon causeways and barges. Since the beaches were unsuitable for beaching LSTs, it was necessary to unload them into LCTs (tank landing craft) and LCMs (mechanized landing craft). Ramp to ramp unloading into LCTs proved difficult, laborious and dangerous because of heavy swells. Ramp to ramp unloading into LCMs under the same conditions was accomplished without difficulty.[10]

At 1216, Area Baker LSTs were directed to move to Area Charlie. By 1700 that evening, LSTs *168*, *703*, *721*, *740*, *935*, *938*, *1016*, *1017*, and *1018* from Area Able had also moved into Area Charlie. Since none of these tank landing ships could beach, all required lighterage.[11]

At 1745, LSTs in Area Charlie came under fire from shore but the destroyer *Conway* (DD-507) soon silenced the enemy gun(s). Damage or casualties were not suffered and work continued, although unloading into LCTs during darkness was next to impossible. Late the following morning, Area Charlie was again subjected to fire from shore and once again, there were no casualties or damage to LSTs.[12]

LSM OPERATIONS

The medium landing ships, with much shallower drafts than the LSTs, were also not able to beach. A UDT beach survey that commander, Balikpapan Attack Force obained the day before the scheduled assault, indicated that the sea floor gradient was too shallow and would be unfavorable even at high tide for unloading LSMs without the use of pontoon causeways. Accordingly, Rear Admiral Noble directed that LSMs be landed "on call" (as ordered and not based on an existing schedule) after a further survey of LSM beaches could be made following the assault landing.[13]

Because the LSMs were not assigned to assault wave(s), as in other amphibious landings, there was sufficient time to construct a pontoon causeway permitting them to discharge their cargo without going into the beach. Although the landing of their cargoes was delayed, this action prevented otherwise almost certain LSM propeller damage by the shallow gradient and an abundance of logs and fragments strewn about from beach defenses demolished by the Underwater Demolition Teams. Having the LSMs unload offshore, undoubtedly saved more of them for use in return supply echelons after they departed Balikpapan.[14]

Photo 20-2

Offshore log barricade immediately east of Green Beach at low water.
Commander Task Group 78.2, Action Report – Balikpapan-Manggar-Borneo June 15-July 6, 1945, 14 August 1945

LAND WARFARE ASHORE

In spite of sporadic fire from enemy artillery, mortars and small arms fire which fell among the boat waves and on the landing beaches, all seventeen assault waves had landed by 1055I [local time] without casualty to a single man. The aggressive manner in which the enemy manned and fought his guns to meet this frontal attack was borne out in the counted 160 enemy dead found in the immediate area of the landing beaches, and 300 additional dead in the area of fortified positions in the high ground to the Northwest of the beaches.

—Commander Task Group 78.2, Action Report – Balikpapan-Manggar-Borneo June 15-July 6, 1945, 14 August 1945.

On 1 July, 7th Australian Division troops landing in assault—two battalions abreast, the 21st Brigade on the right over Green Beaches One and Two, and 18th Brigade on the left over Beaches Red and Yellow—met only light fire in the vicinity of the beaches. They then moved rapidly inland to the north, east and west, and by 1230 had occupied all Phase I objectives. The 2/7 Commando Squadron, which landed over Green One, pushed eastward along the highway with Sepinggang Airfield as its objective, and crossed the Klandasan River before held up by fire from six heavy machine guns north of the airfield.[15]

Photo 20-3

Left: Anti-tank ditch behind Yellow Beach disclosing placement of log pilings.
Right: Damaged concrete pillbox located behind Yellow Beach.
Commander Task Group 78.2, Action Report – Balikpapan-Manggar-Borneo
June 15-July 6, 1945, 14 August 1945

On Assault Day, a total of 10,500 troops, 700 vehicles, and 1,950 tons of stores were landed over very mediocre quality landing beaches, with a 3 to 4 foot surf further impeding ship-to-shore operations. Troop progress inland, although rapid at first, soon met stiffening resistance from prepared tunnel defenses, revetted batteries, trenches, pill boxes and other defended positions.[16]

Once ashore on Assault Day, 7th Division troops had to fight harder to maintain its beachhead than had forces earlier at Tarakan and Brunei Bay. Nevertheless, by the following day, all initial objectives were occupied and advances were made eastward beyond Sepinggang

Airstrip.   Resistance changed as the Australians moved inland. Increased, concerted Japanese resistance lasted for three weeks until the enemy abandoned their positions and withdrew to the rugged hills of the island. The operational tempo decreased thereafter, but daily engagements with the Japanese continued to add to Australian killed and wounded until the war's end, resulting in a total of 229 Australians killed and 621 wounded (850 total casualties).[17]

Photo 20-4

Balikpapan Australian War Cemetery on a rise below Tank Ridge, which overlooks Balikpapan Bay.
Australian War Memorial photograph 119353

LSM BATTLE STARS

Borneo Operation: Balikpapan Operation			
LSM-1	20 Jun-7 Jul 45	LSM-130	26 Jun-6 Jul 45
LSM-2	20 Jun-7 Jul 45	LSM-148	26 Jun-6 Jul 45
LSM-18	26 Jun-6 Jul 45	LSM-150	26 Jun-6 Jul 45
LSM-19	26 Jun-6 Jul 45	LSM-151 (no BS)	26 Jun-6 Jul 45
LSM-21	26 Jun-6 Jul 45	LSM-205	26 Jun-6 Jul 45
LSM-22	26 Jun-6 Jul 45	LSM-223	26 Jun-6 Jul 45
LSM-36	26 Jun-6 Jul 45	LSM-224 (no BS)	26 Jun-6 Jul 45
LSM-37	26 Jun-6 Jul 45	LSM-257	26 Jun-6 Jul 45
LSM-38	26 Jun-6 Jul 45	LSM-258	26 Jun-6 Jul 45
LSM-39	26 Jun-6 Jul 45	LSM-267 (no BS)	26 Jun-6 Jul 45
LSM-40	26 Jun-6 Jul 45	LSM-310	26 Jun-6 Jul 45
LSM-42	26 Jun-6 Jul 45	LSM-311	26 Jun-6 Jul 45
LSM-129	26 Jun-7 Jul 45	LSM-397	26 Jun-6 Jul 45

The RAN's Contribution to Amphibious Warfare in the Pacific
By Commodore Hector Donohue AM RAN (Rtd)

In March 1942, the Australian Government, recognising the importance of an amphibious capability in any effort to drive the Japanese out of the South West Pacific, began exploring the requirements for combined operations training in Australia. Navy and Army planners, both Australian and US, began to examine both the training and organisation requirements. In addition, in late 1942 the RAN commenced converting HMA (His Majesty's Australian) Ships *Manoora*, *Kanimbla* and *Westralia* to infantry landing ships (LSI). The three passenger liners had been requisitioned in late 1939 and following conversion were deployed as armed merchant cruisers.

HMAS ASSAULT

Photo Postscript-1

Training at HMAS Assault. (AWM)

Approval was granted by the Australian War Cabinet in August 1942 to establish HMAS Assault, a RAN Training Centre, in the Port Stephens area of New South Wales. Assault was initially commissioned onboard the armed merchant cruiser *Westralia* on 1 September 1942 and began providing instruction for landing craft crews, beach parties (naval commandos) and combined operations signals teams. Assault transferred ashore on 10 December 1942 with *Westralia* allocated as a temporary accommodation ship and HMAS *Ping Wo* as her tender.

An American Amphibious Training Group was also established nearby and the two facilities were combined as the Amphibious Training Centre (ATC) in February 1943 under Rear Admiral Daniel E. Barbey, USN, the commander of the South West Pacific Amphibious Force, who answered directly to General MacArthur. (The South West Pacific Force was renamed the US 7th Fleet on 15 March 1943, and Barbey's title became Commander, 7th Amphibious Force.) This brought all combined amphibious training in Australia under US command. Training at Assault, from then on, included US soldiers and Marines, as well as Australian army and navy personnel. Training was intense, covering every aspect of landing operations on hostile shores. Assault also provided operational and logistics support to RAN amphibious units.

Meanwhile, the Australian Army had established training facilities in Queensland, initially a Combined Training Centre at Toorbul Point near Bribie Island north of Brisbane. Cairns Trinity Beach was also used to train troops in all aspects of amphibious warfare before heading into war zones north of Australia.

By October 1943, there were 141 ships and landing craft based at Port Stephens. Thirty-six of these ships were controlled by Assault and 105 by the US Navy.

In early March 1944, with operations underway in New Guinea, training at Assault ceased. It had served its purpose well. In August the base was reduced to a 'care and maintenance' status, decommissioning on 7 April 1945. During its short three-year commission more than 22,000 personnel undertook training there. The training expertise was transferred to a 'mobile team' and moved to Milne Bay in mid-1944 and ultimately to Subic Bay in the Philippines the following year.

INTRODUCTION OF LANDING SHIP INFANTRY

Rear Admiral Daniel E. Barbey, USN, was appointed in command of the South West (later 7th Fleet) Amphibious Force at the end of 1942 but because of the pressing need for amphibious ships in other theatres none were immediately available.

HMAS *Manoora*, recommissioned as an infantry landing ship (LSI) in February 1943, was the first ship to join the force. The two other former Australian armed merchant cruisers were converted to LSI with *Westralia* and *Kanimbla* recommissioning in June 1943.

Manoora and *Kanimbla* were motor vessels of some 11,000 gross registered tons (GRT) and 480 feet long, whilst *Westralia* was slightly smaller at 8,000 GRT and 455 feet long. The three ships carried US landing craft – 20-22 LCVP (Higgins boats) plus 2-3 LCMs (mechanized landing craft) and 1,280 troops. As customary for other USN amphibious ships, landing craft were lowered to the waterline, and the troops embarked in these via down rope ladders.

Photo Postscript-2

HMAS *Westralia* configured as an infantry landing ship. (AWM)

In March 1943 the US attack transport USS *Henry T Allen* joined the force; in June the destroyer tender USS *Rigel* joined, and for the remainder of the year was Barbey's flagship.

From the middle of 1943 until April 1944, these three LSIs, with the *Henry T Allen*, were the only transports available to the Seventh Fleet Amphibious Force. They continued to operate with the Force through the South West Pacific Area operations and accomplished all missions assigned them in a most creditable manner.

7TH FLEET AMPHIBIOUS FORCE OPERATIONS

Operations of the Seventh Fleet Amphibious Force in the South West Pacific Area can be divided into three general phases:

- September 1943 - September 1944: Amphibious landings on the Eastern and Northern Coast of New Guinea; in New Britain, Admiralty Islands; and at Morotai in Indonesia's Maluku Islands
- October 1944 - February 1945: Amphibious landings at Leyte, Mindoro, Lingayen and supporting operations in Luzon culminating in the Bataan-Corregidor landings on 15-16 February 1945
- February 1945 - July 1945: Amphibious landings together with extensive minesweeping operations in the Central, and Southern Philippines including Sulu Archipelago; and Borneo

PHASE I: SEPTEMBER 1943 – SEPTEMBER 1944

Map Postscript-1

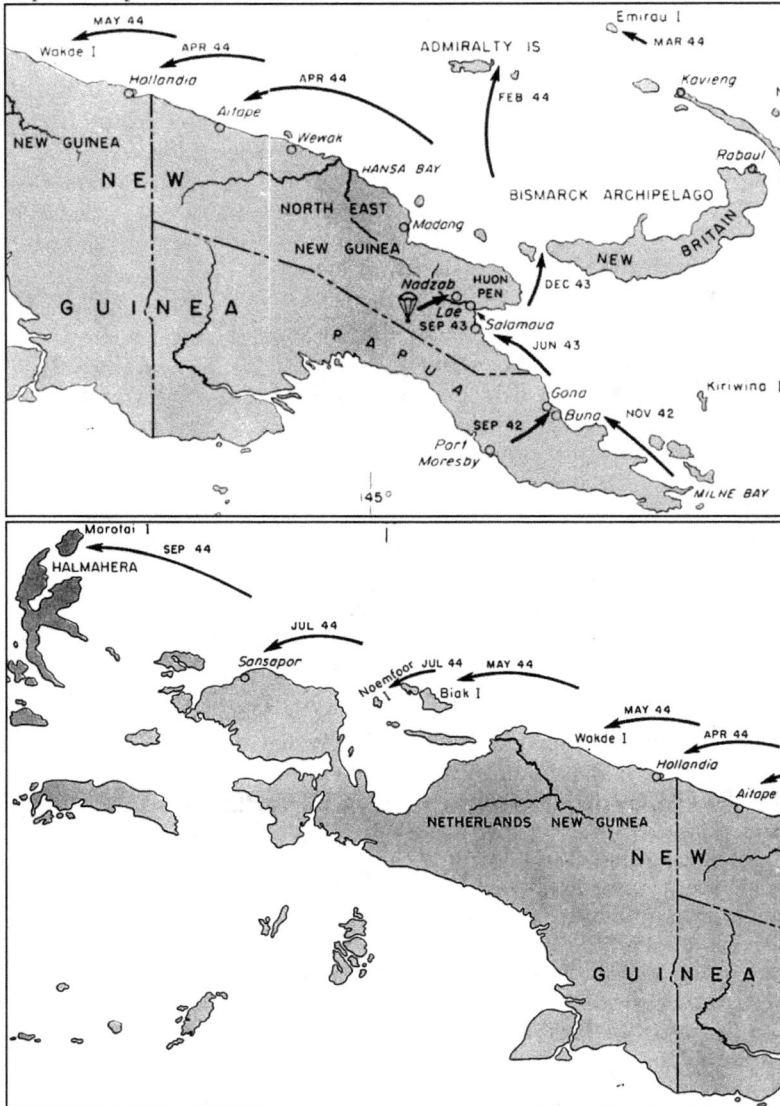

Movement of Allied forces up the Papua New Guinea coast, from Milne Bay (top map, lower right) to Morotai Island (bottom map, upper left)

The amphibious landing at Lae (which may be found on the top map, just to the left of Salamaua) by the 9th Australian Division on 4

September 1943 was the first of a series of assault landings along the New Guinea coast, in the Bismarck Archipelago and in the Halmaheras designed to provide staging areas, minor naval bases, and airfields to support the major assault on the Philippine Islands. From September 1943 to September 1944, the Seventh Amphibious Force made 14 major landings in these areas involving the movement of approximately 300,000 men and 350,000 tons of supplies and equipment.

Following conversion in March 1943, *Manoora* spent the first few months off Port Stephens and Cairns before transporting Australian troops to Milne Bay mid-year. (Following the defeat of the Japanese by Australian forces in September 1942, the first major battle of the war in the Pacific in which Allied troops decisively defeated Japanese land forces, Milne Bay had been developed into a major Allied Base.) *Manoora* transported troops in company with *Kanimbla* to Oro Bay east New Guinea in late August and again in early November. During this period, both ships carried out landing exercises in the Cairns area. *Manoora* returned to Sydney for refit whilst *Kanimbla* remained north.

Westralia conducted a series of training exercises at Port Stephens before transporting US Marines to Goodenough Island near Milne Bay in September. She then conducted further landing exercises and transport of troops to Goodenough Island before being assigned to transport US troops for the landings at Arawe, New Britain on 15 December 1943.

Westralia landed US troops at Cape Cretin (New Guinea) in January 1944. En route from the area on 28 January she was attacked by Japanese aircraft and suffered casualties and damage which was, fortunately, insufficient to put her out of commission. On 5 February she was back at the US base at Cape Cretin south of Finschaven with reinforcements. March and April were spent operating in New Guinea waters including the landings at Hollandia. *Westralia* returned to Sydney on 31 May 1944 for refit.

Kanimbla proceeded to New Guinea in March for exercises with elements of the US 24th Infantry Division at Goodenough Island in preparation for the landings at Hollandia. Allied forces undertook an amphibious landing on 22 April 1944 at Aitape on the northern coast of New Guinea. The amphibious landing was undertaken simultaneously with the landings at Humboldt and Tanahmerah Bays to secure Hollandia to isolate the Japanese 18th Army at Wewak. On 22 April, in company with *Manoora*, five other transports, 16 infantry landing craft and seven tank landing ships, both LSIs participated in the landings at Tanahmerah Bay, Hollandia without incident.

Photo Postscript-3

Landing craft approach the beaches at Tanahmerah Bay, 22 April 1944. (AWM)

In July 1944 *Westralia* again began transporting troops to the forward areas operating from New Guinea bases. August was spent mainly in the Solomon Islands on training exercises, followed by similar duties in the Aitape area in September.

Manoora and *Kanimbla* prepared for the Morotai landings in early September 1944. On 9 September both ships each embarked 1,272 men at Maffin Bay on the northern coast of New Guinea. On 10 September, with 36 other landing ships and supporting vessels of the White Beach Attack Group, they departed for Morotai. The landings took place on 15 September with little opposition and few casualties to the Allied forces. *Manoora* and *Kanimbla* departed for Humboldt Bay (located on the north coast of New Guinea to the east of Hollandia.) arriving 18 September. They were joined by the third Australian LSI, *Westralia*, where they overhauled equipment and embarked troops and supplies for the landings on Leyte.

PHASE II: 2 OCTOBER 1944 – FEBRUARY 1945

The retaking of the Philippines began with an assault on the Leyte Gulf-Surigao Strait area. Planning was complicated by the huge distances involved, for while the Normandy landings on 6 June 1944 were conducted 50 nautical miles across the English Channel, Leyte Gulf was more than 500 nautical miles from the main staging areas in Morotai and Palau. Much of the logistic support had to be sourced from the US west coast, more than 5,000 nautical miles from the front. Because the assault would also take place beyond the range of land-based aircraft, all air support would need to come from US Navy aircraft carriers. The advance from Morotai to Leyte in one bound was a calculated risk, as the Allied forces would be ringed by Japanese airfields and land-based aircraft with greater staying power (time on station) than the aircraft from US Navy aircraft carriers.

Commanded by Vice Admiral Thomas C. Kinkaid, USN, the US Seventh Fleet and assigned elements of the US Third Fleet together formed Task Force 77 and the Central Philippines Attack Force, and comprised 157 combat ships (including 6 battleships, 11 cruisers and 18 escort carriers), 420 amphibious ships and 84 patrol, minesweeping and hydrographic vessels. Another 17 aircraft carriers, 6 battleships, 16 cruisers and 56 destroyers of the Third Fleet, under Admiral William F. Halsey Jr., USN, were tasked with covering the invasion.

The RAN's contribution to Kinkaid's force, under the command of Commodore John A Collins (later Vice Admiral), consisted of the heavy cruisers HMA Ships *Australia* and *Shropshire*; the destroyers *Arunta* and *Warramunga*; the infantry landing ships *Manoora*, *Kanimbla* and *Westralia*; the frigate *Gascoyne*; and the motor launch *HDML 1074*. The RAN was also represented in Task Group 77.7 (the Leyte Gulf Service Force of the Seventh Fleet) by the oiler *Bishopdale*, the provision ship *Merkur* and the ammunition ships *Poyang* and *Yunnan*.

A full-scale rehearsal was carried out at Tanahmerah Bay on 10 October. On 13 October the three Australian LSIs departed for Leyte as part of a large assault convoy escorted by a covering force of US and Australian cruisers and destroyers. The Australian landing ships were part of the Panaon Attack Group which detached from the main group at 0200 on the morning of 20 October arriving off Panaon at 0845. No Japanese resistance was encountered. Within 45 minutes the three Australian ships had disembarked over 2,800 troops of the US 21st Regimental Combat Team on the undefended island. The LSIs then sailed for Humboldt Bay arriving on 25 October 1944.

During November, the three LSIs were engaged in transporting troops from Humboldt Bay to Leyte. On 30 November they, and 15 other ships designated Transport Group 'A', commenced embarking troops and stores for the Lingayen landings. Transport Group 'A' then proceeded to Lae where, in company with Landing Group 'B', practice landings were carried out. The ships then sailed for Manus Island. On

31 December they departed Manus to execute Assault Mike I on Luzon Island in Lingayen Gulf.

Photo Postscript-4

Crewmembers of HMAS *Kanimbla*, watch the ship's landing craft as they proceed towards the beach in the first wave of the landing in Brunei Bay, June 1945. (AWM)

As part of Task Force 79, the Lingayen Attack Force, *Manoora*, *Kanimbla* and *Westralia* passed through Surigao Strait and proceeded up the western side of the Philippine Archipelago to Lingayen Gulf, arriving on 8 January 1945. As the convoy made its final approach to the Gulf, it was subjected to air attack. Following a suicide attack which damaged the escort carrier USS *Kitkun Bay*, *Westralia* was attacked by a Kamikaze (Zero fighter) from astern. The final steep dive indicated it was aimed at the bridge, but the gunners onboard maintained a strong barrage and shot the aircraft down some 10 feet from the stern. There were no casualties, but the steering gear was disabled for a short time. The troops were landed on 9 January, supported by a heavy bombardment. The LSIs discharged their cargoes rapidly and left the area that evening to avoid further air attack, returning via Leyte to Morotai, arriving on 21 January 1945.

The LSIs were now wearing a new paint scheme. Following the landings at Lingayen Gulf a decision was made to apply camouflage paint schemes to all three Australian LSIs. The ships continued conducting transport duties in the area.

Photo Postscript-5

HMAS *Manoora* at Morotai Island, January 1945, with new paint scheme. (AWM)

Kanimbla returned to Sydney for refit on 7 March 1945 and on completion of the refit, in late April she embarked Australian troops in Brisbane and discharged them in Morotai mid-May.

PHASE III: 3 FEBRUARY-JULY 1945 – BORNEO

The Borneo campaign of 1945 was one of the most complex operations involving Australian land, air and sea forces in the war. It was also the last Australian campaign to be planned and undertaken. Initial plans called for six OBOE operations (code name for a series of amphibious assaults). However, as the Allied offensives progressed closer to Japan, OBOE THREE, FOUR and FIVE were cancelled. The remaining three amphibious landings were: OBOE ONE, the invasion of Tarakan Island; OBOE SIX, the invasion of north Borneo at Labuan and Brunei; and OBOE TWO, the invasion of Balikpapan.

Manoora and *Westralia* were engaged in the Australian landings on Tarakan (OBOE ONE). Embarking Australian units for the first time, the LSIs sailed from Morotai on 27 April 1945, each ship towing a tank landing craft (LCT). The transport force arrived off Tarakan on 30 April and the LCTs were slipped. The troops were successfully landed on 1 May and the ships finished discharging their cargoes the next day. They then departed for Morotai where further stores were loaded and brought forward to the landing beaches. By mid-May *Kanimbla* had re-joined the group.

The next operation was the invasion of Brunei, OBOE SIX. The three LSIs departed Morotai on 4 June, in company with a large group of US Navy ships, mostly landing ships and landing craft. They arrived off Brunei on 10 June and commenced landing troops on Green Beach just before 0900 with little or no opposition. After unloading cargo that day they set sail for Morotai on 11 June, arriving on 14 June 1945.

Map Postscript-2

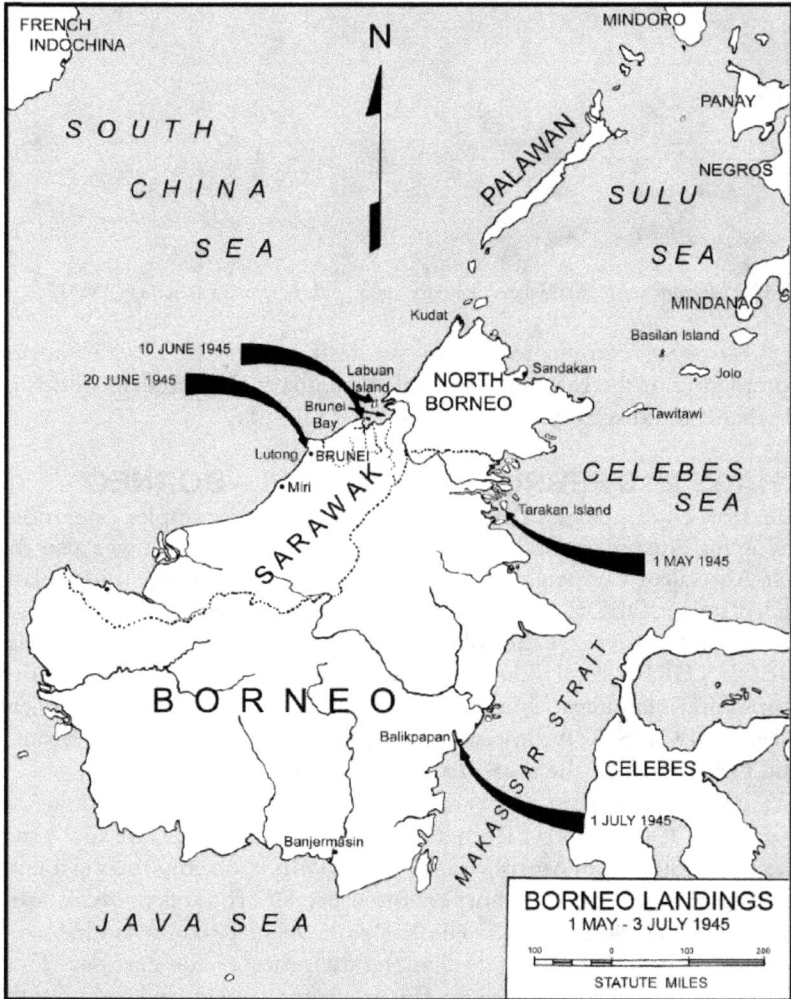

Borneo

The final amphibious operation in which the LSIs took part was the Balikpapan landing, OBOE TWO. It was the largest ever amphibious assault by Australian forces with more than 33,000 personnel landed. After embarking troops and cargo at Morotai, *Manoora*, *Kanimbla* and *Westralia* sailed on 26 June 1945, arriving off Balikpapan on 1 July 1945. That day was spent disembarking troops and unloading the cargo after which the ships sailed for Morotai at 1930. Arriving on 4 July, they embarked reinforcements and departed the same day, returning to Balikpapan on 7 July. It was the LSIs last operation together and the remainder of the war was spent on transport duties around New Guinea, the Philippines and Borneo.

Photo Postscript-6

HMAS *Manoora*, 1944, showing the LCVPs (Higgins boats) carried by davits along her ship's side and on the deck between the bridge and the funnel. (AWM)

Photo Postscript-7

Troops scrambling down nets slung over the side of HMAS *Kanimbla* into landing craft (Higgins boats), for the OBOE SIX Operation Landing, 10 June 1945. (AWM)

THE LSI COMMANDING OFFICERS

During the period they were active as LSIs, each ship had two commanding officers, all being members of the RAN Reserve (Seagoing). It is interesting to briefly review their careers as it offers a snapshot of a typical wartime service for qualified seagoing officers. Of the six officers, three had joined the second entry of the newly formed Royal Australian Naval College in 1914, served briefly in the North Sea in 1918 and ultimately transferred to the reserve, before returning to full time service at the outbreak of World War II. Given the adverse impact on the RAN during the Depression, early retirement of RAN officers was common. Of the remaining three, one was ex-Royal Navy Reserve and merchant marine officer, whilst the other two were ex-merchant marine officers who had enlisted in the RANR(S) in the early 1930s. Four of the six received awards for their time in command of an LSI.

Cecil Claude Baldwin

Cecil Claude Baldwin was born in Kempsey, NSW on 30 September 1900 and joined the RAN College in 1914 as a member of the second college intake, graduating as a midshipman in January 1918. He joined the heavy cruiser HMAS *Australia* in March 1918 for training. He was promoted to Lieutenant in March 1922 and following further training in UK served in the RAN cruisers *Melbourne*, *Sydney*, *Adelaide* and *Australia* during the 1920s and mid-1930s. He was appointed Personal aide-de-camp to the Duke of Gloucester during his Australian visit October/December 1934 and in April 1935 was awarded an MVO (Member Royal Victorian Order) medal.

Baldwin was promoted commander in September 1936 and transferred to the Reserve the next month. At the outbreak of war, Baldwin joined Flinders Naval Depot, the primary RAN Training Establishment (HMAS Cerberus) and assumed command of *Manoora* and as Senior Naval Officer Australian Landing Ships, after her conversion as an LSI on 29 June 1943, as an acting captain. He was involved in training and transporting of troops until her refit in December 1944. He was then appointed as Naval Officer in Charge, Darwin until his death by illness on 10 April 1945.

Norman Hamon Shaw

Norman Hamon Shaw was born in Perth, WA on 9 July 1900 and joined the RAN College in 1914 graduating as a midshipman in January 1918. Following training at sea he was promoted lieutenant in September 1921 and joined the cruiser *Melbourne*. He returned to the UK in November 1924 to qualify as a submariner. In mid-1926 he commanded the RN submarine *H27* before standing by (assigned as part of the crew of) the first RAN submarine HMAS *Oxley* in early 1927. She commissioned in June 1928 and Shaw was posted in command in February 1929. Given the financial constraints at the time the RAN determined not to continue to introduce a submarine capability and returned them to RN service in April 1931. Shaw spent three years exchange service in the RN before returning to Australia in 1934 and shortly after transferred to the RANR(S).

On the outbreak of war, he mobilised and was posted as executive officer of the newly commissioned armed merchant cruiser HMAS *Manoora* and was promoted acting commander in September 1940. Following a short period ashore in Brisbane from mid-1942, he was appointed in command of HMAS *Kanimbla* on commissioning as an LSI in June 1943. He remained in command until June 1944, participating in the amphibious assault by US troops at Hollandia in April. He commanded the naval depot HMAS Kuttabul in Sydney and was confirmed as a commander in January 1946. In July 1949 he was appointed to command the Australian Naval Dockyard Police with the rank of Superintendent – a role he fulfilled until his retirement on 5 August 1958. He was awarded an OBE (Order of the British Empire) in the 1951 New Year's Honours List for his long and distinguished service to the RAN and concurrently the Naval Dockyard Police.

Alfred Victor Knight

Photo Postscript-8

Commander Alfred Victor Knight on the bridge of HMAS *Westralia* holding the ship's mascot, 1943. (AWM)

Alfred Victor Knight was born in Dover, England on 20 February 1897 and joined the merchant marine as a cadet in 1912. Following the outbreak of World War I, he joined the Royal Navy Reserve. As a sub lieutenant, he was awarded the DSC (Distinguished Service Cross) for his conspicuous bravery under heavy enemy fire whilst involved in an assault on Ostende Harbour in April 1918. He also received a MID (Mention in Despatches) as a lieutenant after the war for his service in minesweeping. Post war he returned to the merchant marine and after moving to Australia, he joined the RANR(S) as a lieutenant in 1923. Promotion to lieutenant commander followed in 1931 and commander in 1937.

He mobilised in March 1940, joining the Naval Staff in Melbourne before serving as Commanding Officer of the newly commissioned *Bathurst*-class corvette, HMAS *Lithgow* in June 1941. During this time *Lithgow* swept German-laid mines in Bass Strait, assisted in the sinking of a Japanese submarine off Darwin, escorted the first contingent of Allied troops from Townsville to Milne Bay, and took part in the campaign to recapture Buna in northern New Guinea. For his services in *Lithgow*, Knight was awarded the OBE.

Knight was appointed Commanding Officer of HMAS *Westralia* in February 1943, remaining there until December 1943, taking part in the Allied landings at Arawe, New Britain; Humboldt Bay, New Guinea; and Panaon in the Philippines. For exceptional service in command Knight was awarded the US Legion of Merit. The citation described him as a 'forceful leader,' and by his 'splendid cooperation in the conduct of a vital training programme, aggressive determination and untiring energies' he had 'contributed materially to combined large-scale operations and the successful prosecution of the war' in the South West Pacific Area. He returned to shore duty and was promoted captain on 31 December 1946. He retired from the RANR(S) on 19 February 1952.

Allan Paterson Cousin

Allan Paterson Cousin was born in Clifton, Queensland on 29 March 1900 and joined the RAN College in 1914 graduating as a midshipman in January 1918. Following training at sea he was promoted lieutenant in October 1922 but resigned his commission on 23 April 1923 and joined the Union Steam Ship Co. of New Zealand Ltd. He transferred to the RANR(S) as a lieutenant in April 1925. He was promoted to lieutenant commander in 1930 and commander on 30 June 1936.

He mobilised in March 1941 and in December took command of the newly commissioned *Bathurst*-class corvette, HMAS *Katoomba*. She joined the 24th Minesweeping Flotilla at Darwin and participated in the action in which the Japanese submarine *I-124* was sunk on 20 January 1942. *Katoomba* then began a period of escort duty to New Guinea, shepherding convoys between Townsville and Port Moresby, Milne Bay and Oro Bay.

On 27 January 1944 Cousin was appointed to command *Manoora*, and as Senior Naval Officer, Australian Landing Ships. Between April 1944 and July 1945 *Manoora* landed troops in Netherlands New Guinea at Tanahmerah Bay, Wakde and Morotai; in the Philippines at Leyte and Lingayen Gulf, Luzon; and in Borneo and Brunei at Tarakan, Labuan and Balikpapan. Cousin was awarded the DSO (Distinguished Service Order) in October 1945 for his 'gallantry, fortitude and skill' during the amphibious assaults. He was promoted acting captain in February 1945 and confirmed in the rank on 30 June 1946.

Cousin transferred to command *Kanimbla* in January 1948. She conducted two trips to Japan repatriating prisoners of war and transporting personnel of the British Commonwealth Occupation Force in the first half of 1948. In July, she took personnel and stores to the UK to commission HMAS *Sydney*, returning with British personnel who had enlisted in the RAN as well as 432 displaced persons. After one more voyage to Japan she was decommissioned in Sydney on 25 March 1949. Cousin was demobilised in May 1949.

Andrew Veitch Bunyan

Andrew Veitch Bunyan, born in Leith, Scotland on 17 February 1902, qualified as a master mariner and joined the RANR(S) as a lieutenant in September 1930. He regularly completed Reserve training during the 1930s and mobilised in February 1940. He was promoted to acting lieutenant commander in December 1939 and confirmed in November 1940. In March 1940 he joined the sloop HMAS *Swan* as executive officer and on 6 December assumed command of the newly commissioned corvette HMAS *Bathurst*. After a short period sweeping German mines on Australia's east coast, *Bathurst* deployed to Colombo mid-1941, joining the RN Eastern Fleet for escort and patrol duties in the Indian Ocean, Persian Gulf and Arabian Sea.

Bunyan was relieved in October and after leave joined *Manoora* as executive officer in April 1943. In September 1943, he moved on to command of *Swan* and was promoted to commander in December. *Swan* was assigned to New Guinea waters for escort and patrol duties, and as a fire support ship for military operations ashore. Bunyan was appointed in command of *Kanimbla* in August 1944. She participated in the landings at Morotai, Leyte and Lingayen Gulf and at Tarakan, Labuan and Balikpapan. In October 1945 he was awarded the DSC 'for gallantry, fortitude and skill whilst serving in HMAS *Kanimbla* in numerous amphibious assaults in the South West Pacific Area, including operations in New Guinea, the Philippines and Borneo.' In September 1945 he was posted ashore and demobilised from the RANR(S).

Eric Walton Livingston

Eric Walton Livingston was born in Balmain, Sydney on 27 January 1903 and qualified as a master mariner before joining the RANR(S) as a lieutenant in August 1931. He regularly completed Reserve training during the 1930s and mobilised in February 1940. He was appointed in command of HMAS *Bingen*, an auxiliary anti-submarine vessel and was promoted lieutenant commander in March. In September 1940 he was posted in command of the newly commissioned anti-submarine auxiliary vessel, HMAS *Wyrallah*, which was re-named *Wilcannia* in February 1942, to avoid confusion with the new *Bathurst*-class corvette, HMAS *Whyalla*.

Wyrallah commenced service as an anti-submarine/patrol vessel on the west coast where in November 1941 she participated in the search for HMAS *Sydney* survivors. As *Wilcannia*, she was moved to New Guinea and South Pacific waters to carry out patrols, pilot rescues and transport of stores, returning to the Darwin area in early 1943.

Livingston took command of *Westralia* in December 1943 and continued reinforcing the build-up of troops in Leyte before participating in the Lingayen Gulf landings and ultimately the landings in Borneo. He was in command during the Kamikaze attack in January 1945 when well-aimed fire from *Westralia*'s guns caused the aircraft to disintegrate and crash ten feet astern. He was promoted to acting commander in February 1945. In October 1945 he was awarded the DSC 'for gallantry, fortitude and skill whilst serving in HMAS *Westralia* in numerous amphibious assaults in the South West Pacific Area, including operations in the Philippines and Borneo.' He remained in command of *Westralia* until November 1945, when he was demobilised but remained in the Reserve. He was confirmed as a commander RANR(S) in December 1945 and retired from the Reserve in 1953.

Appendix A: USS *LSM(R)-188* Casualties from Enemy Action on 29 March 1945

Killed in Action:

ADAMS, Gilmer Eugene, 710 35 72, S1c, V6, USNR.
COOPER, William Albert, 961 92 37, S1c, V6 USNR SV.
FLASHER, James Ralph, 923 18 09, RM3/c, USN-I
LEMON, Weldon (n), 931 11 68, StM1/c, V6 USNR SV.
LOOS, Carl Thomas, 612 36 91, GM2/c, V6, USNR.
MC PHERON, Robert Arthur, S1c, 962 53 29, V6 USNR SV.
MILLER, Albert Franklin, GM1/c, 372 42 01, USN.
ZAHN, Harold Carl, 321 70 24, PhM 1/c, USN.
LIGON, Carroll Burton, 848 97 06, FC3/c, V6 USNR SV.
BROOKS, George Edward, S1c, 924 49 04, V6 USNR SV.
MADER, William Paul, S1c, 955 82 58, V6 USNR SV.
OLEWNIK, Joseph Paul, 653 17 82, COX, V6 USNR.
PRADA, Edwin Martin, S1c, 801 46 31, V6 USNR.
SLEASE, Jack Hartford, S1c, 955 82 49, V6 USNR SV.
WRIGHT, William David, S1c, 924 08 63, V6 USNR SV.

Wounded in Action:

Ensign, Frederick Sawyer CLAPPER, 344446, θ(V)S, USNR.
Ensign, Edward Louis CONRAD, 331232, (DE)L, USNR.
ALBERT, Allen Edward, COX, 246 40 16, V6 USNR.
ANDERS, Delbert Relman, S2c, 941 49 27, V6 USNR SV.
ANDERSON, Alvin Martin, S1c, 387 17 61, USN.
ANDERSON, Wesley Greenhill, F2c, 817 02 03, USN-I.
BESSELL, Fredrick August Herman, Sr., SC3/c, 945 22 25, V6S
DELANE, Russell (n), S1c, 656 95 15, USNR.
FIRKINS, George John Jr., QM3/c, 869 56 28, V6 USNR SV.
FERRYMAN, Marlin Milton, F1c, 941 44 14, V6 USNR SV.
GILLIS, Norman Farren, MoMM3/c, 932 66 34, V6 USNR SV.
GROSKINSKY, Elmer Keith, 957 08 33, RM3/c, V6 USNR SV.
GUIANEN, John Joseph, S1c, 924 14 51, V6 USNR SV.
HAMMARBERG, Robert Anton, S1c, 711 97 49, V6 USNR.
HIBBARD, Milton Floyd, COX, 337 03 14, V6 USNR SV.
JOHNSTON, Richard Anthony, SM3/c, 383 21 61, USN.
LINK, Edward John, S1c, 712 32 24, V6 USNR.
LOWERY, Rudolph Valentino, RM3/c, 836 07 42, V6 USNR SV.
MASOKA, Michael Robert, S1c, 256 36 73, USN.
MC CORMIC, Joseph William, COX, 560 71 86, V6 USNR.
MC HUGH, Bernard William, QM3/c, 803 53 81, V6 USNR SV.
PLESKO, Harry Frank, MoMM3/c, 285 62 75, V6 USNR.
RAY, William Claude, BM2/c, 656 25 89, V6 USNR.
READENOUR, Melvin Junior, S2c, 978 44 61, USN-I.
RUDNICK, Michael Jr., COX, 817 52 39, V6 USNR SV.
SANTIAGO, Rafael Louis, S1c, 707 44 35, V6 USNR.
SMITH, "A" "J", S2c, 952 88 26, USN-I.
SMITH, Edward Lyle, SK3/c, 896 26 76, V6 USNR SV.
TETRAULT, Hector Amede, F1c, 803 92 67, USN-I.
VENTERS, Walter Raymond, GM2/c, 706 09 05, V6 USNR.
WEED, Burton, Eugene, MoMM3/c, 246 21 58, USN.
WISE, Robert Riley, S1c, 755 92 48, V6, USNR.

Appendix B: USS *LSM(R)-195* Casualties from Enemy Action on 3 May 1945

PERSONNEL REPORT (As of 6 May 1945).

349463	EALY, "A" "G" ENS.	Surv.
330506	MC KELVEY, James R. ENS.	WIA
396889	MILLIKEN, Thomas H. ENS	MIA
362712	PETERSON, Erik D. ENS	Surv.
348545	SOLOOK, Edward ENS	Surv.
188432	WOODSON, Jr., William E. LT.	Surv.
659 72 61	BABER, Charles H.	Surv.
664 82 45	BELL, Leren F.	Surv.
959 86 16	BERQUIST, Arnold E.	Surv.
343 14 04	BOWLIN, Ronald V.	Surv.
251 44 69	BURKE, William J.	MIA
959 86 86	BUTZKE, Melvin H.	Surv.
322 27 92	CARNICLE, Lewis W.	Surv.
622 82 56	CATCHPOLE, Harold C.	Surv.
726 96 65	COHEN, Albert J.	Surv.
978 36 29	COLLINS, Otis B.	WIA
338 84 97	CRIDER, Russell E.	Surv.
956 18 08	DARLING, Gerald R.	Surv.
338 85 07	DECLUE, John C.	Surv.
577 50 49	DELEON, Odilon (n)	WIA
338 84 10	DENNEY, Lloyd L.	Surv.
314 13 85	DENNY, William R.	Surv.
730 86 50	DENSON, Robert L.	Surv.
577 52 72	DESPAIN, Howard G.	Surv.
577 50 63	DICKENS, Karl L.	MIA
879 80 11	DOSS, Charles A.	Surv.
758 84 47	DOWNES, Vernon J.	WIA
871 49 75	DRAGER, Leslie L.	Surv.
962 63 01	DUVALL, Jr., Leslie L.	Surv.
577 30 03	EDWARDS, Jr., Othe W.	Surv.
609 63 08	ERNST, William J.	Surv.
949 69 45	FRANCIS, John B.	Surv.
927 61 03	GAME, William C.	WIA
868 62 61	GARLICK, Samuel M.	WIA
201 71 54	GOULD, Allan W.	Surv.
952 64 33	GRZESIKOWSKI, Edward (n)	Surv.
943 72 69	GUDGEL, Jesse (n)	WIA
819 68 85	HAAS, Jr., Charles F.	Surv.
861 74 61	HALE, Joseph A.	KIA
293 58 89	HART, Kenneth D.	Surv.
566 20 07	HOLLINGSWORTH, H. L.	Surv.
283 57 39	HOWELL, Ralph B.	Surv.
961 94 50	HOWLETT, Vernon F.	WIA

930 47 20	JACOBS, Walter (n)	WIA
722 24 43	JERNIGAN, James S.	Surv.
727 36 00	JOHNSON, Jr., Edwin H.	Surv.
725 53 18	JOZWIAK, Walter (n)	Surv.
958 93 68	KEETON, Max O.	Surv.
272 96 22	KELLEY, Earl N.	WIA
816 50 31	KERNES, Hyman (n)	MIA
306 82 65	KLUMPP, Donald (n)	Surv.
936 14 00	KORZENDORFER, Roy F.	Surv.
600 72 85	KOWALSKI, Stanley P.	WIA
932 09 15	LEDBETTER, Howard W.	Surv.
656 83 79	LEGGETT, James A.	Surv.
859 98 85	LISTEN, Terence W.	Surv.
895 74 16	LORENZ, Leonard V.	Surv.
614 72 81	MARSH, Russell	Surv.
313 84 61	MASTERS, Charles J.	WIA
896 14 66	MC CHESNEY, Joseph H.	Surv.
905 61 82	MC GORTY, James P.	Surv.
753 32 58	MC MAHAN, Robert (n)	Surv.
948 76 77	MEYERS, Robert E.	WIA
565 22 91	MURILLO, David	Surv.
865 51 48	OVERHOLSER, Junior L.	Surv.
923 55 17	PIZUR, Francis E.	Surv.
906 79 75	PURRMAN, John F.	Surv.
906 76 14	RAFFAELLI, Bruno D.	Surv.
962 62 91	RESTEMEYER, James E.	Surv.
952 62 47	RUHLMAN, George J.	MIA
978 36 40	SHUTTE, Eugene R.	Surv.
647 36 55	STYLES, Daniel W.	MIA
251 57 20	TALLARY, Jr., James	KIA
948 81 79	THOMAS, Vernon E.	WIA
955 81 75	THOMPSON, John E.	WIA
877 33 82	TRAGER, Reinhold V.	Surv.
611 02 51	WESHO, Walter (n)	Surv.
615 83 25	WIERSBICKI, S. T.	Surv.
727 36 37	ZEIGLER, Theodore L.	WIA
285 77 72	ZIMMERMAN, Duane A.	Surv.

Appendix C: USS *LSM(R)-190* Casualties from Enemy Action on 4 May 1945

Personnel Report as of 6 May 1945

NAME	RANK/RATE	FILE/SERVICE NO.	
SAUNDERS, R. H.	Lieutenant	102467	WIA
HARMON, George T.	Lt.(jg)	348361	Surv.
BURKHART, S. E.	Lt.(jg)(mc)	380568	Surv.
TENNIS, L. S.	Ensign	370195	Surv.
BJORKLUND, S. C.	Ensign	361244	KIA
ETTER, G. E.	Ensign	331271	Surv.
BENNER, J. R.	Ensign	401676	WIA
ABBONDANZA, Ralph A.	S2c	908 53 18	WIA
ADAMS, James	S1c	246 06 78	Surv.
ARMSTRONG, Arthur A.	EM2c	706 50 09	KIA
BAILES, Roy N.	S2c	949 69 79	Surv.
BENDER, Harold R.	RdM3c(T)	806 29 89	Surv.
BENZA, Salvatore P.	S2c	713 31 77	Surv.
BERNDT, William D.	MoMM3c	628 03 18	Surv.
BIANUCCI, Alexander	RM3c(T)	923 25 25	Surv.
BLANKENBURG, John E.	S2c	898 75 52	Surv.
BLIESATH, Paul F.	S2c	601 83 81	Surv.
BOZENA, Tadeus V.	GM3c	244 84 66	Surv.
BURTON, Herbert MMN	S2c	958 90 50	Surv.
CARPENTER, Joseph H.	S1c	932 30 44	MIA
CASINO, Anthony W.	RM3c(T)	816 52 31	WIA
CHERNEY, Henry A.	S2c	713 27 73	MIA
COLCLOUGH, Herbert L.	F1c	905 65 35	KIAv.
CONNELLY, Edward W.	F1c	727 05 00	Surv.
COX, Cecil C.	FCO3c	895 48 28	MIA
CROOM, Marion F.	Cox(T)	969 15 51	WIA
DAVIS, Grant R.	F1c	952 27 60	WIA
DUTTON, Thomas J., Jr.	GM1c	707 86 65	MIA
EDSALL, Burnett Jr.	GM3c	825 10 89	WIA
ESCUE, Donald E.	S1c	952 70 84	Surv.
FORET, Eugene T., Jr.	GM3c	645 62 25	Surv.
FOWINKLE, Leon G.	SC3(T)	966 33 50	Surv.
GILLINGHAM, Robert S.	EM3c(T)	413 49 41	Surv.
GLEICH, Norman MMN	S1c	908 21 80	Surv.
GOSNELL, Frank M.	Y1c(T)	626 37 66	Surv.
GOULDEN, Wallace W.	MoMM3c(T)	888 25 90	Surv.
HALL, Donald J.	S1c	313 25 57	Surv.
HALL, Forest G.	S1c	782 00 16	Surv.
HALL, John E.	QM3c(T)	951 41 62	WIA
HALLEY, David (n)	StM2c	908 82 01	Surv.
HARDIN, Ernest G., Jr.	SK3c(T)	764 64 89	Surv.
HASBROUCK, John D.	GM1c	311 54 78	MIA
HEDMAN, Reynolds O.	S1c	952 71 46	Surv.
HOUSTON, Dewey (n)	F1c	882 77 23	WIA
HOWER, William F.	F1c	883 94 52	WIA

JOHNSON, Floyd H.	S2c	955 87 30	Surv.
KARANUTSOS, James Jr.	S1c	874 95 42	KIA
KORORES, Christ (n)	RM2c(T)	611 05 66	Surv.
KONONCHUK, John (n)	F1c	952 66 39	Surv.
LAUGHEAD, Dale E.	S1c	945 22 02	Surv.
MASSI, James A.	S1c	709 58 00	WIA
MC CUSKER, David E.	F1c	923 58 03	Surv.
MC DONNELL, Curtis L.	S1c	245 61 01	WIA
MC NEES, Wilbur Y., Jr.	F1c	251 20 96	Surv.
NADEAU, Normand L.	F1c	803 77 31	Surv.
NEWLAND, Robert W.	S1c	962 53 21	Surv.
NUBER, William J.	RM3c(T)	894 95 57	Surv.
OPAS, Nickolas (n)	Cox(T)	756 00 13	WIA
PERSON, Carl N.	RdM3c(T)	667 66 34	Surv.
PEYRON, Maurice P.	EM1c(T)	660 15 88	Surv.
POOLE, Mark Joseph	F1c	888 34 54	Surv.
POWELL, Lawrence O.	S2c	924 13 64	Surv.
RICKER, Charles E.	QM3c(T)	858 57 39	Surv.
RILEY, James T.	S2c	961 26 34	Surv.
ROBERTS, James K.	S2c	932 33 57	Surv.
SALVATORE, Joseph A.	PhM2c	224 95 43	Surv.
SCHEUERING, Joseph L.	S1c	924 97 85	WIA
SCOTT, Robert (n)	S1c	924 13 65	WIA
SHENEMAN, Ralph Jr.	S2c	635 41 06	WIA
SIMPSON, James S.	B1c	844 94 97	Surv.
SMITH, Edgar E. Jr.	S2c	635 40 98	Surv.
SPENCER, George O.	CMoMM(T)	906 70 40	Surv.
STANDKE, Clarence G.	S1c	959 46 85	Surv.
STURGEON, Ivan L.	S1c	723 66 24	MIA
SWAYNE, Henry F., Jr.	F1c	342 99 42	WIA
TOY, William H.	S1c	932 10 61	KIA
VANDERBECK, James H.	SC1c(B)(T)	654 65 51	Surv.
VANDERHOOF, Leroy L.	SM3c(T)	601 66 11	Surv.
WAY, Norman E.	F2c	961 73 37	Surv.
WEBB, Joseph H.	F1c	557 30 93	WIA
WEBSTER, Ernest M.	SM3c(T)	842 89 57	Surv.
WESTRICH, Richard A.	S1c	874 37 37	Surv.
WHALEY, Francis L.	GM2c	238 87 17	MIA
WILLIAMS, Frederick C.	S1c	955 87 58	WIA

Appendix D: USS *LSM(R)-194* Casualties from Enemy Action on 4 May 1945

HIRSHBERG, Allan M.	Lt.	228315	Surv.
DURHAM, James W.	Ens.	352557	WIA
WICKSER, John P.	Ens.	369349	WIA
STINSON, John M.	Ens.	329953	WIA
KIRKWOOD, Bruce K.	Ens.	367 485	Surv.
MENZEL, Alfred E.	Esn.	393309	Not aboard, previously casualty.

ALEXANDER, Charles J.	GM2c	268 87 11	Surv.
ARNHOLD, Albert J.	S1c	956 43 11	MIA
BABCOCK, George R.	S2c	314 13 32	WIA
BAUMAN, Charles F.	GM1c	821 31 13	Surv.
BELANGER, Stewart F.	S2c	306 55 38	WIA
BENTON, Mervin B.	SK3c	827 57 28	Surv.
BLEAKLEY, Edward T.	S1c	343 14 18	MIA
BOSWORTH, Ralph B.	S1c	952 71 02	Surv.
BRITT, Leon A.	S1c	975 57 42	WIA
BROEKER, Ralph W.	S1c	955 97 41	Surv.
BUTLER, Robert L.	SO3c	820 09 89	Surv.
CALLEN, Joseph B.	S1c	651 77 73	MIA
CANNON, Horace I.	F1c	830 89 84	WIA
CANNON, Lyman L.	RdM3c	885 38 38	Surv.
CARR, Boyd L.	S2c	329 59 83	MIA
COLLINS, Leonard P.	S2c	973 14 81	MIA
CONTRONE, John M. Sr.	S1c	816 35 19	Surv.
COOPER, Russel J.	S2c	313 20 30	Surv.
CROCKER, William L.	S1c	343 13 72	Surv.
DEANE, Rae G.	S1c	893 66 07	WIA
DESCHNER, Donald B.	S1c	306 94 15	Surv.
DESPARD, John R.	MoMM2c	234 43 81	MIA
DICKERSON, Harry L.	S1c	978 44 55	WIA
DRAKE, George G.	CMoMM(T)	670 02 86	Surv.
DURICA, Joseph (n)	S1c	949 70 03	Surv.
DURVETSKY, Metre (n)	S1c	806 52 52	WIA
ECKERMAN, Francis J.	S1c	727 31 06	Surv.
ELLIS, Clarence L.	S1c	314 13 73	MIA
FITTS, Asa E.	MoMM3c	956 60 70	MIA
GARDNER, Jack B.	F1c	923 40 82	Surv.
GATTO, Steve A.	MoMM4c	805 30 57	Surv.
GILBERTSON, Donald L.	EM3c	329 35 61	WIA
GRAHAM, Willie L.	StM1c	885 51 97	Surv.
GROEMAN, Donald L.	EM3c	894 81 43	Sruv.
GROOTHUIS, Peter M.	S1c	952 75 48	Surv.
HABKIRK, Keith H.	FC3c	894 94 43	Surv.
HOUGH, Leroy V.	F1c	924 14 58	Surv.
JOHNSON, Alfred S.	F1c	955 70 95	Surv.
KANNER, Harry (n)	QM3c	828 31 12	Surv.
KEARNEY, John P.	GM2c	651 49 64	Surv.
KULIGOWSKI, Edward J.	F1c	949 44 82	MIA
LANGWIN, Dominic P.	S2c	300 92 47	Surv.
LIEBHART, Ramon A.	S1c	945 38 94	WIA

LUNSFORD, Lloyd E.	S2c	641 87 88	Surv.
LURDING, John B. Jr.	BM2c	634 29 76	Surv.
MAJESKA, Walter H. L.	BM2c	300 23 31	Surv.
MALAGRINO, James (n)	SM3c	816 65 14	Surv.
MC CURRY, William F.	F1c	825 59 82	Surv.
MC LAUGHLIN, Francis A.	BdM3c	245 47 17	Surv.
MC GEHEE, Havey M.	MoMM3c	844 26 32	WIA
MYEROWITZ, Herbert (n)	F1c	713 12 52	MIA
MUELLER, Clifford J.	S1c	727 35 39	WIA
MURPHY, Joseph L.	EM3c	835 89 63	Surv.
NOWAK, Walter M.	QM3c	951 36 97	Surv.
OGDEN, Earl E.	S1c	943 66 05	Surv.
OLMSTED, Earl M.	SC1c	644 21 82	Surv.
PHIPPS, Evans P1	S1c	935 09 29	Surv.
PLACE, Keith A.	F1c	313 50 73	MIA
RAMPAGE, Raymond W.	GM2c	611 52 70	Surv.
RIDGEWAY, Earl D.	PhM1c	623 62 16	WIA
ROSSER, Edward P.	F2c	952 14 19	Surv.
SENDER, Daniel S.	S2c	957 39 61	Surv.
SANDS, Herschel E.	BM2c	724 52 75	WIA
SAYRE, Russell K.	MoMM3c	923 35 62	Surv.
SLAPPEY, Samuel J.	Y2c	830 63 31	WIA
SMITH, John W.	Cox.	212 76 84	MIA
STEFFEN, Carl E.	S1c	579 17 42	WIA
STEWARD, Eugene C.	F2c	945 23 30	Surv.
SULLIVAN, Thomas A.	GM2c	620 99 77	Surv.
SWAB, John A.	S2c	973 08 03	Surv.
VANDERNOORD, John (n)	S1c	955 98 61	Surv.
WILLIAMS, Eine A.	GM1c	203 09 07	WIA
WAJAHN, Albert H.	S1c	285 61 67	WIA
COOK, Paul W.	S2c	727 35 99	WIA
METCALF, Harvey E.	F1c	899 02 70	Surv.

LSM(R) GROUP 27 STAFF (Aboard at time of loss).

PACZAN, Leslie (n)	SK(D) 3c	923 25 88	WIA
THOMAS, Hayden E.	SK3c	962 40 62	MIA
DELLASSANDRO, Frank D.	S1c	823 19 42	WIA

Appendix E: USS *LSM-135* Casualties from Enemy Action on 25 May 1945

The Commanding Officer, Lieutenant Harry Leigh Derby, Jr., U.S.N.R., whose wife, Mrs. Mary Katherine Derby, lives at 426 Kramer Road, Dayton, Ohio, was killed in the flaming conning tower, along with several enlisted men stationed there. Only two are known to have escaped the tower.

They are Lieutenant (junior grade) Rudolph J. Cebull, U.S.N.R., whose wife, Mrs. Marilyn Cebull, lives at 604 North 24th Street, Billings, Montana, and Ensign Sherwin Lane McNair, U.S.N.R., whose father, Grover C. Lane, lives at Gilmer, Texas.

Lieutenant (junior grade) Cebull, the executive officer, had one leg broken and was critically burned when the Kamikaze side-swiped the tower. With a desperate effort he threw himself into the sea to extinguish his burning clothing. He later was assisted to a rescue ship.

Ensign McNair, gunnery officer, seriously burned about the face and hands, also leaped overboard and was picked up. Neither officer could later recall how he escaped from the upper platform of the flaming tower, nearly 40 feet above the sea.

The men killed or missing in the attack on LSM 135 in addition to Lieutenant Derby, Lee and Lawhead, were:

Lawrence Donald Madan, Fireman, First Class, U.S.N.R., whose parents, Mr. and Mrs. Lawrence Madansky, live at 11625 Parkview Avenue, Cleveland, Ohio, (Missing.)

Robert William Washburn, Coxswain, U.S.N.R., whose mother, Mrs. Edith Washburn, lives at 7610 Round Street, Cleveland, Ohio, (Missing.)

Pierce Milton Adams, Seaman, First Class, U.S.N.R., whose parents, Mr. and Mrs. O. F. Adams, live on Route 2, Hogansville, Georgia, (Missing.)

Joseph Crayton Harris, Radioman, Third Class, U.S.N.R., whose parents, Mr. and Mrs. Whitelaw Reid Harris, live at Walnut Cove, North Carolina, (Missing.)

Frank Paul Lombardo, Jr., Electrician's Mate, Third Class, U.S.N.R., whose parents, Mr. and Mrs. Frank Paul Lombardo, Sr., live at 78 Walnut Street, Willimantic, Connecticut, (Missing.)

Frank Meyers Howell, Yeoman, First Class, U.S.N.R., whose parents, Mr. and Mrs. Frank M. Howell, live at 1518 Ward Terrace, Portsmouth, Virginia, (Killed in action.)

Robert Lee Kirk, Jr., Radioman, Second Class, U.S.N.R., whose parents, Mr. and Mrs. Robert L. Kirk, live at 6348 Steadman Avenue, Dearborn, Michigan, (Killed in action.)

John Michael Shea, Signalman, First Class, U.S.N.R., whose parents, Mr. and Mrs. Michael Shea, live at 485 Savoy Street, Bridgeport, Connecticut, (Killed in action.)

The wounded enlisted men, most of whom have returned to duty were:

Hermann Keppeler, Seaman, First Class, U.S.N.R., of 1612 North Fourth Street, Albuquerque, New Mexico.

Eugene Emery Olson, Seaman, First Class, U.S.N.R., whose parents, Mr. and Mrs. Joseph Berg Olson, live at 3776 Southeast Henry Street, Portland, Oregon.

Robert McCoy, Jr., Ship's Cook, Third Class, U.S.N.R., whose parents, Mr. and Mrs. Robert McCoy, live at 320 West 5th Street, Bridgeport, Pennsylvania.

Louis Turrillo, Signalman, Third Class, U.S.N.R., whose mother, Mrs. Marcella Scavetta, lives at 510 East 139th Street, Bronx, New York, New York.

Harry L. Kalish, Seaman, First Class, U.S.N.R., of 1526 Birchwood Street, Chicago, Illinois.

Arthur G. Dupont, Quartermaster, Third Class, U.S.N.R., whose parents, Mr. and Mrs. Albert Dupont, live at 81 Cottage Street, Manchester, Connecticut.

Glin Buford Thompson, Fireman, First Class, U.S.N.R., whose wife, Mrs. Bessie Edna Thompson, lives on South Ironside Street, Florence, Alabama.

John Douglas Gorman, Seaman, Second Class, U.S.N.R., whose parents, Mr. and Mrs. John Gorman, live at 1172 President Street, Brooklyn, New York.

Bibliography / Notes

Bruhn, David D. *Eyes of the Fleet: The U.S. Navy's Seaplane Tenders and Patrol Aircraft in World War II*. Berywn Heights, MD: Heritage Books, 2016.

Bruhn, David D. and Rob Hoole. *Nightraiders: U.S. Navy, Royal Navy, Royal Australian Navy, and Royal Netherlands Navy Mine Forces Battling the Japanese in the Pacific in World War II*. Berwyn Heights, MD: Heritage Books, 2018.

Dyer, George Carroll. *The Amphibians Came to Conquer: The Story of Admiral Richmond Kelly Turner*. Washington, D.C.: Government Printing Office, 1972.

Lott, Arnold S. *Most Dangerous Sea*. Annapolis, MD: Naval Institute, 1959.

MacArthur's General Staff. *Reports of General MacArthur, The Campaigns of MacArthur in the Pacific, Volume I*. Washington, D.C.: U.S. Army, 1966.

Morison, Samuel Eliot. *Leyte June 1944-January 1945*. Edison, NJ: Castle Books, 2001.

—*The Liberation of the Philippines, Luzon, Mindanao, the Visayas 1944-1945*. Boston: Little, Brown, 1959.

—*The Two-Ocean War*. Boston: Little, Brown, 1963.

United States Fleet Headquarters of the Commander in Chief. *Battle Experience, Radar Pickets and Methods of Combating Suicide Attacks Off Okinawa March-May 1945*. Washington, D.C.: Navy Department, 1945.

PREFACE NOTES:

[1] "Amphibious Operations" (https://www.history.navy.mil/our-collections/art/exhibits/conflicts-and-operations/wwii/art-of-naval-amphibious-operations-from-wwii.html: accessed 28 October 2023).

[2] "A Contrast In Capabilities: Amphibious Forces At Inchon And SWA, CSC 1995"
(https://www.globalsecurity.org/military/library/report/1995/DMG.htm#:~:text=Amphibious%20warfare%20came%20of%20age%20during%20World%20War,PERMA%20%28Planning%2C%20Embarkation%2C%20Rehearsal%2C%20Movement%2C%20Assault%29%20planning%20cycle: accessed 28 October 2023).

[3] Ibid.

[4] Ibid.
[5] Ibid.
[6] Ibid.
[7] Ibid.
[8] Office of Naval Operations, *Landing Operations Doctrine United States Navy 1938 F.T.P. 167* (Washington, D.C.: Government Printing Office, 1938).
[9] Ibid.
[10] Ibid.
[11] Ibid.
[12] "A Contrast In Capabilities: Amphibious Forces At Inchon And SWA, CSC 1995."
[13] "Skill in the Surf A Landing Boat Manual February 1945" (https://www.history.navy.mil/content/history/nhhc/research/library/onlin e-reading-room/title-list-alphabetically/s/skill-in-the-surf-a-landing-boat-manual.html: accessed 24 October 2023).
[14] Ships of the U.S. Navy, 1940–1945 (www.ibiblio.org/hyperwar/USN/ships/ships-lcv.html: accessed 24 February 2012); Com7thPhibFor, FINSCHHAFEN Operation—Report upon, dated 23 October 1943; "The Higgins Boat" (www-cs-faculty. stanford.edu/~eroberts/courses/ww2/projects/fighting-vehicles/ higgins-boat.htm: accessed 24 February 2013); Jared Bahr, "Higgins: The Forgotten Man: The LCVP (Landing Craft, Vehicle, Personnel): A Strategic Military Innovation with Impact" (http://andrewjacksonhiggins. weebly.com/wwii-impact.html: accessed 25 February 2013).
[15] Ut supra.
[16] Ut supra.
[17] "Skill in the Surf A Landing Boat Manual February 1945."
[18] "LCI Facts" (http://usslci.org/facts/: accessed 31 October 2023).
[19] Ibid.
[20] "DUKW" (https://www.britannica.com/technology/DUKW: accessed 29 October 2023).
[21] Joint Publication 3-02 Amphibious Operations, 04 January 2019 Validated on 21 January 2021.
[22] "Adventures of a Landing Craft Coxswain" (https://www.usscalvert.com/wp-content/uploads/2013/02/The-Adventures-of-a-Landing-Craft-Coxswain.pdf: accessed 28 October 2023).
[23] "Perilous Ordeal Off Leyte: A pair of LSMs—landing ships, medium— proved their resilience during a December 1944 odyssey in which the vessels' determined crews faced one setback after another" by Joe Johnston, *Naval History Magazine*, February 2016 Volume 30, Number 1
[24] Ibid.
[25] "LSM Class, Allied Landing Ships" (http://pwencycl.kgbudge.com/L/s/LSM_class.htm: accessed 19 October 2023).
[26] "Perilous Ordeal Off Leyte"; "US Navy Landing Ship Medium (Early)" (https://www.scalehobbyist.com/manufacturers/Revell_of_Germany/Ship_

Models/us-navy-landing-ship-medium-early/RMG00005123/product.php:
accessed 6 October 2023).
[27] "Perilous Ordeal Off Leyte."
[28] Ibid.
[29] Ibid.
[30] "Perilous Ordeal Off Leyte"; "Pray for a Miracle" by Burton G. Wright
(https://www.usni.org/magazines/naval-history-
magazine/2007/august/contact: accessed 28 October 2023.
[31] "The Infantry Organization for Combat, World War II
(https://www.trailblazersww2.org/history_infantrystructure.htm: accessed 11
December 2023).

CHAPTER 1 NOTES:

[1] USS *Hugh W. Hadley* War Diary, May 1945; Samuel Eliot Morison, *The
Two-Ocean War* (Boston: Little, Brown, 1963), 555.
[2] United States Fleet Headquarters of the Commander in Chief, *Battle
Experience, Radar Pickets and Methods of Combating Suicide Attacks Off Okinawa
March-May 1945* (Washington, D.C.: Navy Department, 1945).
[3] Ibid.
[4] Ibid.
[5] Ibid.
[6] Ibid.
[7] "LSMR Landing Ship, Medium (Rocket)"
(https://www.globalsecurity.org/military/systems/ship/lsmr.htm#:~:text=A
n%20LSMR%20%28landing%20ship%2C%20medium%2C%20rocket%29%
20was%20not,of%20guns%20and%20rockets%20to%20perform%20this%2
0task: accessed 29 September 2023).
[8] Ibid.
[9] Ibid.
[10] Ibid.
[11] Commanding Officer, USS *Hugh W. Hadley* (DD-774), Action Report –
Action against enemy aircraft attacking this ship, while on Radar Picket
Station Fifteen, off Okinawa, Nensei Shoto, 11 May 1945.
[12] Commanding Officer, USS *LSM(R) 193*, Action Report – Battle of
Okinawa 11 May 1945.
[13] United States Fleet Headquarters of the Commander in Chief,
*Battle Experience, Radar Pickets and Methods of Combating Suicide Attacks Off
Okinawa March-May 1945.*
[14] Commanding Officer, USS *LSM(R) 193*, Action Report – Battle of
Okinawa 11 May 1945.
[15] Ibid.
[16] Ibid.
[17] Ibid.
[18] Ibid.
[19] Ibid.
[20] Ibid.

[21] Ibid.
[22] Ibid.
[23] Ibid.

CHAPTER 2 NOTES:

[1] Commanding Officer, USS *LSM 138*, History of the USS *LSM 138*, 31 October 1945.
[2] Ibid.
[3] USS *LSM-139* War Diary, June 1944.
[4] Ibid.
[5] USS *LSM-139* War Diary, July 1944.
[6] Commanding Officer, USS *LSM 138*, History of the USS *LSM 138*, 31 October 1945.
[7] Ibid.
[8] Ibid.
[9] Ibid.
[10] Ibid.
[11] Ibid.
[12] Ibid.

CHAPTER 3 NOTES:

[1] Samuel Eliot Morison, *History of the United States Naval Operations in World War II: Leyte June 1944-January 1945* (Edison, NJ: Castle Books, 2001), 142.
[2] Ibid, 55-56.
[3] Ibid, 55.
[4] Ibid, 116.
[5] Commander Transport Division Twenty-Four War Diary, October 1944.
[6] Ibid.
[7] Commander Transport Division Twenty-Four War Diary, October 1944; Commanding Officer, USS *LSM 257*, Shore Battery Action Report of *LSM 257* on 20 October 1944, 28 October 1944; Morison, *Leyte June 1944-January 1945*, 134.
[8] Commanding Officer, USS *LSM 257*, Shore Battery Action Report of *LSM 257* on 20 October 1944, 28 October 1944.
[9] USS *LSM-19* War Diary, October 1944.
[10] Commanding Officer, *USS LSM 257*, Shore Battery Action Report of *LSM 257* on 20 October 1944, 28 October 1944.
[11] Commander Transport Division Twenty-Four War Diary, October 1944; Morison, *Leyte June 1944-January 1945*, 134.
[12] Commander Transport Division Twenty-Four War Diary, October 1944.
[13] Morison, *Leyte June 1944-January 1945*, 130-131.
[14] Ibid, 135.
[15] Commander LSM Flotilla Two War Diary, October 1944; Commander Task Group 78.2, Action Report – Leyte Operation – Report on, 29 November 1944; Commanding Officer, USS *LSM 18*, Action Report, 1 November 1944.

[16] Commander LSM Flotilla Two War Diary, October 1944.
[17] Ibid.
[18] Ibid.
[19] Ibid.
[20] Ibid.
[21] Landing Attack Order ComTransDiv 18 No. A20-44.
[22] Commander Task Unit 79.6.14, Action Report, 30 October 1944.
[23] Ibid.
[24] Ibid.
[25] Ibid.
[26] Ibid.
[27] Ibid.
[28] Ibid.
[29] Ibid.
[30] Ibid.
[31] Ibid.
[32] Ibid.
[33] Morison, *The Two-Ocean War*, 435.

CHAPTER 4 NOTES:
[1] USS *LSM-22* and USS *Lamson* War Diary, December 1944.
[2] Commander Task Unit 78.3.10, Action Report, Task Unit 78.3.10 – Amphibious Movement from Leyte Gulf to Baybay, Leyte – 4-5 December, 1944, 11 December 1944; LSM Group Four War Diary, December 1944; Morison, *Leyte June 1944-January 1945*, 372-373.
[3] Commander Task Unit 78.3.10, Action Report, Task Unit 78.3.10 – Amphibious Movement from Leyte Gulf to Baybay, Leyte – 4-5 December, 1944, 11 December 1944.
[4] Ibid.
[5] Commander Task Unit 78.3.10, Action Report, Task Unit 78.3.10 – Amphibious Movement from Leyte Gulf to Baybay, Leyte – 4-5 December, 1944, 11 December 1944; LSM Group Four War Diary, December 1944.
[6] Commanding Officer, USS *LCI(L) 1017*, Action – report of, 7 December 1944; Commander Task Unit 78.3.10, Action Report, Task Unit 78.3.10 – Amphibious Movement from Leyte Gulf to Baybay, Leyte – 4-5 December, 1944, 11 December 1944.
[7] Commander Task Unit 78.3.10, Action Report, Task Unit 78.3.10 – Amphibious Movement from Leyte Gulf to Baybay, Leyte – 4-5 December, 1944, 11 December 1944; LSM Group Four War Diary, December 1944; USS *LSM-22* War Diary, December 1944.
[8] Commander Task Unit 78.3.10, Action Report, Task Unit 78.3.10 – Amphibious Movement from Leyte Gulf to Baybay, Leyte – 4-5 December, 1944, 11 December 1944.
[9] Ibid.
[10] LSM Group Four War Diary, December 1944.

[11] Commanding Officer, USS *LCI(L) 1017*, Action – report of, 7 December 1944.

[12] LSM Group Four War Diary, December 1944.

[13] LSM Group Four War Diary, December 1944; Commanding Officer, USS *LCI(L) 1017*, Action – report of, 7 December 1944.

[14] LSM Group Four War Diary, December 1944.

[15] Commanding Officer, USS *LCI(L) 1017*, Action – report of, 7 December 1944.

[16] LSM Group Four War Diary, December 1944.

[17] Commanding Officer, USS *LSM-20*, USS *LSM-20* – Loss of, 29 May 1945.

[18] LSM Group Four War Diary, December 1944.

[19] Commanding Officer, USS *LSM-20*, USS *LSM-20* – Loss of, 29 May 1945.

[20] Commanding Officer, USS *LCI(L) 1017*, Action – report of, 7 December 1944; Commanding Officer, USS *LSM-20*, USS *LSM-20* – Loss of, 29 May 1945.

[21] Commanding Officer, USS *LCI(L) 1017*, Action – report of, 7 December 1944.

[22] USS *LSM-23* War Diary, December 1944.

[23] Ibid.

[24] Ibid.

[25] Ibid.

[26] Commanding Officer, USS *LCI(L) 1017*, Action – report of, 7 December 1944.

[27] LSM Group Four War Diary, December 1944.

[28] Commander Task Unit 78.3.10, Action Report, Task Unit 78.3.10 – Amphibious Movement from Leyte Gulf to Baybay, Leyte – 4-5 December, 1944, 11 December 1944.

[29] Commander Task Unit 78.3.10, Action Report, Task Unit 78.3.10 – Amphibious Movement from Leyte Gulf to Baybay, Leyte – 4-5 December, 1944, 11 December 1944; LSM Group Four War Diary, December 1944.

CHAPTER 5 NOTES:

[1] Morison, *Leyte June 1944-January 1945*, 376-377.

[2] Morison, *Leyte June 1944-January 1945*, 375; Commander in Chief, U.S. Pacific Fleet and Pacific Ocean Areas, Operations in Pacific Ocean Areas – December 1944, 25 June 1945.

[3] Commander in Chief, U.S. Pacific Fleet and Pacific Ocean Areas, Operations in Pacific Ocean Areas – December 1944, 25 June 1945.

[4] Morison, *Leyte June 1944-January 1945*, 375, 377.

[5] Commanding Officer, USS *LSM 34*, Action Report, 8 December 1944.

[6] Ibid.

[7] USS *LSM-20* War Diary, December 1944.

[8] Commander in Chief, U.S. Pacific Fleet and Pacific Ocean Areas, Operations in Pacific Ocean Areas – December 1944, 25 June 1945; Arnold S. Lott, *Most Dangerous Sea* (Annapolis, MD: Naval Institute, 1959), 141.

[9] Commander in Chief, U.S. Pacific Fleet and Pacific Ocean Areas, Operations in Pacific Ocean Areas – December 1944.

[10] Commanding Officer, USS *LSM 318*, Report of Action – Ormoc Bay, P.I., Amphibious Operation, 16 January 1944.

[11] Ibid.

[12] Ibid.

[13] Ibid.

[14] Ibid.

[15] Ibid.

[16] Commanding Officer, USS *LSM 318*, Report of Action – Ormoc Bay, P.I., Amphibious Operation, 16 January 1944; Commanding Officer, *LCI(L) 970*, Action Report – Ormoc Operation on west coast of Leyte Island, Philippine Islands, 9 December 1944.

[17] Commanding Officer, USS *LSM 318*, Report of Action – Ormoc Bay, P.I., Amphibious Operation, 16 January 1944.

[18] Ibid.

[19] Ibid.

[20] Ibid.

[21] Ibid.

[22] Ibid.

[23] LSM Group Four War Diary, December 1944.

[24] Commander, Task Group Seven Eight Point Three, Action Report – Ormoc Landing, 7 December 1944, 30 December 1944.

[25] Morison, *Leyte June 1944-January 1945*, 385.

CHAPTER 6 NOTES:

[1] Commander Task Group Seven Eight Point Three (Commander Amphibious Group Nine), Mindoro Action Report – 15 December 1944, 7 March 1944; Commander Task Unit 78.3.3, Action Report – Mindoro Operation, 30 December 1944.

[2] Commander Task Group Seven Eight Point Three (Commander Amphibious Group Nine), Mindoro Action Report – 15 December 1944, 7 March 1944.

[3] Commander Task Group Seven Eight Point Three (Commander Amphibious Group Nine), Mindoro Action Report – 15 December 1944, 7 March 1944; Commander Task Unit 78.3.3, Action Report – Mindoro Operation, 30 December 1944.

[4] Commander Task Group Seven Eight Point Three (Commander Amphibious Group Nine), Mindoro Action Report – 15 December 1944, 7 March 1944.

[5] Ibid.

[6] Commander Task Unit 78.3.3, Action Report – Mindoro Operation, 30 December 1944.

[7] Commander Task Group Seven Eight Point Three (Commander Amphibious Group Nine), Mindoro Action Report – 15 December 1944, 7 March 1944.

[8] Commander Task Unit 78.3.3, Action Report – Mindoro Operation, 30 December 1944; Commanding Officer, USS *LSM-258*, Action Report – Mindoro Operation, 17 December 1944.

[9] Commanding Officer, *LSM 258*, Action Report – Mindoro Operation, 17 December 1944.

[10] Ibid.

[11] Ibid.

[12] Ibid.

[13] Ibid.

[14] Commanding Officer, USS *LSM 34*, Action Report, 17 December 1944.

[15] Ibid.

[16] Ibid.

[17] Ibid.

[18] *LSM-311* War Diary, December 1944.

[19] Ibid.

[20] Commander in Chief, U.S. Pacific Fleet and Pacific Ocean Areas, Operations in the Pacific Ocean Areas – December 1944, 25 June 1945.

[21] Commanding Officer, USS *LSM 34*, Action Report, 17 December 1944.

[22] Ibid.

[23] Commander in Chief, U.S. Pacific Fleet and Pacific Ocean Areas, Operations in the Pacific Ocean Areas – December 1944, 25 June 1945.

[24] Seventh Amphibious Force Command History, 10 January 1943 - 23 December 1945.

CHAPTER 7 NOTES:

[1] Command History Seventh Amphibious Force.

[2] Commander in Chief, U.S. Pacific Fleet and Pacific Ocean Areas, Operations in Pacific Ocean Areas – January 1945, 31 July 1945.

[3] Commander in Chief, U.S. Pacific Fleet and Pacific Ocean Areas, Operations in Pacific Ocean Areas – January 1945, 31 July 1945; Commander Luzon Attack Force, Action Report – Luzon Attack Force, Lingayen Gulf – Musketeer Mike One Operation, 15 May 1945.

[4] Commander in Chief, U.S. Pacific Fleet and Pacific Ocean Areas, Operations in Pacific Ocean Areas – January 1945, 31 July 1945.

[5] Ibid.

[6] Ibid.

[7] Ibid.

[8] Commander Luzon Attack Force, Action Report – Luzon Attack Force, Lingayen Gulf – Musketeer Mike One Operation, 15 May 1945.

[9] Ibid.

[10] Commander Luzon Attack Force, Action Report – Luzon Attack Force, Lingayen Gulf – Musketeer Mike One Operation, 15 May 1945; "80-G-273158 HMAS Australia" (https://www.history.navy.mil/content/history/nhhc/our-collections/photography/numerical-list-of-images/nara-series/80-g/80-G-270000/80-G-273158.html: accessed 12 November 2023).

[11] Commander Luzon Attack Force, Action Report – Luzon Attack Force, Lingayen Gulf – Musketeer Mike One Operation, 15 May 1945.
[12] Ibid.
[13] Ibid.
[14] Commander Third Amphibious Force (Commander Task Force 79), Lingayen Gulf Operations – Report of participation of Task Force 79), 5 February 1945.
[15] Commander Task Group Seventy-Nine Point One (Commander Amphibious Group Seven), Report of Task Group 79.1 participation in Amphibious Operations for the assault in the Lingayen Gulf Area of Luzon, P.I., 20 January 1945.
[16] Ibid.
[17] Ibid.
[18] Ibid.
[19] Commander LSM Flotilla Three, Action Report – Submission of, 30 January 1945.
[20] Ibid.
[21] Commander Task Group 79.2 (Commander Amphibious Group Six), Amphibious Attack on Lingayen, Luzon – Report of, 1 February 1945.
[22] Commander LSM Flotilla Three, Action Report – Submission of, 30 January 1945.
[23] Ibid.
[24] Ibid.
[25] Ibid.
[26] LSM Group Nineteen War Diary, January 1945; Commander Task Unit 78.5.6, Action Report – San Fabian, Luzon, Blue Beach Attack Operation, 29 January 1945.
[27] Commander Task Unit 78.5.6, Action Report – San Fabian, Luzon, Blue Beach Attack Operation, 29 January 1945.
[28] Commander Task Group 78.5, Action Report – Lingayen Gulf, Luzon Operation – Report on, 14 February 1945.
[29] Commander Task Group 78.5, Action Report – Lingayen Gulf, Luzon Operation – Report on, 14 February 1945; Commander Task Unit 78.5.6, Action Report – San Fabian, Luzon, Blue Beach Attack Operation, 29 January 1945.
[30] Ut supra.
[31] Commander Task Group 78.5, Action Report – Lingayen Gulf, Luzon Operation – Report on, 14 February 1945.
[32] Ibid.
[33] Commander Task Unit 78.5.6, Action Report – San Fabian, Luzon, Blue Beach Attack Operation, 29 January 1945.
[34] Commander LSM Group Nineteen War Diary, January 1945.
[35] Commander Task Force Seventy-Eight, Report of the Lingayen Operation – San Fabian Attack Force, 12 February 1945.
[36] Ibid.

[37] Commanding Officer, USS *LSM-41*, Action Report – Invasion of Luzon at Lingayen Gulf, 17 January 1945.

[38] Commander Task Force Seventy-Eight, Report of the Lingayen Operation – San Fabian Attack Force, 12 February 1945; Commanding Officer *LSM-127*, Action Report – Lingayen Gulf, P.I., 11 January 1945.

[39] Commanding Officer, USS *LSM 219*, Action Report – San Fabian, Lingayen Gulf Operation, 17 January 1945.

[40] Ibid.

[41] Ibid.

[42] Ibid.

[43] Ibid.

[44] Ibid.

[45] Commander LSM Group Nineteen War Diary, January 1945.

[46] Ibid.

[47] Commanding Officer, *LSM-269*, Action Report – Luzon Operation, 17 January 1945.

[48] Ibid.

[49] Commander Luzon Attack Force, Action Report – Luzon Attack Force, Lingayen Gulf – Musketeer Mike One Operation, 15 May 1945.

[50] Commander Third Amphibious Force (Commander Task Force 79), Lingayen Gulf Operations – Report of participation of Task Force 79), 5 February 1945.

[51] Commander Luzon Attack Force, Action Report – Luzon Attack Force, Lingayen Gulf – Musketeer Mike One Operation, 15 May 1945.

[52] Ibid.

CHAPTER 8 NOTES:

[1] Commander in Chief, U.S. Pacific Fleet and Pacific Ocean Areas – January 1945, 31 July 1945.

[2] Ibid.

[3] Commander in Chief, U.S. Pacific Fleet and Pacific Ocean Areas – January 1945, 31 July 1945; Samuel Eliot Morison, *The Liberation of the Philippines, Luzon, Mindanao, the Visayas 1944-1945* (Boston: Little, Brown, 1959), 184-189.

[4] "Operation Mike VII" (https://codenames.info/operation/mike-vii/: accessed 14 November 2023); Morison, *The Liberation of the Philippines, Luzon, Mindanao, the Visayas 1944-1945*, 187.

[5] Commander Task Group 78.3, Report of Amphibious Landings in Zambales Province, Luzon, P.I., 4 March 1945.

[6] Ibid.

[7] Commander Task Group 78.3, Report of Amphibious Landings in Zambales Province, Luzon, P.I., 4 March 1945; Commander LSM Group Nineteen, Action Report – Amphibious Assault Landing in Zambales Province Area of Luzon, P.I., 3 February 1945.

[8] Ut supra.

[9] Commander Task Group 78.3, Report of Amphibious Landings in Zambales Province, Luzon, P.I., 4 March 1945.

[10] Commander LSM Group Nineteen, Action Report – Amphibious Assault Landing in Zambales Province Area of Luzon, P.I., 3 February 1945.

[11] Commander Task Group 78.3, Report of Amphibious Landings in Zambales Province, Luzon, P.I., 4 March 1945.

[12] Morison, *The Liberation of the Philippines, Luzon, Mindanao, the Visayas 1944-1945*, 188-189.

[13] Commander Task Unit 78.2.4 (ComLSM Flot 7), Action Report of Task Unit 78.2.4 Operation M-6, 3 February 1945.

[14] Commander Task Group 78.2, Action Report – Nasugbu, Luzon Operation – Report on, 8 March 1945.

[15] Commander Task Group 78.2, Action Report – Nasugbu, Luzon Operation – Report on, 8 March 1945; Morison, *The Liberation of the Philippines, Luzon, Mindanao, the Visayas 1944-1945*, 190-191.

[16] Commander Task Group 78.2, Action Report – Nasugbu, Luzon Operation – Report on, 8 March 1945.

[17] Ibid.

[18] Commanding Officer, USS *LSM 203*, Action Report, Nasugbu, Luzon, Operation, 1 February 1945.

[19] Commander Task Group 78.2, Action Report – Nasugbu, Luzon Operation – Report on, 8 March 1945.

[20] Ibid.

[21] Commander Task Group 78.2, Action Report – Nasugbu, Luzon Operation – Report on, 8 March 1945; Morison, *The Liberation of the Philippines, Luzon, Mindanao, the Visayas 1944-1945*, 192.

[22] USS *Lough* War Diary, January 1945.

[23] Morison, *The Liberation of the Philippines, Luzon, Mindanao, the Visayas 1944-1945*, 192.

CHAPTER 9 NOTES:

[1] Commander Task Group Seventy Eight point Three, Action Report – Mariveles-Corregidor Landings, 15-16 February 1945, 29 June 1945.

[2] Commander in Chief, U.S. Pacific Fleet and Pacific Ocean Areas – February 1945, Operations in Pacific Ocean Areas – February 1945, 27 August 1945.

[3] Ibid.

[4] Ibid.

[5] Ibid.

[6] Ibid.

[7] Commanding Officer, USS *YMS-48*, Loss of Vessel in Action – report of, 1 March 1945.

[8] Commander in Chief, U.S. Pacific Fleet and Pacific Ocean Areas – February 1945, Operations in Pacific Ocean Areas – February 1945, 27 August 1945; Commanding Officer, USS *YMS-48*, Loss of Vessel in Action – report of, 1 March 1945.

[9] Ut supra.

[10] Commanding Officer, USS *YMS-48*, Loss of Vessel in Action – report of, 1 March 1945.

[11] Commander in Chief, U.S. Pacific Fleet and Pacific Ocean Areas – February 1945, Operations in Pacific Ocean Areas – February 1945, 27 August 1945.

[12] Commander Task Group Seventy Eight point Three, Action Report – Mariveles-Corregidor Landings, 15-16 February 1945, 29 June 1945.

[13] Commander LSM Group Six War Diary, February 1945.

[14] Ibid.

[15] Commander LSM Group Six War Diary, February 1945; Commander Task Group Seventy Eight point Three, Action Report – Mariveles-Corregidor Landings, 15-16 February 1945, 29 June 1945.

[16] Commander Task Group Seventy Eight point Three, Action Report – Mariveles-Corregidor Landings, 15-16 February 1945, 29 June 1945.

[17] USS *Grasp* War Diary, February 2023; Commanding Officer, USS *LSM 39*, Action Report, Landing at Mariveles Harbor, Luzon, 17 February 1945.

[18] Acting Commanding Officer, *LSM 169* [Ens. H. H. Foley], Report of Action, 24 February 1945.

[19] Ibid.

[20] USS *Grasp* War Diary, February 2023; USS *LSM 39*, Action Report, Landing at Mariveles Harbor, Luzon, 17 February 1945.

[21] Commander LSM Group Six War Diary, February 1945.

[22] Commander Task Group Seventy Eight point Three, Action Report – Mariveles-Corregidor Landings, 15-16 February 1945, 29 June 1945.

[23] Commanding Officer, USS *LSM 18*, Action Report – Mariveles Operation, 16 February 1945.

CHAPTER 10 NOTES:

[1] Commander LSM Flotilla Two War Diary, February 1945.

[2] "History of the U.S. Army's 1st Filipino Regiment and 2d Filipino Battalion (Separate)"
(https://history.army.mil/html/topics/apam/filipino_regt/filipino_regt.html: accessed 17 November 2023).

[3] Ibid.

[4] Ibid.

[5] Commander LSM Flotilla Two War Diary, February 1945.

[6] Ibid.

[7] Ibid.

[8] "A History of the 1st and 2nd Filipino Regiment"
(https://www.nps.gov/goga/blogs/a-history-of-the-1st-and-2nd-filipino-regiment.htm: accessed 17 November 2023).

[9] "A History of the 1st and 2nd Filipino Regiment"; "California's Filipino Infantry" by Alex S. Fabros (https://www.militarymuseum.org/Filipino.html: accessed 17 November 2023).

[10] Ut supra.

CHAPTER 11 NOTES:

[1] Morison, *The Two-Ocean War*, 513.

[2] Ibid.

[3] Ibid.

[4] Ibid, 514.

[5] Commander in Chief, U.S. Pacific Fleet and Pacific Ocean Areas, Operations in Pacific Ocean Areas – February 1945, 27 August 1945.

[6] Ibid.

[7] Commander Task Group 53.4, Action Report, Attack on Iwo Jima, 19 February 1945, 7 March 1945; Commander in Chief, U.S. Pacific Fleet and Pacific Ocean Areas, Operations in Pacific Ocean Areas – February 1945, 27 August 1945.

[8] Commander in Chief, U.S. Pacific Fleet and Pacific Ocean Areas, Operations in Pacific Ocean Areas – February 1945, 27 August 1945.

[9] Ibid.

[10] Ibid.

[11] Ibid.

[12] Commander Task Group 53.4, Action Report, Attack on Iwo Jima, 19 February 1945.

[13] Ibid.

[14] Ibid.

[15] Ibid.

[16] Ibid.

[17] Ibid.

[18] Ibid.

[19] Ibid.

[20] Ibid.

[21] David D. Bruhn and Rob Hoole, *Nightraiders: U.S. Navy, Royal Navy, Royal Australian Navy, and Royal Netherlands Navy Mine Forces Battling the Japanese in the Pacific in World War II* (Berwyn Heights, MD: Heritage Books, 2018), 241.

[22] Ibid, 242.

[23] "William Hubbard Carpenter 29 January 1904-4 December 1948" (https://www.history.navy.mil/research/library/research-guides/modern-biographical-files-ndl/modern-bios-c/carpenter-william-hubbard.html: accessed 26 November 2023).

[24] George Carroll Dyer, *The Amphibians Came to Conquer: The Story of Admiral Richmond Kelly Turner* (Washington, D.C.: Government Printing Office, 1972), 1002-1003.

CHAPTER 12 NOTES:

[1] Commander Task Group 78.2, Action Report – Puerto Princessa, Palawan Operation, Report on, 25 March 1945.

[2] Morison, *The Liberation of the Philippines Luzon, Mindanao, the Visayas 1944-1945*, 216-217.

[3] Ibid, 217.

[4] MacArthur's General Staff, *Reports of General MacArthur, The Campaigns of MacArthur in the Pacific, Volume I* (Washington, D.C.: U.S. Army, 1966), 328-329.

[5] Ibid, 329.

[6] Commander Task Group 78.2, Action Report – Puerto Princessa, Palawan Operation, Report on, 25 March 1945.

[7] Commander Task Unit 78.2.4 (ComLSMFlot 7), Action Report of Task Unit 78.2.4, Operation V-3, 4 March 1945.

[8] Commander Task Group 78.2, Action Report – Puerto Princessa, Palawan Operation, Report on, 25 March 1945; *Reports of General MacArthur, The Campaigns of MacArthur in the Pacific, Volume I*, 332.

[9] Commander Task Group 78.2, Action Report – Puerto Princessa, Palawan Operation, Report on, 25 March 1945.

[10] Ibid.

[11] Ibid.

[12] Ibid.

[13] Commander Task Unit 78.2.4 (ComLSMFlot 7), Action Report of Task Unit 78.2.4, Operation V-3, 4 March 1945.

[14] Ibid.

[15] Commander Task Group 78.2, Action Report – Puerto Princessa, Palawan Operation, Report on, 25 March 1945.

[16] Ibid.

CHAPTER 13 NOTES:

[1] Commander Task Group 78.1, Amphibious Attack on Zamboanga, Mindanao – Report of, 26 March 1945; Commander Task Unit 78.1.12, Action Report – Victor-Four Operation, 16 March 1945.

[2] Commander Task Group 78.1, Amphibious Attack on Zamboanga, Mindanao – Report of, 26 March 1945.

[3] Commander Task Group 78.1, Amphibious Attack on Zamboanga, Mindanao – Report of, 26 March 1945; Commander Task Unit 78.1.5, Report of Minesweeping Operations – Basilan Strait and Zamboanga, P.I., 20 March 1945.

[4] Commander Task Unit 78.1.5, Report of Minesweeping Operations – Basilan Strait and Zamboanga, P.I., 20 March 1945.

[5] Commander Task Group 78.1, Amphibious Attack on Zamboanga, Mindanao – Report of, 26 March 1945.

[6] Ibid.

[7] Ibid.

[8] Commander Task Unit 78.1.12, Action Report – Victor-Four Operation, 16 March 1945.

[9] Commander Task Group 78.1, Amphibious Attack on Zamboanga, Mindanao – Report of, 26 March 1945.

[10] Commander Task Unit 78.1.12, Action Report – Victor-Four Operation, 16 March 1945.

[11] Ibid.

[12] Ibid.
[13] Ibid.
[14] Ibid.
[15] *Reports of General MacArthur, The Campaigns of MacArthur in the Pacific, Volume I*, 336-337.
[16] Ibid.
[17] Ibid.

CHAPTER 14 NOTES:

[1] Commander in Chief, U.S. Pacific Fleet and Pacific Ocean Areas, Operations in Pacific Ocean Areas – March 1945, 31 August 1945.
[2] Commander Task Unit 78.1.1, The attack on Basilan Island, Philippine Islands on 16 March, 1945 by Task Unit 78.1.2, 20 March 1945; Commander in Chief, U.S. Pacific Fleet and Pacific Ocean Areas, Operations in Pacific Ocean Areas – March 1945, 31 August 1945.
[3] Commander in Chief, U.S. Pacific Fleet and Pacific Ocean Areas, Operations in Pacific Ocean Areas – March 1945, 31 August 1945.
[4] Commander Task Group 78.3, Panay (Victor-One Operation) Action Report – 18 March 1945, 25 May 1945.
[5] Commander Task Unit 78.3.3, Action Report, Task Unit 78.3.3 – V-1 Operation, 18 March 1945, 31 March 1945; Operations in Pacific Ocean Areas – March 1945, 31 August 1945; Commander Task Group 78.3, Panay (Victor-One Operation) Action Report – 18 March 1945, 25 May 1945.
[6] Commander Task Unit 78.3.3, Action Report, Task Unit 78.3.3 – V-1 Operation, 18 March 1945, 31 March 1945; Operations in Pacific Ocean Areas – March 1945, 31 August 1945; Commander Task Group 78.3, Panay (Victor-One Operation) Action Report – 18 March 1945, 25 May 1945.
[7] Commander Task Unit 78.3.3, Action Report, Task Unit 78.3.3 – V-1 Operation, 18 March 1945, 31 March 1945.
[8] Ibid.
[9] Ibid.
[10] Commander Task Unit 78.3.3, Action Report, Task Unit 78.3.3 – V-1 Operation, 18 March 1945, 31 March 1945.
[11] Commander Task Group 78.3, Panay (Victor-One Operation) Action Report – 18 March 1945, 25 May 1945; Commander in Chief, U.S. Pacific Fleet and Pacific Ocean Areas, Operations in Pacific Ocean Areas – March 1945, 31 August 1945; *Reports of General MacArthur, The Campaigns of MacArthur in the Pacific Volume I*, 341.
[12] Commander in Chief, U.S. Pacific Fleet and Pacific Ocean Areas, Operations in Pacific Ocean Areas – March 1945, 31 August 1945.
[13] Commander in Chief, U.S. Pacific Fleet and Pacific Ocean Areas, Operations in Pacific Ocean Areas – March 1945, 31 August 1945; *Reports of General MacArthur, The Campaigns of MacArthur in the Pacific Volume I*, 341.

CHAPTER 15 NOTES:

[1] Commander in Chief, U.S. Pacific Fleet and Pacific Ocean Areas, Operations in Pacific Ocean Areas – March 1945, 31 August 1945.

[2] "Americal Legacy Foundation" (https://americalfoundation.org/cmsalf/americal-history/world-war-ii.html: accessed 22 November 2023).

[3] Ibid.

[4] "Albert T. Sprague" (https://catholiceducator.blogspot.com/2015/12/albert-t-sprague.html: accessed 22 November 2023).

[5] Commander in Chief, U.S. Pacific Fleet and Pacific Ocean Areas, Operations in Pacific Ocean Areas – March 1945, 31 August 1945.

[6] Commander LSM Group 20 Flotilla War Diary, March 1945.

[7] Commander LSM Group 20 Flotilla War Diary, March 1945; Commander Task Group 78.2, Action Report – Cebu City, Cebu Operation, 4 April 1945.

[8] Commander Task Group 78.2, Action Report – Cebu City, Cebu Operation, 4 April 1945.

[9] Ibid.

[10] Ibid.

[11] Ibid.

[12] Ibid.

[13] Ibid.

[14] Ibid.

[15] Ibid.

[16] Ibid.

[17] Ibid.

[18] "Japanese Midget Submarine Operations 1942-45 II" (https://thehistoryfiles.com/japanese-midget-submarine-operations-1942-45-ii/: accessed 22 November 2023).

[19] Commander Task Group 78.2, Action Report – Cebu City, Cebu Operation, 4 April 1945.

[20] Ibid.

[21] "Japanese Midget Submarine Operations 1942-45 II."

[22] Commander LSM Group 20 Flotilla War Diary, March 1945; Commander Task Group 78.2, Action Report – Cebu City, Cebu Operation, 4 April 1945.

[23] Commander Task Group 78.2, Action Report – Cebu City, Cebu Operation, 4 April 1945.

CHAPTER 16 NOTES:

[1] Commander Task Group 32.2 (52.2), Report of Capture of Okinawa Gunto – Phases One and Two, 23 July 1945.

[2] David D. Bruhn, *Eyes of the Fleet: The U.S. Navy's Seaplane Tenders and Patrol Aircraft in World War II* (Berwyn Heights, MD: Heritage Books, 2016), 361-362.

[3] Morison, *The Two-Ocean War*, 555.

[4] Morison, *The Two-Ocean War*, 556; "Okinawa: The Costs of Victory in the Last Battle" (https://www.nationalww2museum.org/war/articles/okinawa-costs-victory-last-battle: accessed 12 December 2023).

[5] "Casualties: U.S. Navy and Coast Guard Vessels, Sunk or Damaged Beyond Repair during World War II, 7 December 1941-1 October 1945: (https://www.history.navy.mil/content/history/nhhc/research/histories/ship-histories/casualties-navy-and-coast-guard-ships.html: accessed 2 December 2023).

[6] CTG 52.21, Action Report – Ie Shima and Southeastern Okinawa, 2 April through 20 April 1945, 21 April 1945.

[7] "LSMR Landing Ship, Medium (Rocket)" (https://www.globalsecurity.org/military/systems/ship/lsmr.htm: accessed 2 December 2023).

[8] CTG 52.21, Action Report, Battle of Kerama Retto and Okinawa Shima, 26 March through 1 April 1945, 2 April 1945.

[9] Ibid.

[10] CTG 52.21, Action Report, Battle of Kerama Retto and Okinawa Shima, 26 March through 1 April 1945, 2 April 1945; *Halligan, DANFS*.

[11] CTG 52.21, Action Report, Battle of Kerama Retto and Okinawa Shima, 26 March through 1 April 1945, 2 April 1945.

[12] Commanding Officer, USS *LSM(R) 189*, Attack by enemy small boats on 29 March 1945 off Okinawa Island, 3 April 1945.

[13] Ibid.

[14] Commanding Officer, USS *LSM(R) 189*, Attack by enemy small boats on 29 March 1945 off Okinawa Island, 3 April 1945; Commanding Officer, USS *Barton* (DD 722), Report of Capture of Okinawa Gunto 21 March 1945 to 17 May 1945, 12 June 1945.

[15] Commanding Officer, USS *LSM(R) 189*, Attack by enemy small boats on 29 March 1945 off Okinawa Island, 3 April 1945.

[16] Ibid.

[17] Ibid.

[18] Commanding Officer, USS *LSM(R) 188*, Battle Report, 30 March 1945.

[19] Commanding Officer, USS *LSM(R) 188*, Battle Report, 30 March 1945; CTG 52.21, Action Report, Battle of Kerama Retto and Okinawa Shima, 26 March through 1 April 1945, 2 April 1945.

[20] Commanding Officer, USS *LSM(R) 188*, Battle Report, 30 March 1945.

[21] CTG 52.21, Action Report – Ie Shima and Southeastern Okinawa, 2 April through 20 April 1945, 21 April 1945; Commanding Officer, USS *LSM(R) 188*, Battle Report, 30 March 1945.

[22] CTG 52.21, Action Report, Battle of Kerama Retto and Okinawa Shima, 26 March through 1 April 1945, 2 April 1945.

[23] Ibid.

[24] Ibid.

[25] Ibid.

[26] CTG 52.21, Action Report – Ie Shima and Southeastern Okinawa, 2 April through 20 April 1945, 21 April 1945.

[27] Commanding Officer, USS *LSM(R) 195*, Action Report – Battle of Okinawa, 3 May 1945, 5 May 1945.

[28] Ibid.

[29] Ibid.

[30] Ibid.

[31] Ibid.

[32] Executive Officer, USS *LSM(R) 190*, Action Report – Battle of Okinawa, 4 May 1945, 18 August 1945.

[33] Ibid.

[34] Ibid.

[35] Ibid.

[36] Ibid.

[37] Ibid.

[38] Ibid.

[39] Navy and Marine Corps Awards Manual Department of the Navy NAVPERS 15,790 (Rev. 1953). The Navy Awards Manual identifies USS *LSM 877* as well as a Navy Unit Commendation recipient. Apparently the hull number results from a keystroke error, because there was no LSM-877.

[40] Commanding Officer, USS *LSM(R) 194*, Action Report – Battle of Okinawa – 4 May 1945, 6 May 1945.

[41] Ibid.

[42] Ibid.

[43] Ibid.

[44] Senior Surviving Officer, Action Report – Attack by Japanese Suicide Plane, 25 May 1945, Ie Shima, Ryukyu Rhetto, Resulting in Loss of Ship – U.S.S. *LSM 135*, 1 June 1945.

[45] Senior Surviving Officer, Action Report – Attack by Japanese Suicide Plane, 25 May 1945, Ie Shima, Ryukyu Rhetto, Resulting in Loss of Ship – U.S.S. *LSM 135*, 1 June 1945; Navy Department Immediate Release Press and Radio, Kamikaze Attack Sank LSM 135 off Ie Shima, July 28, 1945.

[46] Ut supra.

[47] Navy Department Immediate Release Press and Radio, Kamikaze Attack Sank LSM 135 off Ie Shima, July 28, 1945.

[48] Ibid.

[49] Ibid.

[50] Ibid.

[51] Ibid.

[52] Ibid.

[53] Senior Surviving Officer, Action Report – Attack by Japanese Suicide Plane, 25 May 1945, Ie Shima, Ryukyu Rhetto, Resulting in Loss of Ship – U.S.S. *LSM 135*, 1 June 1945.

[54] Navy Department Immediate Release Press and Radio, Kamikaze Attack Sank LSM 135 off Ie Shima, July 28, 1945.

[55] Commanding Officer, USS *LSM-59*, Action Report – Sinking of USS *LSM 59* by Japanese suicide plane on 21 June 1945, 23 June 1945; "USS *Barry*

(APD-29)" (https://www.navsource.org/archives/10/04/04029.htm: accessed 5 December 2023).

[56] Commanding Officer, USS *LSM-59*, Action Report – Sinking of USS *LSM 59* by Japanese suicide plane on 21 June 1945, 23 June 1945.

[57] Ibid.

[58] Ibid.

[59] Ibid.

[60] Ibid.

CHAPTER 17 NOTES:

[1] Commanding Officer USS *LSM 51*, Action Report – Submission of – Fort Drum (El Fraile) Operation, 14 April 1945.

[2] Commanding Officer USS *LSM 51*, Action Report – Submission of – Fort Drum (El Fraile) Operation, 14 April 1945; "The Blasting of Fort Drum," *Yank the Army Weekly*, August 3, 1945.

[3] Commanding Officer USS *LSM 51*, Action Report – Submission of – Fort Drum (El Fraile) Operation, 14 April 1945.

[4] Commanding Officer USS *LSM 51*, Action Report – Submission of – Fort Drum (El Fraile) Operation, 14 April 1945; "The Blasting of Fort Drum," *Yank the Army Weekly*, August 3, 1945.

[5] Commanding Officer USS *LSM 51*, Action Report – Submission of – Fort Drum (El Fraile) Operation, 14 April 1945.

[6] USS *Phoenix* War Diary, April 1945.

[7] Ibid.

[8] "Fort Drum: The Unsinkable Concrete Battleship That Guarded the Philippines" by Ryan McLachlan (https://www.warhistoryonline.com/world-war-ii/fort-drum-philippines.html: accessed 23 November 2023).

[9] Ibid.

[10] "Fort Drum, the unsinkable concrete 'battleship' of Manila Bay" by Jack Beckett (https://www.warhistoryonline.com/featured/fort-drum.html: accessed 23 November 2023).

[11] "Fort Drum – The Concrete Battleship" by Mark Milligan (https://www.heritagedaily.com/2023/08/fort-drum-the-concrete-battleship/148307: accessed 23 November 2023).

[12] Ibid.

[13] "El Fraile Island" (https://www.concretebattleship.org/fort_drum_History.htm: accessed 23 November 2023).

[14] Ibid.

[15] "The Blasting of Fort Drum," *Yank the Army Weekly*, August 3, 1945.

[16] Ibid.

[17] Ibid.

[18] Ibid.

[19] Commanding Officer USS *LSM 51*, Action Report – Submission of – Fort Drum (El Fraile) Operation, 14 April 1945.

[20] Ibid.

[21] Ibid.

CHAPTER 18 NOTES:

[1] Commanding Officer, USS *Philip* (DD-498), Action Report, USS *Philip* – Sadau and Tarakan Operations, 30 April to 3 May 1945, 6 May 1945.

[2] Bruhn and Hoole, *Nightraiders: U.S. Navy, Royal Navy, Royal Australian Navy, and Royal Netherlands Navy Mine Forces Battling the Japanese in the Pacific in World War II*, 297.

[3] Commanding Officer, USS *Philip* (DD-498), Action Report, USS *Philip* – Sadau and Tarakan Operations, 30 April to 3 May 1945, 6 May 1945.

[4] Commanding Officer, USS *LSM 151*, Action Report – USS *LSM 151*, 9 May 1945.

[5] Commanding Officer, USS *LSM 151*, Action Report – USS *LSM 151*, 9 May 1945; Commanding Officer, USS *Philip* (DD-498), Action Report, USS *Philip* – Sadau and Tarakan Operations, 30 April to 3 May 1945, 6 May 1945.

[6] Commanding Officer, USS *LSM 151*, Action Report – USS *LSM 151*, 9 May 1945.

[7] Commanding Officer, USS *LSM 151*, Action Report – USS *LSM 151*, 9 May 1945; Commanding Officer, USS *Philip* (DD-498), Action Report, USS *Philip* – Sadau and Tarakan Operations, 30 April to 3 May 1945, 6 May 1945.

[8] Commanding Officer, USS *LSM 151*, Action Report – USS *LSM 151*, 9 May 1945; Commander Task Group 78.1, Action Report, CTG 78.1 (ComPhibGruSix) – Tarakan, Borneo, Operation (1-3 May 1945), 5 May 1945.

[9] Commander in Chief, U.S. Pacific Fleet and Pacific Ocean Areas, Operations in Pacific Ocean Area – May 1945, 5 November 1945.

[10] Commander in Chief, U.S. Pacific Fleet and Pacific Ocean Areas, Operations in Pacific Ocean Area – May 1945, 5 November 1945; Commander Task Unit 78.1.5, Minesweeping Operations, Tarakan Island Netherlands East Indies – Report of, 9 May 1945.

[11] Commander in Chief, U.S. Pacific Fleet and Pacific Ocean Areas, Operations in Pacific Ocean Area – May 1945, 5 November 1945.

[12] Ibid.

[13] Ibid.

[14] Ibid.

[15] Commander Task Unit 78.1.14, Action report, vessels of Task Unit 78.1.14 – Tarakan Operation – 1 May 1945, 30 May 1945.

[16] Ibid.

[17] Ibid.

[18] Ibid.

[19] "Borneo 1945 - An Amphibious Success Story" by Nial Wheate and Gregory P. Gilbert (https://www.navy.gov.au/history/feature-histories/borneo-1945-amphibious-success-story#:~:text=The%20amphibious%20assault%20on%20Tarakan%20%28O BOE%20ONE%29%20commenced%2C,defences%2C%20the%20landing%

20was%20accomplished%20with%20marked%20success.: accessed 28 November 2023).

CHAPTER 19 NOTES:

[1] Commander in Chief, U.S. Pacific Fleet and Pacific Ocean Areas – June 1945, 21 November 1945.
[2] Ibid.
[3] Lott, *Most Dangerous Sea*, 158.
[4] Ibid.
[5] Commander Task Group 78.1, Action Report, CTG 78.1 (ComPhibGrpSIX) – Brunei Bay, Borneo, Operation (10-17 June 1945), 19 June 1945.
[6] Ibid.
[7] "RAN Beach Commandos" by Petar Djokovic (https://www.navy.gov.au/history/feature-histories/ran-beach-commandos: accessed 29 November 2023).
[8] Commander Task Group 78.1, Action Report, CTG 78.1 (ComPhibGrpSIX) – Brunei Bay, Borneo, Operation (10-17 June 1945), 19 June 1945.
[9] Commander Task Group 78.1, Action Report, CTG 78.1 (ComPhibGrpSIX) – Brunei Bay, Borneo, Operation (10-17 June 1945), 19 June 1945; Commander Task Unit 78.1.14, Action Report, OBOE-6, Brunei Operation, 19 June 1945.
[10] Commander Task Unit 78.1.14, Action Report, OBOE-6, Brunei Operation, 19 June 1945.
[11] Commanding Officer, USS *LSM 64*, Action Report – OBOE Six Operation, 14 June 1945.
[12] Commander Task Group 78.1, Action Report, CTG 78.1 (ComPhibGrpSIX) – Brunei Bay, Borneo, Operation (10-17 June 1945), 19 June 1945.
[13] Ibid.
[14] Ibid.

CHAPTER 20 NOTES:

[1] Commander Task Group 78.2, Action Report – Balikpapan-Manggar-Borneo June 15-July 6, 1945, 14 August 1945.
[2] Ibid.
[3] Commander, Task Unit 78.2.9, Action Report, Minesweeping Unit Balikpapan, Borneo, NEI, 11 June to 1 July 1945, 11 July 1945.
[4] Commander Underwater Demolition Team Unit (78.2.11), Action Report C.T.U. 78.2.11 – 25 June to 1 July 1945 Operation OBOE TWO, 2 July 1945.
[5] Commander Task Group 78.2, Action Report – Balikpapan-Manggar-Borneo June 15-July 6, 1945, 14 August 1945.
[6] Ibid.
[7] Commander Task Group 78.2, Action Report – Balikpapan-

Manggar-Borneo June 15-July 6, 1945, 14 August 1945; Commander Task Unit 78.2.5, Action Report – Manggar – Balikpapan Area of Eastern Borneo, 12 July 1945.

[8] Commander Task Unit 78.2.5, Action Report – Manggar – Balikpapan Area of Eastern Borneo, 12 July 1945.

[9] Ibid.

[10] Ibid.

[11] Ibid.

[12] Commander Task Group 78.2, Action Report – Balikpapan-Manggar-Borneo June 15-July 6, 1945, 14 August 1945.

[13] Commander Task Unit 78.2.4, Action Report – OBOE TWO, Balikpapan, Borneo Operation, 8 July 1945.

[14] Ibid.

[15] Commander Task Group 78.2, Action Report – Balikpapan-Manggar-Borneo June 15-July 6, 1945, 14 August 1945.

[16] Ibid.

[17] "Balikpapan"
(https://www.awm.gov.au/collection/PL1913#:~:text=The%20government%2C%20however%2C%20stood%20behind%20the%20Commander-in-Chief%20of,deaths%20of%20229%20Australians%20and%20around%201%2C800%20Japanese: accessed 1 December 2023).

Index

Archer, Robert John, 12
Arnold, Archibald V., 35
Arnold. Henry H., 28
Australia/Australian
  2/4 Commando Squadron, 183, 186
  2/7 Commando Squadron, 209
  2/17 Infantry Battalion, 198, 201
  7th Infantry Division, 204, 209
  9th Infantry Division, 190-201,
  HMAS Assault (RAN Training Centre), 211
  Matilda tank, 201
  Mk1 Folding Assault Boat, 191
  Royal Australian Engineers
    11th Field Company, 191
    158th Field Battery, 2/7 Field Regiment, 186
Baker, George F., 150
Baldwin, Cecil Claude [Capt., MCO RANR(S)], 222
Barbey, Daniel E., 24, 28-29, 32, 51, 70, 73, 80
Barrett, John P. B., 76, 78
Beary, Donald B., 116
Beierl, Peter G., 12
Benner, J. R., 167
Berkey, Russell S., 62, 73, 103, 149, 188
Bjorklund, S. C., 167
Blanche Jr., J. G., 35-37, 76
Blandy, William H. P., 116
Bowman, Horace A., 161
Boynton, Donald E., 8, 10, 12-13
Bradley, James L., 35
Bradley, John R., 45, 47
Brittain, Thomas B., 29
Browne, Milton C., 180
Bruce, Andrew D., 52
Bukovics, Steve, 182
Bunyan, Andrew Veitch [Comdr., DSC RANR(S)], 225
Burgett, William A., 80, 82, 85, 91, 192
Burns Jr., Harmon, 84-85
Carpenter, William Hubbard, 117, 123
Callaghan, William M., 116
Carter, Worrall R., 116
Cole, William M., 40-42, 48

Collins, John Augustine (Vice Adm., KBE, CB RAN), 217
Coney (Capt.), 62
Conolly, Richard L., 35, 73
Cousin, Allan Paterson (Capt., DSO, RAN), 196, 205, 224-225
Cronin, Joseph C., 73
Davis (Comdr.), 62
Decker, James H., 16
Derby Jr., Harry L., 171
Deutermann, William V., 53, 62
Dewey, George, 177-178
Doe, Jens A., 127
Durgin, Calvin T., 73
Eichelberger, Robert L., 132
Erwin, William D., 5
Etter, G. E., 167
Faddis, James Morris, 12
Fazer, C. H., 174
Fechteler, William M., 28, 33, 80-81, 95, 125, 149
Fields, Thomas M., 122
Foley, H. H., 105, 107
Francis, Dennis L., 157-159, 163, 206
Freseman, W. L., 53
Frey, C. W., 174
Fulweiler, John H., 158, 163
Glover, Robert Ogden, 73
Gorchov, S. J., 172
Gray, Charles W., 185
Griswold, T. F., 117
Hall Jr., John L., 156
Halsey, William, 23-24, 28
Harada, Kaku, 153
Harmon, George T., 166
Hawley, D. C., 124, 173
Hickman, Kark K., 47
Hicks, Howard J., 67-69
Higgins, Ronald D., 78
Hill, Harry W., 116
Hirshberg, Allan M., 170
Holt, P. C., 53
Hoover, John H., 116
Huie (Comdr.), 73
Irving, Frederick A., 28
Jacob, Richard G., 44
Japan/Japanese
    Fourteenth Area Army, 90
    32nd Army, 156

33rd Naval Special Base, 153
  Kerama Retto, 10-11, 156-161, 173
    Mae Shima, 163
  Okinawa, 1-13, 114-115, 155-174
  Tokyo, 114-115
Jenkins Jr., B. N., 172
Johnson, Ralph C., 104
Johnson, Reginald C., 24, 28, 42, 48, 53, 55, 59
Kaiser, Howard A., 102
Kay, K. E. H., 202
Keefer, James R., 188
Ketcham, Dixwell, 116
Kiland, Ingolf N., 75-76
Kinkaid, Thomas C., 26-28, 73
Knight, Alfred Victor [Capt., OBE, DSC, MID, RANR(S)], 223-224
Knowles, Herbert B., 79
Krueger, Walter, 26, 60, 125
Lawhead, Ralph W., 171-172
Lee, Robert J., 171-172
Lind, A. E., 117
Linthicum (Comdr.), 62
Livingston, Eric Walton [Comdr., DSC RANR(S)], 226
Loud, Wayne R., 73
MacArthur, Douglas, 23-28, 33, 38, 90, 114-115, 125, 141, 193
Martin, F. B. C., 109
Martin (Capt.), 62
McComb, Edward L., 28, 31
McEathron, Ellsworth D., 53, 62
McGuffle, William B., 180
McKittrick, Frederick William, 183
McLean, J. B. (Capt.), 73
McVay III, Charles B., 116
Mee, Francis J., 206
Mitscher, Marc A., 116
Montgomery, G. C., 116
Morrison, F. W., 75
Moss, J. A., 75
Mudge, Verne D., 28
Mullaney, Baron Joseph, 10, 12
Naye, John A., 12
Nimitz, Chester W., 28, 60, 114-115
Noble, Albert G., 204, 207
Nuber, William J., 166
Oldendorf, Jesse B., 73
Osmena, Sergio, 35
Pacific Islands

Admiralty Islands, 23-24, 28
  Los Negros, 24
  Manus, 23-24, 28, 78
Bismarck Archipelago, 23
Borneo
  Balikpapan, 125, 184-188, 193, 203-210
  Brunei Bay, 125, 130, 184-185, 195-202
    Brunei Town, 201
    Labuan Island, 184, 195-201
    Muara Island, 197, 201
  Sadau Island, 183-195
  Tarakan Island, 125, 130, 183-196
Formosa Island (today Taiwan), 114, 156
  Emirau, 23
Mariana Islands
  Saipan, 114, 120
Netherlands East Indies
  Morotai Island, 185, 188, 192, 200, 204
New Caledonia
  Noumea, 22-23
Society Islands
  Bora Bora, 20-22
Solomon Islands
  Green Island, 23
Papua New Guinea
  Hollandia, 29, 37
  Milne Bay, 23
  Port Moresby, 23
Philippines
  Basilan Island, 126, 141
  Bohol Island, 91, 125-126, 143
  Camotes Sea, 41
  Canigao Island, 41, 43, 53
  Cebu Island, 79, 125-126, 141-154
  Guimaras Island, 141-146
  Inampulugan Island, 141, 146
  Leyte Island, 25-38
    Ormoc Bay, 40, 51-60
    Leyte Gulf, 27-41, 53, 62, 69, 73, 95, 112, 150
      San Pedro Bay, 41, 44, 64, 112
  Luzon Island
    Bataan Peninsula, 91, 99-103, 108
    Corregidor (Fort Mills), 99-103, 108, 141, 175-188
    Grande Island, 89-92, 178
    Manila Bay
      Caballo Island (Fort Hughes), 100, 103, 141, 178

Carabao Island (Fort Frank), 100, 178
El Fraile Island (Fort Drum), 100, 103, 175-182
Mariveles Bay, 99-108
Nasugbu Bay, 89-99
Olongapo, 91-93, 99
Subic Bay, 90-92, 98-99, 103-107, 175-178, 182
Negros Islands
Occidental, 126, 143
Oriental, 126, 146
Mindanao Island/Sea, 73, 125, 131-141, 153
Zamboanga, 125-153
Mindoro Island, 61-73, 88, 91, 96, 127-132, 139, 141
Lingayen Gulf, 71-78, 82, 88, 143
Lingayen Town, 72
San Fabian Beaches/Town, 72-89
Palawan Island, 125-130, 140
Puerto Princesa, 125-129
Panay Island, 83, 91, 125-126, 141-146
Panaon Island, 41
Samar Island, 64, 109-112, 143
Catbalogan, 109-112
Sulu Archipelago, 126-127, 142
Surigao Straits, 39, 41, 73, 91, 153
Tawi-Tawi Island, 204
Parsons, W. S., 53, 62
Pattie, Samuel H., 176
Passowski, J. R., 47
Patch, Alexander, 149
Potts Jr., James, 176
Powers, Carrell R., 33
Prinkey, Merle, 16
Rairden Jr., Percy W., 55-59
Reifsnider, Lawrence F., 156
Richardson, C. G., 82
Riggs, Ralph S., 92
Rodgers, Bertram J., 116
Rodgers, H. R., 83
Roosevelt, Franklin D., 25
Royal, Forrest B., 35, 76, 131-132, 188, 196
Saltmarsh, Ernest, 135
Saunders, Richard H., 165
Schmidt, Harry, 123
Seay, Erskine A., 91
Sharp Jr., Alexander, 155
Shaw, Norman Hamon (Comdr., OBE RAN), 222-223

Ships and Craft

Australian
  Adelaide, 222
  Arunta, 217
  Australia, 73-74, 81, 217, 222
  Bathurst, 224-225
  Bingen, 226
  Bishopdale, 217
  Gascoyne, 217
  H27, 223
  HDML 1074, 217
  Kanimbla, 29, 196, 211-226
  Katoomba, 224-225
  Lithgow, 224
  Manoora, 29, 192, 196, 200, 205, 211-225
  Merkur, 217
  Melbourne, 222
  Oxley, 223
  Ping Wo, 212
  Poyang, 217
  Shropshire, 217
  Swan, 225
  Sydney, 222, 225-226
  Warramunga, 217
  Westralia, 29, 192, 196, 205, 211-226
  Wyrallah (renamed *Wilcannia*), 226
  Yunnan, 217
Dutch
  Koda Enten, 170-171
Japanese
  Akagi, 8
  Chiyoda, 153
  I-124, 225
United States
  Coast Guard
    Ingram, 104
  Navy
    amphibious/troop ships
      Arneb, 83
      Banner, 81
      Barry, 173
      Biscayne, 159
      Blue Ridge, 51, 182
      Bowie, 86
      Carter Hall, 205
      Cofer, 139, 154, 188
      Egeria, 83, 162

Eldorado, 120
Fayette, 29
General R. E. Callan, 112
Gosper, 174
Henry T. Allen, 213
Kephart, 139, 154
Kline, 204
LCFF-789, 205
LCI(A)-755, *LCI(A)-974*, 35
LCI(G)-589, 160
LCI(G)-961, *LCI(G)-964*, *LCI(G)-1015*, *LCI(G)-1016*, *LCI(G)-1017*,
   LCI(G)-1018, *LCI(G)-1060*, 42
LCI(L)-365, 87
LCI(L)-547, 175-176, 182
LCI(L)-578, *LCI(L)-579*, *LCI(L)-607*, *LCI(L)-611*, *LCI(L)-612*,
   LCI(L)-613, *LCI(L)-685*, *LCI(L)-687*, *LCI(L)-758*, *LCI(L)-759*,
   LCI(L)-962, *LCI(L)-963*, *LCI(L)-966*, *LCI(L)-972*, *LCI(L)-976*,
   LCI(L)-977, *LCI(L)-978*, *LCI(L)-981*, *LCI(L)-983*, 62
LCI(L)-609, 62, 68
LCI(L)-628, 117
LCI(L)-635, *LCI(L)-653*, 110
LCI(L)-674, 87
LCI(L)-686, 62, 69
LCI(L)-688, *LCI(L)-699*, 106
LCI(L)-701, 110
LCI(L)-710, 136
LCI(L)-712, 185-186
LCI(L)-771, 137
LCI(L)-779, 136
LCI(L)-964, 42, 62
LCI(L)-965, 62, 154
LCI(L)-970, 56-59, 62
LCI(L)-980, 62, 154
LCI(L)-982, 42
LCI(L)-984, 154
LCI(L)-1003, 110
LCI(L)-1014, 40, 47, 49, 62
LCI(L)-1017, 40, 42-50, 62
LCI(L)-1018, 40-49, 62, 68
LCI(L)-1021, *LCI(L)-1022*, *LCI(L)-1065*, 62
LCI(L)-1025, *LCI(L)-1071*, *LCI(L)-1075*, 136
LCI(M)-353, 173
LCS(L)-14, 164
LCS(L)-21, 169-170
LCS(L)-23, 170
LCS(L)-25, 164

LCS(L)-50, 185
LCS(L)-81, 165
LCS(L)-82, 2, 12
LCS(L)-83, 2, 8, 10, 12, 164
LCS(L)-84, 2, 8, 12, 165, 167
LCS(L)-118, 165
LCT-1331, 185
Leedstown, 31
Liddle, 60
Little, 164
Lloyd, 139
LSM-1, LSM-2, 210
LSM-8, LSM-10, LSM-11, LSM-13, LSM-15, LSM-25, LSM-31, LSM-32, LSM-33, 75, 88
LSM-12, 75, 88, 157
LSM-14, 76, 78-79, 88
LSM-18, 28, 33, 38, 40, 42, 46-48, 53, 55-60, 88, 104, 107-108, 138, 140, 210
LSM-19, 28-31, 33-34, 38-40, 49, 53, 56-57, 59-60, 88, 104, 108, 137, 139-140, 210
LSM-20, 28, 33-34, 38-41, 45-49, 157
LSM-21, 28-30, 33, 38, 40, 49, 62, 65, 70, 104, 108, 137, 140, 210
LSM-22, 28, 33-34, 38, 40-41, 43, 48, 53, 62, 65, 70, 110, 137, 140, 210
LSM-23, 28, 33-34, 38-40, 45-48, 50
LSM-24, 35-38, 76, 78, 86, 88
LSM-27, 75, 88, 137
LSM-28, 76, 78, 88
LSM-29, 35-38, 76, 78, 88
LSM-30, 76, 78, 88
LSM-34, 28, 33-34, 38, 40, 45, 48-50, 53, 62, 65-70, 104, 108, 140
LSM-35, 80-81, 88, 146, 150, 154
LSM-36, 80-81, 88, 210
LSM-37, 62, 65, 70, 104, 108, 140, 210
LSM-38, 104, 108, 137, 140, 210
LSM-39, 104, 106, 108, 137, 140, 210
LSM-40, 62, 65, 69-70, 104, 108, 137, 140, 210
LSM-41, 80, 82, 84, 93, 95, 98, 129-130
LSM-42, 104, 108, 137, 140, 210
LSM-43, LSM-44, LSM-47, LSM-48, LSM-49, LSM-60, LSM-92, LSM-202, LSM-206, LSM-207, LSM-238, LSM-239, LSM-241, LSM-242, LSM-260, LSM-261, 117, 124
LSM-46, 117, 121, 124
LSM-50, 76, 78, 88, 129-130, 146, 150, 154, 198, 202
LSM-51, 38, 53, 88, 175-182, 198, 202
LSM-52, 76, 78, 88, 93, 95, 98, 104, 108, 198, 202
LSM-53, 76, 78, 88, 93, 95, 98, 129-130, 145-146, 198, 202

LSM-54, 75, 88, 93, 95, 98, 128-130, 145-146, 198, 202
LSM-59, 117, 124, 157, 168, 173-174
LSM-63, 80, 82, 91, 129-130, 145-146, 198, 202
LSM-64, 80, 82, 85, 91, 98, 104, 108, 198, 200, 202
LSM-65, 76, 78, 88, 93, 95, 98, 129-130, 145-146, 198, 202
LSM-66, 80, 82, 85-86, 91, 98, 129-130, 145-146
LSM-67, 80, 82, 85, 91, 98, 129-130, 198, 202
LSM-68, 80, 82, 85, 91, 98, 198-199, 202
LSM-70, LSM-74, 117, 119-120, 124
LSM-126, 15, 117, 119-120, 124
LSM-127, 15, 80, 82-86, 129-130
LSM-128, 129-130, 145-146, 198, 202
LSM-129, 129-130, 210
LSM-130, 140, 210
LSM-131, 129-130, 145-146
LSM-133, 129-130, 198, 202
LSM-134, 35, 38
LSM-135, 35, 37-38, 75, 88, 157, 168, 170-173, 235-236
LSM-136, 35-38
LSM-137, 75, 86, 88
LSM-138, 16-17, 19-22, 24, 28, 33-34, 38, 53, 62, 65, 68, 70, 104, 108,
    138, 140, 198, 202
LSM-139, 16-17, 28, 33-34, 38, 53, 62, 65, 68, 70, 104, 108, 140, 198,
    202
LSM-140, LSM-141, 117, 126
LSM-143, 121, 126
LSM-144, 17, 75, 88
LSM-145, 17, 117, 126
LSM-148, 62, 65, 70, 110, 210
LSM-150, 62, 65, 70, 110-111, 146, 150, 154, 210
LSM-151, 110, 146, 150, 154, 185-187, 192-193, 210
LSM-168, 79, 130, 146, 150, 152, 154, 198, 202
LSM-169, 80, 88, 93, 95, 98, 104-108
LSM-201, 88, 117, 124
LSM-203, 80, 88, 93, 95, 98, 104-105, 108, 198-199, 202
LSM-205, 80, 88, 140, 210
LSM-210, 76, 78, 88
LSM-211, LSM-216, 117, 119-120, 124
LSM-217, 80, 88
LSM-218, 80, 88, 93, 95, 98, 104, 107-108, 140
LSM-219, 80, 82, 84-86, 129-130, 150, 154, 198, 202
LSM-223, 80, 210
LSM-224, 129-130, 145-146, 192-193, 210
LSM-225, 129-130, 150, 154, 198, 202
LSM-233, 35, 37-38, 76, 78, 88
LSM-234, LSM-235, 75, 88

LSM-237, 129-130, 150, 154, 198, 202
LSM-257, 17, 28-30, 33, 38, 53, 68, 104, 108, 140, 192, 210
LSM-258, 17, 28, 33, 38, 53, 62, 65-68, 70, 110-111, 137, 140, 210
LSM-259, 17, 76, 78, 88
LSM-264, 113, 117, 124
LSM-265, 146
LSM-266, 124
LSM-267, 145-146, 192-193, 210
LSM-268, 80, 82, 91, 98, 129-130, 150, 154
LSM-269, 80, 82, 85-86, 91, 98, 129-130, 145-146, 192-193, 198, 202
LSM-310, 53, 62, 65, 70, 104, 108, 140, 210
LSM-311, 23, 26, 28, 32-33, 38, 53, 62, 65, 68, 70, 104, 108, 140, 171,
   210
LSM-312, 76, 79, 88
LSM-313, 75, 88
LSM-314, 80, 88, 110, 140
LSM-315, 80, 88
LSM-316, *LSM-317*, 110, 146, 150, 154
LSM-318, 38, 40, 49, 53, 55-60, 157
LSM-319, 104, 108, 137, 140
LSM-323, 117, 119-120, 124
LSM-397, 210
LSM(R)-188, 158-162, 167-168, 227
LSM(R)-189, 158-161, 163, 167-168
LSM(R)-190, 157-158, 163, 165-168, 231-232
LSM(R)-191, *LSM(R)-192*, *LSM(R)-196*, *LSM(R)-197*, *LSM(R)-198*,
   LSM(R)-199, 158, 163
LSM(R)-193, 1-12, 158, 163, 168
LSM(R)-194, 5, 157-159, 163, 165, 167-171, 233-234
LSM(R)-195, 5, 157-158, 163-165, 229-230
LST-168, *LST-397*, *LST-454*, *LST-457*, *LST-632*, *LST-639*, *LST-694*,
   LST-703, *LST-721*, *LST-740*, *LST-777*, *LST-935*, *LST-938*,
   LST-1016, *LST-1017*, *LST-1018*, 207
LST-171, *LST-181*, 32
LST-245, 83
LST-269, *LST-270*, 35
LST-737, 60
LST-452, 32, 207
LST-472, 68
LST-548, *LST-610*, 87
LST-615, 35
LST-630, 132
LST-667, 105, 185
LST-724, *LST-760*, *LST-779*, *LST-788*, *LST-808*, 113
LST-736, 69
LST-738, 66-69

LST-742, 67
LST-753, 132
LST-912, 129
LST-915, 73
LST-1028, 87
LST-1035, 148
Newman, 139, 154
Ozark, 77
Rocky Mount, 132, 188
Rushmore, 132-133
Schmidt, Titania, 205
Ward, 60
Warhawk, 87
auxiliaries
  ATR-14, 10
  ATR-23, 10
  Grasp, 105-107
  Hercules, 31
  Lipan, 173
  Mango, 203
  Menominee, 37
  Rigel, 213
  Tekesta, 173
combatants
  aircraft carriers
    Kitkun Bay, 218
    Ranger, 94
  battleships
    Mississippi, 81
    New Jersey, 175
  cruisers
    Boise, 33
    Boston, 177
    Nashville, 63-64
    Phoenix, 103, 177, 182, 188
    Raleigh, 177
  destroyers
    Abbot, 154
    Barton, 64
    Conway, 207
    Conyngham, 154
    Dashiell, 64
    Drayton, 40, 42, 45, 48, 125
    Eaton, 87
    Evans, 2-3, 6-9, 12
    Fletcher, 100-103

Flusser, 40, 45, 49-50, 154
Halligan, 158-159
Hopewell, 67, 100, 102
Hugh W. Hadley, 2-3, 7, 9-13
Ingraham, 64, 169
Lamson, 40-42, 48, 50, 60
La Vallette, 45, 49
Lough, 97
Luce, 165, 167
Mahan, 60
Moale, 66
Morrison, 169
Mugford, 45, 49-50
Nicholas, O'Bannon, 177
O'Brien, 67
Philip, 87, 183-187
Renshaw, Robinson, 87
Sampson, 49
Shaw, 40, 48
Sigourney, 139
Stanly, 64
Swearer, 174
William C. Cole, 173
cutter
  McCulloch, 177
sub-chasers
  PC-1120, 185-186
  PC-1128, 158
  PC-1129, 96-97
  PC-1133, 104, 154
  PC-1134, 154
  PC-1603, 37
motor torpedo boats
  Portunus (tender), 145
  PT-376, 182
  PT-490, 141
gunboat
  Concord, 177
mine warfare
minelayers
  Aaron Ward, 164
  Smith, 2
minesweepers
  Pursuit, Requisite, Sage, Saunter, Scrimmage, Triumph, 53
  Salute, 53, 196, 204
  Scout, Sentry, 53, 204

Scuffle, 204
Spectacle, 170-171
Steady, 174
YMS-6, YMS-8, 102
*YMS-9, YMS-10, YMS-39, YMS-47, YMS-49, YMS-52, YMS-84,
    YMS-95, YMS-196, YMS-314, YMS-315, YMS-329, YMS-335,
    YMS-336, YMS-339, YMS-365, YMS-366, YMS-368,
    YMS-392*, 204
YMS-46, 102, 204
YMS-48, 100-103
YMS-50, 135, 204
YMS-51, YMS-334, YMS-363, YMS-364, YMS-481, 189, 204
YMS-53, 102, 104
YMS-71, 135
YMS-176, 37
YMS-311, 77, 171

Sibert, Franklin C., 28
Smith, E. G., 80-81
Smith, Holland McTyeire, 116
Sprague, Albert T., 149
Spruance, Raymond A., 115-116
States, L. A., 205
Stewart, James M., 159-160
Stillwell, Joseph W., 28
Stimson, Henry L., 111
Struble, Arthur D., 28-29, 51, 60-64, 91, 99, 103, 105, 143
Studley, Robert A., 5
Sultan of Brunei and wife, 202
Tennis, Lyle S., 165-168
Townsley, Forrest L., 95
Turner, Blaney C., 97
Turner Jr., H. T., 86
Turner, Richmond K., 116, 120
Turner, W. H., 161
United States
  Army
    Americal Division, 148-150
    1st Cavalry Division, 24, 28, 33, 52
    1st Filipino Regiment, 109-112
    2nd Filipino Regiment, 112
    6th Infantry Division, 73, 81
    6th Ranger Battalion, 28
    7th Infantry Division, 35, 52, 156
    11th Airborne Division, 93, 97
    13th Air Depot Group, 22
    23rd Infantry Division, 148-149

24th Infantry Division, 28-29, 33, 52, 62, 69-70, 91, 106
25th Infantry Division, 73
26th, 33rd, 34th Infantry Divisions, 149
32nd Infantry Division, 52
37th Infantry Division, 73, 76
38th Infantry Division, 91-92
40th Infantry Division, 73, 78-79, 143, 146
41st Infantry Division, 127, 129, 131, 139-140
43rd Infantry Division, 73
77th Infantry Division, 52, 54, 59-60, 68
96th Infantry Division, 35, 52, 156
113th Engineer Combat Battalion, 176, 180
129th, 148th Infantry Divisions, 72, 76
151st Infantry Division, 176, 180
162nd, 163rd, 186th Infantry Divisions, 127
503rd Parachute Regiment, 62, 69-70
Camp Beale (today Beale Air Force Base), 111
Camp Stoneman, 109, 112
Army Air Force
Fifth Air Force, 63
Marine
1st, 6th Marine Divisions, 156
3rd Marine Division, 123
4th, 5th Marine Divisions, 118-119, 122-123
Navy
Amphibious Training Base, Little Creek, Virginia, 16
"Black Cat" PBY Catalina patrol aircraft, 64
Cruiser Division Fifteen, 50
Underwater Demolition Team (UDT), 81, 152, 207
UDT 11, UDT 18, 204-205
Ushijima, Mitsuru, 156
Venters, Walter R., 162
Verge, William E., 75, 93, 95, 128-129, 145
Walter (Lt.), 62
Webb (Capt.), 62
Weintraub, Daniel J., 109-111, 131, 137, 205
Weire, Everett E., 104
Whitehead, S. B., 200
Wilkinson, Thomas S., 35, 38, 73, 75, 87-88
Williams, Willard W., 82
Woodson, William E., 165
Wootten, George F., 201
Yamashita, Tomoyuki, 90

About the Author

Commander David D. Bruhn, U.S. Navy (Retired) served twenty-two years on active duty and two in the Naval Reserve, as both an enlisted man and as an officer, between 1977 and 2001.

He is a graduate of California State University, Chico, and has Masters degrees from the U.S. Naval Postgraduate School and U.S. Naval War College.

During his career, Bruhn served aboard six ships including command of the mine countermeasures ships USS *Gladiator* (MCM-11) and USS *Dextrous* (MCM-13) in the Persian Gulf. Ashore, he did two three-year tours in the Pentagon. During the first one, he was assigned to Secretary of the Navy and Chief of Naval Operation staffs as a budget analyst and resources planner. His final assignment was to the Secretary of Defense staff as executive assistant to a senior (SES 4) executive at the Ballistic Missile Defense Organization in Washington, D.C.

Following military service, he was a high school teacher and track coach for ten years, and remains an avid Track & Field fan. He lives in northern California with his wife Nancy and has two grown sons, David and Michael.

Bruhn has authored twenty-eight books on naval history; one on shipboard engineering; four related to sports, *Toe the Mark*, *Stride Out*, *Distant Finish*, and *Beavers* about competitive running; and two devoted to leisure activities, *Land Yacht Seaward*, and *Stand Easy*.

www.ingramcontent.com/pod-product-compliance
Lightning Source LLC
Chambersburg PA
CBHW071837270326
41929CB00013B/2019